More praise for *Global Vision*

"*Global Vision* focuses on the centrality of national institutions—political, economic, and cultural—in facilitating or constraining a company's global expansion. This unique strength of the book also makes it a must read for corporate leaders charged with designing and managing a firm's global strategy."
—Anil K. Gupta, Michael Dingman Chair in Strategy and Globalization, Smith School of Business, The University of Maryland, and Co-author, *The Quest for Global Dominance* and *Getting China and India Right.*

"A must read for anyone contemplating cross-border transactions. Robert Salomon has highlighted the myriad of pitfalls that CEOs forget in their eagerness to expand their markets around the world. Large and small corporations become oblivious to the real risks of globalization. Understanding the mistakes made by these corporations is sobering…and avoidable. This book is a checklist on how to avoid those pitfalls and properly evaluate risk."
—Stanley P. Gold, Chairman, Shamrock Holdings, Inc.

"*Global Vision* is a must read manual for any company considering international expansion. I wish that I had read it long ago, as it would have helped our company avoid many of the costly mistakes that we experienced along the way."
—Leonard S. Marcovitch, President and CEO, White Wave Sportswear, Inc., and Harvard MBA

"*Global Vision* is an insightful discussion of the tangible and intangible factors that must be understood before any business entity attempts to expand globally. Salomon provides an important straightforward recipe to help get it right!"
—Barry Alperin, Former COO and Vice Chairman, Hasbro; Director at Several Large, Publicly-traded Multinationals

Global Vision

How Companies Can Overcome the Pitfalls of Globalization

Robert Salomon

palgrave
macmillan

GLOBAL VISION
Copyright © Robert Salomon 2016

First published 2016 by
PALGRAVE MACMILLAN

The author has asserted their right to be identified as the author of this work in accordance with the Copyright, Designs and Patents Act 1988.

Palgrave Macmillan in the UK is an imprint of Macmillan Publishers Limited, registered in England, company number 785998, of Houndmills, Basingstoke, Hampshire, RG21 6XS.

Palgrave Macmillan in the US is a division of Nature America, Inc., One New York Plaza, Suite 4500, New York, NY 10004-1562.

Palgrave Macmillan is the global academic imprint of the above companies and has companies and representatives throughout the world.

Hardback ISBN: 978–1–137–50281–0
E-PUB ISBN: 978–1–137–50283–4
E-PDF ISBN: 978–1–137–50282–7
DOI: 10.1057/9781137502827

Distribution in the UK, Europe and the rest of the world is by Palgrave Macmillan®, a division of Macmillan Publishers Limited, registered in England, company number 785998, of Houndmills, Basingstoke, Hampshire RG21 6XS.

Library of Congress Cataloging-in-Publication Data

Salomon, Robert, 1973– author.
    Global vision : how companies can overcome the pitfalls of
  globalization / Robert Salomon.
        pages cm
    Includes bibliographical references and index.
    ISBN 978–1–137–50281–0 (alk. paper)
      1. International business enterprises. 2. International trade.
  3. International economic relations. 4. Globalization—Economic
  aspects. I. Title.

HD2755.5.S237 2016
658′.049—dc23   2015032487

A catalogue record for the book is available from the British Library.

Printed in the United States of America.

Contents

List of Tables vii

List of Figures ix

Acknowledgments xi

Introduction xiii

Chapter 1 Globalization: A Cautionary Tale 1

Chapter 2 The Globalization Process 17

Chapter 3 The Impact of National Institutions on Globalization 35

Chapter 4 Political Institutions and Globalization 49

Chapter 5 Economic Institutions and Globalization 69

Chapter 6 Cultural Institutions and Globalization 93

Chapter 7 Using Global Acumen to Account for Risk 115

Chapter 8 Global Acumen in Practice 143

Chapter 9 Using Global Acumen in Other Contexts 159

Chapter 10 The End of the Beginning for Global Acumen 183

Notes 195

Bibliography 207

Index 215

Tables

2.1 Business Projections for Newlandia 23

2.2 Business Projections for Newlandia: Assuming
an Upfront Investment 24

2.3 Business Projections for Newlandia: Assuming
an 8.5% Discount Rate 25

4.1 Political Data Sources 67

5.1 Economic Data Sources 90

6.1 Culture Data Sources 111

7.1 Risk to US Companies Expanding Abroad 135

7.2 Risk to Foreign Companies Expanding to
the United States 137

7.3 Bilateral Risk Spreads for a Set of Eight Countries 139

8.1 Business Projections for Newlandia: Assuming
an 8.5% Discount Rate 145

8.2 Business Projections for Newlandia: Assuming
an 18.5% Discount Rate 149

8.3 Business Projections for Newlandia: Assuming
a 28.5% Discount Rate 150

8.4 Business Projections for Newlandia: Estimating
Liability of Foreignness Costs 156

9.1 Business Projections for Newlandia: Assuming
Shared Profit for Joint Venture (JV)
and a 13.5% Discount Rate 168

9.2 Business Projections for Newlandia: Assuming
Partial Profit for Export and a 9.5% Discount Rate 170

Figures

1.1 Global Corporate Investment 9
7.1 Institutional Distance Illustration 118
7.2 The Architecture of Global Acumen 134
9.1 The Architecture of Global Acumen 171
9.2 Learning Curves and Institutional Risk Premiums 175

Acknowledgments

Writing this book required me to expend considerable effort and energy, but I benefited tremendously from the generosity of a constellation of contributors along the way. I could not have climbed this mountain without their help, encouragement, and guidance, for which I am forever grateful.

I wrote this book during my year's sabbatical in Spain, and I thank the Instituto de Estudios Superiores de la Empresa (IESE) Business School for providing me with office space in Madrid. The good folks at IESE—Jose Campa, Pascual Berrone, Joan Enric Ricart Costa, and Almudena Maceira Suarez, among many others—were a great help in facilitating my efforts. Over this past year I experienced what a world-class institution IESE is, and I am honored to have been affiliated with IESE, even if only for a short time and in a limited capacity.

I am tremendously grateful to New York University (NYU) and the NYU Stern School of Business, my academic home and my alma mater, for granting me a sabbatical so that I could write this book. In particular, I thank the NYU Stern Center for Global Economy and Business and its directors Kim Schoenholtz and Jennifer Carpenter for providing critical funding that made it possible to complete the book. The NYU Stern Center for Global Economy and Business has supported a number of my research projects over the years, including prior work on institutions and institutional distance—the foundation upon which I built *Global Vision*.

I am also eager to acknowledge my academic colleagues, starting with Myles Shaver, Xavier Martin, and Bernard Yeung, who fed and nurtured my passion for international business. They were instrumental to my education and contributed immeasurably to my development as a globalization scholar. My coauthors, especially Jin-Hyun Bae, Yunok Cho, and Zheying Wu, helped round out my knowledge of institutions and institutional distance. I learned a great deal from each of them and appreciate their willingness to act as a sounding board to help refine many of the ideas I present in *Global Vision*. I am also indebted to numerous colleagues upon whose work my own work builds and to the thousands of students and business executives who helped me test and sharpen the ideas in this book.

Alison Rooney, editor extraordinaire, has helped me with countless projects over the past 15 years, none more involved than nor as demanding as this one. I always benefit from Alison's astute editorial insight and input, and this time I relied on her suggestions for substantive improvement. The book is much improved thanks to her gift for logical storytelling and her uncanny ability to translate technical academic writing into accessible, engaging prose.

I am indebted to friends and family scattered across the globe, who have been instrumental at all stages of my development as a person and as a professional. In particular, I appreciate the incredible support and encouragement of my family in Spain. They really looked out for me during my time there. I thank Barry and Mimi, who have always treated me like family. I am grateful to my siblings—Gene Jr., Maria Randazza, and Henry—who always provide a fertile and supportive training ground to test my half-baked intellectual ideas. And of course, I am eternally indebted to my parents, Bea and Gene, for providing me the raw materials from which to draw; from my early years on, they have opened doors to a world of intellectual pursuits and educational possibilities.

Finally, I thank Ben, Sophie, and Julie. My children, Ben and Sophie, inspire me daily and gave me the courage to see this project through. Julie, my confidante, my companion, and best friend, has been steadfast with her love and support throughout the entire book-writing process. She made incredible personal sacrifices to move to Spain so that I could write this book, and words can never express the depths of my gratitude to her. I certainly know I would have achieved far less without Ben, Sophie, and Julie in my life, and so in however small a gesture, I dedicate this book to them, in recognition of all they have done for me and for all they have sacrificed on my behalf.

Introduction

I see the impact of globalization and global business all around us, every day, and not just because it's my day job to research, publish articles, and teach the subject. I am fascinated by how global business activity connects us on so many levels. To our benefit as well as our detriment, the impacts of globalization are everywhere, and this dynamic is only becoming more powerful. And while it is not my objective with this book to make judgments about which impacts are good and which are bad, I do feel an urgency to unpack any crucial insights that might empower those in business—central players on an international stage—to make better global strategy decisions. This book therefore provides a lens through which to view globalization in a new and compelling way.

I have been interested in globalization and the dynamics of how businesses expand across national borders for almost 25 years. The maneuvers and decisions that managers make as they build their businesses in this way have fascinated me, including, eventually, how and why some ventures turned out to be successful and others disastrous. This began as a casual interest when I was a young person growing up in the shadow of New York City. I grew up with a father who was born and raised in Spain, lived for a number of years in Cuba, and traveled the globe as a businessman orchestrating global deals on behalf of a US-based company. My mother was born to Italian immigrants, was raised in an Italian neighborhood in Brooklyn, and taught English as a second language to elementary school students who had emigrated to the United States from all over the world. In our household an international perspective was required and discussions about global current events were routine.

My parents nurtured this international perspective even further when they sent me at the age of seven to spend the first of 11 consecutive summers with our extended family in Spain. There I began to appreciate firsthand the differences between countries. During my first summer in Spain in 1980 I was not prepared for the scale of these differences. My seven-year-old brain brimmed with questions: why Spaniards looked different, why everyone did not speak English, why people in Spain used an unfamiliar and strange-colored currency, why I could not find the same foods to eat, and why people did not wear the same style of clothes.

Over subsequent summers I developed new and refined questions based on my observations of more subtle distinctions, such as why the Spanish frowned upon some behaviors that were commonplace in the United States. I was also struck by how among my family and their friends as well as more broadly, out in cafes and other public places, it was taboo to discuss domestic politics openly and candidly. This especially stood out for me given how ubiquitous vigorous political debate was among the adults I had observed both in my family at home and in US society more generally.

Later, with the benefit of hindsight, I was able to appreciate how the Spain I had come to know starting in the early 1980s was a country still dealing with the aftermath of a Franco dictatorship that ended abruptly in 1975. It became clear to me then why from that period on and through the late 1980s, as Spain was transitioning to a democracy, political discussions among those on both sides of the Franco debate were imbued with intense emotion and how this was a function of historical circumstances during a unique transitional era. Even in my own family, there were strong opinions on both sides, which could lead to conversations that could easily become incendiary, and so Spanish politics was a topic often avoided.

My summers in Spain offered countless invaluable experiences that forever shaped my perspective on what it means to be raised in a particular country with a unique and distinct political, economic, and cultural context. This interest in and curiosity about the differences between nations—even those as relatively similar as the United States and a Western European country like Spain—stayed with me throughout my formative years.

As I traveled more widely and came to know other countries across the globe, my observations about these differences continued to evolve. As a young adult, I had the good fortune to work in Mexico, first as a summer intern at a small import-export company following the ratification of NAFTA and later as a university graduate in an entry-level position with a large, US-based multinational corporation. Given that I had spent 11 consecutive summers in Spain, I expected that even from when I first arrived, it would be a cinch to adapt to life and work in Mexico. Given that Spanish is the dominant language, I assumed there would be only minimal differences. I quickly became aware that my impressions were patently wrong. Beyond some basic similarities, there were innumerable differences—some so pronounced that I was never quite able to adapt.

This experience of working in another country sparked an interest in phenomena beyond my own personal trials and tribulations with adaptation. Interacting with senior managers at my company and with expatriate managers from other multinationals led to a more nuanced perspective. I learned that businesses also struggle to adapt in foreign countries. It turned out that the same differences in politics, economics, and culture I had experienced as an individual had a profound influence not only on how expatriate managers behaved, but also on the outcomes for their companies in foreign markets.

This personal background and work history was the seed of my desire to enter academia and devote my career to the broader study of globalization and global strategy. I was committed to studying how businesses globalize and how political, economic, and cultural differences influence the risks companies face in global markets. I wanted to understand why some companies are able to overcome risks and perform well in global markets while others stumble in the face of seemingly insurmountable obstacles.

As with all scholarly work, this endeavor has required building upon the best research from a variety of disciplines—economics, psychology, sociology, international business, and business strategy—to develop an original perspective. And the more I immersed myself in research and interacted with high-ranking executives, the more I realized that global companies, even the successful ones, struggle to manage institutional—political, economic, and cultural—differences across countries. I began to see with greater clarity and in greater detail how these institutional differences are at the root of the risks global companies face.

I first came up with the idea for this book about 10 years ago when I began to develop what I now call Global Acumen: a comprehensive global risk management tool. I devised this book and Global Acumen out of one simple insight: that there is a profound disconnect between what managers believe in real time about the risks inherent in globalization and what we academics have learned about the realities of those risks.

My academic peers have long understood the extent to which institutional differences create risks for global companies that, if managed poorly, can lead to disaster. Through my many conversations with high-level managers across a range of industries at companies both large and small, I began to notice that managers intuitively understand the risks that institutional distance creates, but struggle to meaningfully account for those risks. Moreover, although we academics have developed a sophisticated understanding of institutions, institutional distance, and institutional risk, we had not developed an effective tool to help practitioners manage globalization's institutional risks. Our inability to inform and guide managerial practice has therefore let down the management community.

The body of academic work I have built upon and contributed to has emboldened me to see that we in the field have the knowledge to build such a tool. We are finally in a position to take that next step and improve the practice of global strategy in a meaningful and tangible way, and this book and its accompanying Global Acumen tool represent one step toward that end.

As a professor at a business school, it is my job to make research comprehensible and accessible while explaining to students in the classroom its real-world value. And yet I believe this charge should extend well beyond the classroom to our most important audiences: practicing managers in the thick of crucial global business decisions. Accordingly, I have tried to use less scientific and more practical and direct language here than in my other work. Though certainly less technical than my usual fare, there is plenty of meat here for those interested in a dense, complex analysis (especially in chapter 7 as well as in the endnotes throughout), where I lay out the findings in the context of years of rigorous academic research and voluminous scientific findings.

I built the overarching approach I lay out in this book on insights I have gleaned over decades from many fields: economics, psychology, sociology, international business, and business strategy. In this book I translate, extend, and convert research findings on institutional differences into a practical, powerful set of risk management tools with a set of step-by-step instructions that managers can immediately apply to help overcome globalization's most stubborn challenges. Up until I decided to write this book, I dedicated my career to research, scholarship, scientific inquiry, and scholarly publications; however, I sincerely hope that this book sparks a dialogue and builds a bridge between two worlds: the towers of academia and the trenches of global business management.

CHAPTER 1

Globalization: A Cautionary Tale

Managers tend to speak optimistically about the prospects of globalization, and for good reason. Globalization has fostered an increasingly interconnected world, with nearly $30 trillion in goods and services traded and more than $1 trillion in corporate investment in 2013 alone.[1] Advances in information technology and transportation have helped facilitate globalization—connecting developed and developing worlds, lifting some 400 million people out of poverty along the way.[2]

Nations are now inextricably linked through global trade and investment. There is no turning back. Accordingly, managers often view globalization as a powerful and inevitable force, and they tend treat it with reverence—speaking of it as if it were a breakthrough technology, the wave of the future that will change the world, if not their companies' fortunes. And they tend to think of themselves as the champions of globalization, akin to explorers embarking on a mission to discover and conquer far-off, unexplored lands.

Managers express their optimism for globalization in terms of the profitability it can generate. They salivate at the potential for double-digit sales growth. They are seduced by opportunities that promise to slash costs by half or more, simply by shifting operations overseas. And they lead their companies on journeys to global markets in search of untapped and untold riches.

However, opportunity and reality do not always coincide. Although globalization certainly holds promise, it is also rife with hazards. It presents risks that managers fail to appreciate and that they often overlook. Sadly, in the high-stakes world of global strategy, companies regularly fail to convert potential into profits. Most companies are poorly positioned to capitalize on globalization's potential, and many are spectacularly unsuccessful in their attempts to globalize. In reality, failure in global markets is an epidemic with no signs of abating, characterized by otherwise well-intentioned, ambitious managers who make predictable—but avoidable—mistakes.

When it comes to globalization, managers are not just optimists; all too often, they are *unbridled* optimists. They habitually overestimate the benefits of globalization and underestimate its costs. In evaluating globalization opportunities, managers often forget the other side of the opportunity equation: risk. Risk goes hand in hand with opportunity, and managers fail to accurately account for the risks they face in global markets.

Managers often make dangerous assumptions about what it takes to succeed in global markets. They tend to assume that their current business model, one they successfully and profitably exploit in their home country, will translate simply and effectively to other countries, yielding similar levels of profitability. These same managers fail to account for real and salient differences between nations and to consider how those differences generate operational risks that may negatively impact their business. Unfortunately, they end up learning the hard way that the risk borne out of cross-country differences can overwhelm even the best-laid globalization plans. And there is no shortage of examples.

In just the past 20 years, high-profile companies, such as AES, IKEA, Tesco, and Walmart (among others), have been hobbled by globalization. AES fatally underestimated political risk in the Republic of Georgia. IKEA experienced a setback brought on by Russian corruption. Tesco demonstrated a fatal ignorance of US consumers. Even the behemoth Walmart suffered from a toxic cocktail of problems in China, where it tried to force-fit its business model into an immensely varied and misunderstood market with a dramatically underdeveloped infrastructure.

While it is helpful to learn from the struggles that have beset these high-profile companies, it is important to realize that globalization's challenges do not afflict just large companies in specific industries from specific countries. The harsh reality is that no business is immune from the kinds of globalization mistakes I describe below. It matters little whether the company is large or small, whether it is expanding abroad for the first time or has a long history of operating in global markets, whether it operates in new or mature industries, or whether it hails from developed or developing countries. The one irrefutable constant is that companies struggle with globalization.

The irony in all of this is that there are mountains of data and research documenting the risks and challenges associated with globalization, but the lessons of struggle have not been learned, and they have not effectively crossed over into mainstream management. As a result, managers tend to repeat past mistakes in routine fashion—lather, rinse, repeat.

Global Vision unlocks the mysteries of globalization and presents a framework and a tool—Global Acumen—that managers can immediately apply to navigate globalization's hazards successfully. The book will help us learn from the past and avoid common globalization mistakes.

Four Examples of Flawed Expansion

Let's begin by walking through a handful of examples of familiar companies. I have chosen these companies because each of them struggled with a different set of factors—all of which will come into play in discussions in later chapters.

Faltering from Political Instability: AES in Georgia

The US-owned, multinational power company AES attempted to enter the Republic of Georgia shortly after that country's independence from the Soviet Union; the endeavor ultimately was a staggering failure in globalization as a result of a gross underestimation of risk.

AES entered Georgia in 1999, following the country's establishment as post-Soviet state, when Georgia was working its way through political upheaval and civil unrest. AES negotiated a deal with the Georgian government to provide power to residential and commercial customers in the city of Tbilisi and its surrounding area. At the time, the company's analysts estimated that if the government made good on its promises, the deal would yield AES an annual return of approximately 20 percent. However, local political actors thwarted AES's business at every turn, largely as a result of the corruption that is endemic not only to Georgian society but especially to Georgian politics.

From the very start, AES had trouble collecting payment from residential customers who were unaccustomed to paying for electricity, which they had enjoyed free of charge under the Soviet regime. In addition, AES had an especially difficult time collecting payment from commercial customers, many of which were owned by the Georgian government. This was, of course, the same government that had contracted with AES for the provision of electricity in the first place. As AES struggled to collect from its customers, its financial losses mounted.

At the same time, and over a period of several years—from 1999 to 2003—the political situation in Georgia deteriorated. The country was once again teetering on the edge of civil war. At one point, the political environment became so unstable that the mere presence of AES became a symbol of Western imperialism, as Georgian citizens increasingly felt that their government was ceding control over its most important national resources to foreign interests. It became more and more clear to AES that the Georgian government was not likely to live up to its end of the bargain and allow the company to (1) charge market rates for electricity and (2) collect on outstanding electricity bills from residential and commercial customers. As a result, AES decided to abandon the Georgian market after only four years, losing its entire investment along the way—nearly $300 million. What is more, as a part of a settlement brokered between AES and the Georgian government, the company was forced to pay $30 million to the government just for the right to terminate the contract early and leave the country.

There is no doubt that AES made a number of mistakes in the Republic of Georgia, but its cardinal error was being seduced by the country's market potential while underestimating its extreme political risk. In spite of the financial maxim that when it comes to business investments, high risk reaps big rewards, the risks of expanding into Georgia were just too great, and for AES, the rewards did not justify the risks.[3]

Fighting the Home-Field Advantage: IKEA in Russia

For IKEA in Russia, corruption, coupled with a legal system that favors local interests over foreign interests, was the culprit in its underwhelming results. In the 15 years since the Swedish home furnishings giant first entered that country, it has struggled to generate sufficient profitability, a struggle largely due to Russia's legal system and its political and social makeup, in which corruption and graft are commonplace. IKEA opened its first outlet in Moscow in 2000, and almost immediately the local utility company demanded bribes in exchange for maintaining an uninterrupted electricity supply to the store. IKEA managers—determined to do things aboveboard and accustomed to a political and social environment that disdains bribes and kickbacks—opted to rent generators to protect itself against the threat to its power supply.

Renting generators to circumvent the threat of electricity outages seemed like a clever solution. Only later would IKEA discover that its own employee charged with managing the company's relationship with the Russian generator company was involved in a kickback scheme to artificially inflate the price of the generator service. When IKEA sought redress in Russian civil court, the judge not only ruled against IKEA but also slapped the company with a fine for breach of contract with the generator company. IKEA learned a hard lesson: Even when laws exist to protect the interests of foreign investors, local courts do not always enforce them. There remains a large and unwritten home-field bias in the local court system, and IKEA suffered an expensive—and avoidable—loss that has prevented the company from achieving profitability targets in Russia.[4]

Lost in Cultural Translation: Tesco in the United States

For British grocery retailer Tesco—one of the largest in the world—failure in its expansion to the United States was largely the result of its insufficient understanding of the US consumer market. The company opened a chain of small-format grocery stores in Arizona, California, and Nevada in 2007 at a cost of $436 million.[5] It positioned its new "Fresh & Easy" stores in a niche between typical US convenience stores (such as 7-Eleven and Circle K) and local supermarket chains (such as Kroger, Safeway, and Albertson's), hoping to appeal to what it perceived as an underserved middle market. Tesco's Fresh & Easy store format offered a wider selection of staple products than convenience stores and yet more convenience than supermarkets (for customers who wanted to get in and out of the store quickly). It also offered a mix of products between that of upscale, high-end stores (such as Whole Foods) and mass-market stores (such as Walmart).

Unfortunately, Tesco misread the needs of American shoppers, who became confused by its mix of branded and private-label products. Instead of appealing to an underserved niche, Tesco got stuck in the middle, offering neither enough variety to draw customers away from convenience stores nor adequate gains in convenience to woo customers from supermarkets.

Tesco learned the hard way that it is important to understand the local consumer culture. Management was overconfident about its business model and the benefits of imposing what it knew about English customers onto the market in the United States. There was a good reason the middle-market niche had not been filled: It did not appeal to local cultural tastes. Customers were already being well served by the two distinct categories—convenience stores and supermarkets—based on selection, price point, and accessibility. Ultimately, Tesco's mistake—misreading the local cultural environment—cost it dearly. It chose to exit the US market in 2013 after year-over-year operating losses and total losses of nearly $2 billion.[6]

Misreading the Overall Environment: Walmart in China

In some cases a company's difficulty with global expansion stems not solely from a poor understanding of the host country's social, political, or economic environment but from a combination of circumstances that interfere with the company's business model.

Walmart's ongoing troubles in China, since opening its first super-store in Shenzhen in 1996, reflect a fundamental misunderstanding of China's overall environment, one that demonstrates the company's failings in multiple areas.

As Tesco did in the United States, Walmart has struggled to understand Chinese consumers and Chinese culture. Chinese consumers, unlike those in the United States, differ widely from city to city in their needs and tastes. Walmart therefore struggles to find the right product mix to offer in all 117 cities and 25 provinces in which it operates. This makes it challenging to sell a core set of products nationwide.

Like IKEA and AES, Walmart has also suffered from troubled relationships with politicians—both local and national—and the company has had its fair share of run-ins with the law. On one occasion the Chinese government fined Walmart for violating local and national laws and even forced it to close stores temporarily for purported product violations. Walmart paid the fines, in spite of the fact that the company believed the claims to be unfounded.

Even if Walmart could harmonize its product offerings with consumer needs in China and avoid cultural and political missteps, the company's greatest challenge remains an economic infrastructure that is problematic and underdeveloped. China simply cannot accommodate one of Walmart's greatest strengths: an ultraefficient and technologically advanced supply chain. What was largely responsible for Walmart's success in the United States has led to its downfall in the Chinese economic environment; the company did not anticipate that scaling up its business model there would present so many problems.

Since 1996, Walmart has opened 400 stores in China, and maintaining a retail footprint this large in a country that is so complex presents numerous logistical challenges. Wal-Mart's struggles highlight the difficulties inherent in transferring a competitive advantage rooted in supply-chain efficiency—that is, logistics—to a country lacking a sophisticated technological and physical infrastructure.

Although China has led the globe in infrastructure investment over the past several years, outside of its largest cities (e.g., Shanghai, Beijing, Tianjin, Guangzhou, and Shenzhen), its infrastructure remains more than problematic.[7] The efficient transport of goods from one region to another is a challenge for Walmart not just because of China's sheer physical size, but also because its air, ground, and rail infrastructure is not up to the company's standards. To date, Walmart has not been able to supply its stores efficiently enough to generate a profit, and its China business has struggled to generate profits for nearly two decades.

Unlike Tesco, IKEA, and AES, which each faced one prominent issue, Walmart in China faced a number of cultural, political, and especially economic obstacles that, combined, have persistently dogged it. As a result, Walmart has consistently underperformed in this huge and potentially lucrative market. Worst of all, had it taken a more tempered approach to China, Walmart's losses could have been avoided.

Failure to Globalize Effectively: Some Common Ground

These high-profile failures reveal corporate misjudgment that is, unfortunately, more the norm than the exception. Globalizing companies habitually underperform in foreign markets, and more often than not, they fail to achieve desired performance targets in global markets. The performance statistics are staggering. Globalizing companies take about three months longer and spend anywhere from 5 to 25 percent more than domestic companies just to get their businesses off the ground. Foreign companies pay higher wages, on average, than their domestic competitors. They are also more likely to get sued than domestic companies and more likely to lose local lawsuits. All of this translates into a higher general cost structure for foreign firms and significantly higher rates of failure for global business expansions compared to domestic business expansions.

Even those companies that are lucky enough to achieve profitability in global markets tend to earn lower returns in their foreign-market operations than in their domestic ones. Starbucks, for example, which has been relatively successful in global markets, has operating margins in Japan—its second-largest market in terms of revenue—that are half those of its US business.[8] Similarly, Lincoln Electric, one of the world's largest and most profitable welding equipment manufacturers, has been making profits in Asia that are only one-third of those in the United States. Its profitability in South America is about half that in the United States.[9]

The global financial crisis has even exposed flaws in the business models of global banks. The banking industry, which has embraced globalization more than other industries, suffers from widespread global mismanagement, fierce local competition, and regulatory challenges that have caused industry-wide global profitability to decline. Studies show that foreign banks tend to achieve lower levels of profitability than similar domestic banks, and large banks such as Citibank and HSBC are no exception. They have significantly eroded profit margins through global expansion. Less formidable global competitors such as ABN-AMRO and Royal Bank of Scotland have been felled by misguided attempts to globalize.[10]

Despite the precedent of these high-profile global failures and struggles, global expansion continues apace. Companies have increased their globalization at a rate far greater than the rate of inflation. The gray line in figure 1.1 illustrates annual corporate global investment (foreign direct investment) flows from 1995 through 2013. Although there have been some notable declines in the wake of the dot-com crash and the global financial crisis, foreign direct investment has almost quadrupled (from $360 billion to

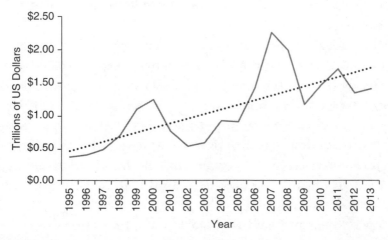

Figure 1.1 Global Corporate Investment.

$1.4 trillion per year). This represents growth of about 389 percent, or 8 percent compound growth on an annualized basis (illustrated by the dashed trend line). That is nearly double the growth rate of global gross domestic product (GDP) over that same time span.[11]

Opening up markets by reducing trade barriers and relaxing investment restrictions has certainly helped to fuel this growth, but ultimately managers are the ones who commit investment dollars to global expansion and are thus responsible for it. These same managers reap what they sow when it comes to global expansion, and it seems they have bought into Thomas Friedman's message that the world is flat. There is one crucial path to success in a flat world: Managers *must* grow their companies into global champions. Unfortunately, this is a flawed thesis, with potentially disastrous consequences.

Reimagining the Globalization Landscape

Thomas Friedman is renowned for claiming that the world is flat, in not one but two best-selling, highly lauded, and widely quoted books—*The World is Flat* (2005) and *Hot, Flat, and Crowded* (2008).[12] Friedman posits that information technology is revolutionary in that all people and countries bear an increasing resemblance; he suggests that borders between countries are becoming increasingly irrelevant. It follows that companies that fail to globalize and capitalize on this convergence trend will be left behind.

While advances in information technology are indeed increasing at a rapid rate, and those advances have certainly facilitated the coordination, connectedness, and efficiency of communications across borders, it does not follow that all peoples and countries will converge so as to become nearly indistinct. Despite what business pundits who exhort globalization would have us believe, important differences between countries remain, and information technology simply does not fully bridge the political, economic, and cultural divides between countries.[13]

Pankaj Ghemawat and Richard Florida, for example, have demonstrated that the world is not as flat as Friedman purports.[14] There is still substantial difference in the world. People are not the same the world over. Countries vary on a host of dimensions, and the ways in which they differ have important implications for how companies ought to globalize and how globalizing businesses will perform. These differences make it incredibly challenging to manage far-flung global corporations.

And therein lies the managerial challenge. It seems that managers of global and globalizing companies have taken Friedman's words to heart, and as a result they are either unsure or unaware of how differences between countries will impact their business. They therefore make dangerous assumptions, underestimating the extent to which such differences are likely to negatively influence the bottom (or top) line, only to learn through a series of costly and painful lessons that the challenges of globalization are real and complex. Building on what research has shown again and again, I reveal a different framework that managers will need if they are to help their firms succeed in expanding across borders and across continents.

Ultimately, institutional factors (political, cultural, and economic) that distinguish countries are at the root of the poor performance of so many global enterprises. In the examples I provide above, AES, IKEA, Tesco, and Walmart all struggled with global expansion, and each faced a unique set of pressures and obstacles specific to the countries in which they operated that impeded their global expansion efforts. Each faced challenges that grew out of differences in institutions between countries. For AES, the problem was political; for IKEA, the issue was also largely political. For Tesco, the challenge was cultural, and Walmart encountered largely economic challenges as well as a combination of other difficulties. Had the managers of each of these firms focused less on the "flatness" of the economic landscape and more on the specific terrain of each market into which they were expanding, these globalization anecdotes would have had much happier—and more profitable—endings. This is not a question of hindsight being 20/20, but rather of well-documented cautionary tales that offer overarching lessons managers have largely ignored.

Institutional Distance: A Key Factor

To improve your understanding of global business, to make better international expansion decisions, and to better manage the complexities inherent in an organization with geographically far-flung operations, you need a more sophisticated understanding of institutions. You need to appreciate how nations differ in institutional makeup, how institutional differences between nations support or impede business practices, and how those differences manifest as increasing risks (and costs). More important, you need to be able to assess the risks so as to account for them in strategic and financial analyses. This book tackles these issues head on to help you improve your "global acumen" and increase the likelihood that your company will thrive in global markets.

I begin with a detailed, research-based examination of how countries differ in critical institutional factors, both formal and informal. I explore how a country's laws, regulations, and political structures lead to behavioral edicts that distinguish between permitted (and not permitted) activity. I explain how economic market structures create patterns of behavior that can either promote or constrain certain types of business activity. Finally, I reveal how cultural institutions such as languages and religions shape social norms, providing a guide for socially acceptable or unacceptable conduct.

As you might expect, it is easier to conduct business in countries that share commonalities in institutional profile. Successful global expansion is more likely in a country that is institutionally similar to your own—where you not only speak the language, but also understand the culture as well as the political and economic environments. Many managers make the mistake of assuming a certain degree of similarity between their firm's home country and host country (the one it seeks to expand to). It is, of course, trickier to conduct business in a country that varies significantly from your own. Managers often find themselves lost in such situations—struggling to understand local norms, customs, and cultural nuances. They make costly and unnecessary mistakes when they misread or misjudge the local cultural, political, and economic environments.

There is a long history of studying institutions and institutional differences in academic circles in the fields of economics, psychology, sociology, and anthropology. The academic literature has even devised terminology to describe institutional differences across countries. We scholars refer to such differences as *institutional distance*. When institutions are similar across countries, institutional distance is small. For example, institutional distance is relatively small between Canada and the United States, between Spain and Mexico, and between the United Kingdom and Australia. (There are obvious cultural, political, and economic similarities that make this seem like common sense.) When institutions differ substantially between countries, institutional distance is great. For example, institutional distance is relatively great between China and the United States, between India and Brazil, and between Indonesia and Spain.

What Is Your Company's Institutional Distance?

If you're a manager or a business owner, think about institutional distance in the context of your own business. What are the factors that make your business a success in your home market? Are these factors similar in other regions to which you seek to expand? Of course, this could apply even to expansion into another town, city, or state or to expansion from a rural market to an urban one or vice versa. But do a thought experiment that begins to break down the institutional (political, cultural, and economic) features of your own home country and consider those features in terms of institutional distance to other countries in which you are considering doing business. The greater the differences between your current context and the context into which you would like to expand, the greater the institutional distance, and the more challenging it will be to expand there.

It should be clear that institutional distance relates to but is not the same as geographic distance. Some countries that are geographically close resemble one another in institutional profile, as with Canada and the United States. However, other countries that are geographically close are not institutionally similar, as with the United States and Mexico. Countries that are geographically distant can be also institutionally close, such as the United States and the United Kingdom. In fact, some pairs of countries are institutionally closer than other pairs that are closer geographically. For example, the United States shares more institutional commonality with the United Kingdom and Australia than it does with Mexico.

Moreover, institutional distance is relative. Institutional proximity by no means guarantees success in global expansion, as the Tesco example illustrates. Tesco hails from the United Kingdom, a country that shares an institutional history with and is institutionally similar in many respects to the United States, and yet Tesco still struggled with cultural differences between the two countries. While it would be far easier for Tesco to operate in the United States than in China, globalizing to an institutionally similar country still requires overcoming numerous institutional obstacles.

Why Managers Are Unfamiliar with Institutional Distance

Institutional distance is not a new concept in academic literature on globalization; we have long understood the challenges institutional distance can pose, and we have made great strides in measuring it. And yet the ways in which we academics have conceptualized institutional distance has been of very little use to managers; we have not developed a good way to convey the toll this distance can take on global and globalizing companies. We academics have done little to help guide managerial practice.

The result of this lack of communication is that managers tend to underestimate the risks of globalization; they focus on the measurable—the top-line growth potential or the headline cost savings associated with globalization—rather than on the potential (and, in fact, likely) downside risks that we know go hand in hand with expansion to institutionally distant countries. That lack of communication ends here.

How This Book Can Help You

Global Vision first helps you gain an appreciation for how countries differ and a solid understanding of the critical institutions underpinning those differences. It then teaches you how to measure those differences—that is, institutional distance—across political, cultural, and economic dimensions. Once you understand institutions and the risks that institutional distance creates for global and globalizing companies, you will understand how to use measures of institutional distance to generate risk spreads (Global Acumen) that help to account for globalization risk. Managers can easily incorporate the outputs of Global Acumen into existing corporate strategy analyses and financial decision models.

Ultimately, using the institutional distance framework this book provides and the Global Acumen risk spreads can help you make better globalization decisions and avoid costly globalization mistakes. Global Acumen will:

- help you appreciate that *differences in political, cultural, and economic institutions are at the root of globalization's challenges;*
- help *guide your globalization decisions* regardless of the country, industry, stage, or size of your business—or even its globalization history;
- help you *make better informed, smarter globalization decisions by taking institutional differences into account;*
- help you *determine which countries it makes sense to enter and which to avoid,* based on institutional profiles and institutional distance;
- provide a means to accurately price globalization risk and *build in safeguards* to help protect against that risk;
- teach you how to *incorporate globalization risk into existing financial decision models* (e.g., financial benchmarking, breakeven analysis, internal rate of return, or discount rate techniques);
- help you *select the appropriate mode of entry into foreign markets;*
- help you determine how to *optimally structure your global operations;*

- help you make better *management and staffing decisions* in ongoing foreign operations;
- help you *think through strategies for global sourcing and supply chains.*

The world of international business is an exciting one with plenty of opportunities. But it is also precarious. Managers need a new set of tools that will empower them to make smart decisions about globalization. Unfortunately, managers run into problems when they use globalization strategies that are simply extensions of their domestic strategy. In order to play the complicated and high-stakes game of global strategy and have any chance at winning, managers need to awaken from this desultory approach. There are facts and data about what it takes to succeed: how to identify, assess, and manage the risks managers will encounter as they globalize. Global Acumen can help unlock the secrets to successful globalization that until now have remained within the walls of academia. *Global Vision* can be your guide. The next chapter begins the journey toward developing the mindset and the tools you need to become "globalization savvy"—allowing you to capitalize on globalization's opportunities while adroitly avoiding its costly and well-documented mistakes.

CHAPTER 2

The Globalization Process

Before we set off on our journey to explore the complexities of globalization, I want to set the stage with a couple of basic concepts that are fundamental to a discussion of how businesses function and how they globalize. This chapter explains my view of globalization in the context of profitability and the role that managers play in that process, given the globalization-related decisions they make on behalf of their companies. The perspective I adopt is not unique to this book but reflects an approach that is shared broadly. However, it is helpful to revisit it here because it is essential to building the framework for globalization that I explore in later chapters.

A Preface on Profits

This book's most basic assumption relates to profitability and the role of managers in generating profits for their companies. I refer to profit, generally, as the financial gains to a business. It is what is left over after a company has collected all of its receipts and paid all of its bills. We can therefore express profit as a residual of its underlying components: revenues and costs. Any profits that exist after a company has subtracted its costs from its revenues rightfully belong to the shareholders (owners) of the corporation.

With that in mind, we can view profit generation as the principal responsibility of managers. As agents and fiduciaries of shareholders, managers are preoccupied with and acutely attuned to how business activities affect revenues, costs, or both. Indeed, many of the decisions managers make are guided by profitability concerns, with a specific focus on increasing revenues or reducing costs.

When it comes to profits, you will notice I refer to "principal" managerial responsibility rather than to "sole" responsibility. I am not suggesting that managers consider *only* the desire of shareholders and always put profits first. Given that managers must balance the demands of various other stakeholders—customers, employees, suppliers, governments, local communities—there will be instances when the interests of two or more of the constituents (i.e., shareholders and other stakeholders) will be in conflict. In fact, there are likely to be times when managers will put the needs of certain stakeholders above the profitability requirement of shareholders. The point is simply that, though stakeholder voices matter, profits are incredibly important to managers, and therefore I focus my discussion of globalization largely on its role in generating profits for companies.

Globalization and Profits

Against this backdrop, the process of globalization generally starts with managers identifying an opportunity to increase profits. At some point, managers recognize that operating globally has the potential to generate additional revenues or lower costs.

Expanding globally allows companies to reach far-flung customers and generate foreign sales. And these days, it seems all the rage to penetrate fast-growing emerging markets, like those in China and India, to reach a vast consumer base. Managers are often lured to China by the potential to reach its more than one billion consumers, and the automobile industry is one such example.

Drawn by China's massive demand-side market potential, foreign automobile manufacturers first entered the Chinese market in 1978, with Volkswagen leading the charge. Other foreign auto manufacturers (GM, Mercedes, BMW, Nissan, Ford, and Toyota) followed suit soon after, piling into China to such an extent that foreign brands now make up more than 50 percent of all new automobiles sold there. In fact, GM has reached record levels of sales in China, selling more cars in China than in the United States.[1]

Managers also identify opportunities to decrease costs via global expansion. For example, companies can shift value-added activities to countries where they can access cheap, abundant labor. Many US companies take advantage of NAFTA tax provisions that allow them to move operations (in the form of maquiladoras) to Mexico, where wage rates are about 20 percent of equivalent rates in the United States.[2] Mattel, one of the largest toy companies in the world, has long operated a maquiladora manufacturing facility near Tijuana.

Similarly, in the textile industry, many large companies source products from countries with low-cost labor, such as China, Indonesia, Thailand, and Vietnam, where they can pay wages that are only a fraction of those they would have to pay in the United States. H&M, a Swedish concern that is one of the largest retailers in the world, outsources more than 60 percent of its production to Asia to keep its input costs down.

Of course, opportunities for revenue enhancement or cost savings are not reserved for large companies. Companies of all types can increase revenues and/or reduce costs via globalization. Logoplaste, for example, a relatively small Portuguese packaging company has been able to lower its operating costs by manufacturing in Eastern Europe. Similarly, the Selkirk Group, a small, family-owned Australian building materials company, has been able to effectively tap into the Japanese export market to increase its overall revenues by 10 percent.

The Impetus for Expansion

Managers come across opportunities to increase sales or decrease costs in a variety of ways. Sometimes an opportunity simply falls into a company's lap. Companies often see demand for their products and services pop up in unexpected places. The kinds of expansion where local customers pull a company into a foreign market are known as "follow-the-customer" globalization strategies. They are fairly typical in the service sector, where retailers, banks, accounting firms, consulting companies, and law firms follow clients from the home country into global markets to serve them there.

Gliding into a Niche: L.L. Bean in Japan

In the late 1980s and early 1990s, when L.L. Bean first started to expand globally, Japan's economy was flourishing, and Japanese citizens were enjoying a surge in personal wealth, with more leisure time and an increased interest in outdoor recreational activities. Tourism from Japan to the United States was at its peak. Japanese consumers exhibited an affinity for L.L. Bean's products, buying not only when they visited the United States, but also over the phone from L.L. Bean's catalog. The company was more than happy to fill orders to Japan, especially given that Japanese customers paid full freight for the goods (absorbing the company's transportation costs) and even agreed to a "no returns/no exchange" policy. By the early 1990s sales to Japan via the catalog accounted for nearly 10 percent of L.L. Bean's overall sales. Ultimately, in 1992, L.L. Bean established physical stores in Japan—a market into which it had not purposely sought to expand—licensing Seiyu and Matsushita to run the Japanese operations. L.L. Bean successfully capitalized on an opportunity that arose suddenly and quite unexpectedly.[3]

There are also cases in which opportunity arises on the cost side of business operations. Managers might not be looking specifically to globalize their supply chain to reduce costs, but sometimes foreign suppliers will approach a company with offers in hand.

Partnering with a Mexican Supplier

The CEO of a large, US-based food ingredient company explained to me how a Mexican producer unexpectedly approached him with an offer to manufacture an ingredient under license in the Mexican company's facilities, an ingredient his firm had been producing in the United States—at a significant cost savings (even after factoring in the additional transportation costs from Mexico to the United States). After several months of negotiations, the US company ultimately decided to cease production of the product domestically and license the manufacture of the product to the Mexican supplier for resale in the United States. Shifting production to Mexico not only lowered the company's overall operating costs, but it freed up the company's manufacturing capacity in the United States such that the company was then able to repurpose its facility to manufacture products that had a higher value-added and were more profitable.

Happenstance notwithstanding, managers more often than not make decisions about globalization proactively and deliberately. Globalization strategies typically are devised by managers who are continually scanning the environment, looking for an opportunity to pounce. Many managers spend a good portion of their time considering opportunities to generate additional sales and/or drive costs down through globalization. They often carry out or commission studies of foreign markets in advance, looking for opportunities to grow the business and streamline operations. They even regularly schedule exploratory fact-finding tours to assess opportunities in global markets. One high-level executive at a large retailer in the United States told me that he tours current and prospective markets at least twice per year, not only to meet with his current suppliers but also to identify new suppliers to source products from in order to reduce operating costs.

This is not to suggest that global tours are exclusively the domain of large, deep-pocketed companies. Even small, family-owned companies, such as the Selkirk Group, use regularly scheduled tours of foreign markets as a strategic tool to generate global business. Selkirk executives typically tour several Asian markets per year to meet with existing (and potential) sales agents and customers as a means to drum up business.

Building Globalization Business Plans

Regardless of how globalization opportunities arise—by chance or by design—global expansion requires careful analysis. Managers must be able to justify the revenue and cost benefits associated with globalization, and they are wise to factor a host of considerations into their calculations. Based on those factors, managers can build a business plan to justify their globalization efforts, comprehensively projecting revenues and costs to assess whether they can profitably globalize. They can express their business plan in financial terms reflecting:

- the duration of the opportunity,
- the projected revenues and operating costs,
- the investment costs,
- the residual value of the business (should the company decide to sell the business),
- the exchange-rate considerations (should the company do business in a foreign currency),
- the tax implications (associated with tax policies in both the home country and the host country),
- the overall profitability associated with the opportunity.

"Newlandia": A Concrete Example

We can put this all together in the form of a concrete example to consider how a typical financial analysis influences managers' decisions to expand globally. You might explore these ideas if you were taking a class on global strategy or international corporate finance, and I am providing them here so we are working from the same foundation. Though simplified in nature, these considerations are not too far removed from those that managers use in their real world financial models. And this will serve you well in subsequent chapters, where I revisit the example to illustrate certain principles and dynamics of globalization. As an added benefit, you can compare the approach adopted in this example to the one your company typically takes in managing its globalization efforts.

Let us consider a fictitious (but representative) example: global expansion for a US-based company into a country I call "Newlandia."

Consistent with the case in which managers proactively seek opportunities in new markets, the company's managers believe that there is an opportunity to increase revenues (and, ultimately, profitability) by selling to a new set of customers in Newlandia.

Initial Assumptions

For the sake of simplicity, this example contains several assumptions, namely, the following:

1. The business opportunity in Newlandia exists for five years.
2. The company can generate a $1,000 in constant revenues per year.
3. The company has constant operating costs of $800 per year.
4. There are no investment costs (i.e., the company can start up its operations in Newlandia for free).
5. There is also no residual value for the business (i.e., at the end of the five-year period the opportunity disappears and the company cannot sell the business for additional monies).
6. The company will conduct business in Newlandia in US dollars (i.e., there is no currency risk).[4]
7. There are no taxes.

Table 2.1 reflects the overall financial implications for the Newlandia business plan, expressed in the form of a standard income statement. Assuming all the revenues and costs in the table are the only ones associated with the company's global expansion plan and that these are absolutely certain, this investment seems like a no-brainer. Just about every manager would be willing to move forward with the Newlandia opportunity, as it generates a return of 20 percent ($200/$1,000) per year. Anyone making even basic investments would agree that 20 percent is an excellent return, far outpacing what could reasonably be expected in the US stock market

Table 2.1 Business Projections for Newlandia

	Year 1	Year 2	Year 3	Year 4	Year 5
Revenues	$1,000	$1,000	$1,000	$1,000	$1,000
Costs	$800	$800	$800	$800	$800
Profit	$200	$200	$200	$200	$200

(which has traditionally fallen in the 7–9% range). And in this theoretical example the return comes with zero risk, because we know all the costs and revenues with certainty.

Introducing More Real-World Factors

Given that the world is much more complicated than this simple model, let's add a tinge of complexity: start-up costs and the time value of money. This makes it possible to compare our profits from globalization into Newlandia to those we could reasonably expect if we invested the company's money otherwise.

The modified example in table 2.2 assumes a $550 investment in Newlandia.[5] (After all, if we want to manufacture products, we would need to buy [or rent] land, build a factory, purchase equipment, etc.) Once we factor in these start-up investment costs, it is not immediately clear that Newlandia presents a good business investment. We must assess whether it makes sense to invest $550 today (in year zero) for $200 in profits over each of the next five years.

To answer that question in a fiscally prudent way—one that would satisfy most managers and shareholders—we need to think about alternative ways in which we could invest those $550, and the likely returns that amount would generate. We could, for example, invest the $550 in the stock market (with nearly a 7–9% historical return) or give the $550 to our shareholders in the form of dividends—it is their money, after all—and let them invest it as they see fit.

To determine whether the Newlandia opportunity provides shareholders adequate benefit in exchange for the initial investment, we should discount the cash flows associated with the investment

Table 2.2 Business Projections for Newlandia: Assuming an Upfront Investment

	Year 0	Year 1	Year 2	Year 3	Year 4	Year 5
Revenues		$1,000	$1,000	$1,000	$1,000	$1,000
Costs		$800	$800	$800	$800	$800
Initial Costs	$550					
Profit	–$550	$200	$200	$200	$200	$200

(factoring in the time value of money, recognizing that $1 today is not the same as $1 tomorrow). We will discount the future profits associated with the Newlandia investment so that they are faithfully reflected in terms of present-day cash values in order to make an apples-to-apples comparison with the initial investment. The interest rate we will use to discount the cash flows will be the one we could earn otherwise if we had used the amount dedicated to Newlandia for an alternative purpose. We can then add the discounted inflows of cash (the future profits) to the outflows of cash (the initial investment) to determine the net present value (NPV) of the Newlandia opportunity.

Table 2.3 reflects a scenario that assumes an opportunity cost of capital of 8.5 percent based on the capital asset pricing model (CAPM), where the 8.5 percent represents the long-run average interest rate (more or less) of investing in the stock market, and therefore an appropriate benchmark for the rate of return for a company with average riskiness.[6] In other words, the 8.5 percent discount rate assumes that if we did not invest in Newlandia, we (or the shareholders who would receive a dividend in the form of cash) could alternatively invest that $550 in an investment with a level of risk similar to that in the stock market—one that generates about 8.5 percent compound interest per year.

Table 2.3 implies that the discounted cash flow associated with the year 1 profit of $200 is equivalent to $184 expressed in terms of today's present value dollars ($200/1.085). That is to say, if I invested $184 in the stock market today, I would expect—assuming an 8.5 percent historical return on investment—for it to yield about $200 by this time next year. Similarly, the $200 profit from year 2

Table 2.3 Business Projections for Newlandia: Assuming an 8.5% Discount Rate

	Year 0	Year 1	Year 2	Year 3	Year 4	Year 5
Revenues		$1,000	$1,000	$1,000	$1,000	$1,000
Costs		$800	$800	$800	$800	$800
Initial Costs	$550					
Profit	−$550	$200	$200	$200	$200	$200
Present Value	−$550	$184	$170	$157	$144	$133
Overall NPV	$238					

would be worth only $170 today ($200/(1.085)^2). That is, if I were to invest $170 today at 8.5 percent compound interest for two years, I should expect to have $200 two years hence. And so on.[7]

Based on these calculations—adding all of the present values of the future cash flows and subtracting the initial investment—the Newlandia opportunity generates a positive net present value that exceeds the initial investment by $238 (where the NPV equals the total across discounted cash flows for years 1 through 5 [$184 + $170 + $157 + $144 + $133] minus the initial investment cost in year 0 [$550]). This reveals that the total future discounted profits from investing in Newlandia are greater than the opportunity cost alternative of investing the $550 in the stock market. Given this, the manager is wise to invest in Newlandia on behalf of the company.

Real-World Complexity

The Newlandia example can be helpful in thinking through the impact of globalization on profitability. Companies typically use some variant of the modeling technique I describe above to evaluate global business opportunities. However, real-world complexity often creeps into the model because Newlandia—or its real-world equivalent—is likely to be very different from the United States. Its government and legal systems, laws and regulations, economic system, and culture are all likely to be different from those in the United States. If we relax some of the simplifying assumptions from the tables above to account for some of these differences, we can begin to examine how the latter impact the financial projections.

Revenues

Let's start with revenues. One key question revolves around the confidence with which managers can project revenues. For example, how sure can managers be that customers in Newlandia will like the products the company sells? Will the product or service suit local tastes?

Years ago, I consulted for a company in Mexico that was attempting to import fudge from the United States to the Mexican market. The company had a plan for how to sell the fudge and developed detailed financial projections accordingly, but as the firm began to sell the product, the consumers did not react well to the taste; they said the fudge was too sweet. Sales ended up being way off from the projections, failing to meet revenue targets, and failing to generate profits. As a result, the company stopped selling the product in Mexico, ultimately losing money on that product line.

Given that managers often know significantly less about the foreign country to which they wish to expand than they do about their home country, it is far more difficult to know how foreign customers will react to new products and how industry dynamics will play out in the host country and how competitors will react to market entry. Critical factors therefore extend beyond the product's compatibility with the local culture to whether the company can sell its products in the same way, through the same sales channels, and with the same level of success as in its domestic market.

Industry norms in the host country could differ such that the company's standard approach for reaching customers might not be an option. In India, for example, Apple does not sell iPhones through its familiar Apple stores, but rather, through resellers. An inability to reach customers through sales channels with which the company is familiar can certainly add uncertainty to revenue projections. Similarly, should local competitors significantly reduce prices in the face of foreign competition, it could be more difficult to meet revenue projections. A variety of factors therefore make accurately projecting revenues a challenge.

Costs

The same issues apply to the cost side of the equation; unforeseen costs can cut into profitability. It could be that start-up costs are greater than expected. For example, when we build our plant, it is likely to be hard to identify an appropriate location, to determine a fair price for the real estate, and to select contractors best suited to build it.

Similarly, it is a difficult to identify the "right" people (expats or managers hired locally) to run the business and determine the appropriate amount to pay those people. We can easily calculate how much labor costs in a particular location, based on average hourly wages and salaries, and factor them into any model; however, it is much more challenging to ensure that the productivity of those employees will match their cost. For these and other reasons, it is likely that despite our best intentions, our cost projections will be imprecise.

Discount Rate

There are similar important questions to ask about the appropriate cost of capital, such as why 8.5 percent would be the right discount rate to use in Newlandia. The 8.5 percent rate is one that is more characteristic of a US context, and so it is appropriate to ask whether an investment in Newlandia would be equally risky as an investment in the US stock market. A more appropriate cost of capital for discounting purposes might reflect the company's actual/historical cost of capital—the cost at which the company can finance (or has financed) projects. We can determine this alternative cost of capital by using a weighted average cost of capital (WACC) based on the company's cost of debt plus its cost of equity. Alternatively, we could turn to some historical internal rate of return (IRR) hurdle to discount cash flows.

Unfortunately, the alternative discount rates (WACC or IRR) are likely to suffer shortcomings similar to rates we could generate using CAPM approaches. This is because IRR and WACC rates are generally skewed to the company's historical domestic market activity, and so it is unclear that we can apply them effectively to global projects. In concrete terms, because operating in Newlandia is likely to present much more risk to the company than operating in the United States, WACC, IRR, and CAPM approaches are likely to underestimate the various risks the company will face. For this reason, these approaches are not appropriate for use in Newlandia.

The Bottom Line

It is by no means easy to quantify risks to revenue and cost projections in the United States, but it is certainly easier to quantify those risks in our home country than in Newlandia. As outsiders in Newlandia, we are at an informational disadvantage compared to local companies. Our projections are therefore messier and our business riskier than if we were simply considering a new business opportunity in the United States. Newlandia poses unique risks that we, as outsiders, cannot fully appreciate, and therefore we cannot appropriately quantify them in terms of revenue and costs.

Financial theory tells us that if we know Newlandia is different from the United States, we can factor those differences into our revenue and cost projections. However, this is where the problem lies. We live in an uncertain world. It is incredibly difficult to specify how Newlandia is different so as to translate those differences into revenue and cost equivalents. And it is next to impossible to adjust projections when we are unsure of the possible contingencies. For example, how can we adjust projected revenues in situations where

- the government in Newlandia is unstable;
- local laws and rules put foreigners at a disadvantage compared to local companies;
- Newlandia is characterized by extreme economic volatility—rampant inflation, currency instability, recession;
- Newlandia's culture is significantly different from that in our home country?

Factors such as these complicate the use of financial models for the evaluation of global expansion. Risk and uncertainty can complicate the best globalization plans, even in markets we think we understand relatively well.

Keeping It Real: Personal Experience with Country Differences

I spent the 2014–15 academic year on sabbatical in Madrid, Spain. I know the country fairly well. My father is from Spain; I have close family living in Madrid; I have spent extended periods of time in Spain; I am fluent in Spanish; and I even have a solid understanding of Spanish politics, economics, and culture. Despite those advantages, there were some surprises that caught me off-guard and that made it difficult for me to adapt to life in Spain.

Initially, it was challenging for me to establish residency. I paid an immediate visit to an office of the Ministry of Exterior to present documentation registering myself as a foreigner living in Spain. I waited in line for several hours, only to discover (when I reached the front of the line) that I had gone to the wrong office for my type of visa. After locating the appropriate office, my next attempt to register with the Ministry of Exterior was thwarted because the documents I had brought had not been formatted properly for the Spanish authorities. I finally broke down after several failed attempts and hired a lawyer to help me through what turned out to be a rather involved residency process.

Due to my inability to properly register as foreigner living in Spain, I lacked the appropriate documentation to open a local bank account. This made it inordinately difficult to procure even the most basic services, because providers of electric, water, gas, mobile phone, fixed-line telephone, television, and Internet services require a local bank account to establish a customer account. This delayed my integration into the Spanish economy.

Finally, although I am familiar with Spain's culture, the cultural significance of vacation, and the tendency of Spaniards to take vacation during the month of August, I misjudged just how difficult it would be to get things done by planning my move to Madrid for August. Even after I provisionally registered myself as a foreigner living in Spain and successfully opened a local bank account, it was impossible to schedule appointments in August to connect in-home utility services. Nearly all of the technicians were away on vacation, and there was a substantial waiting list for prospective customers. Indeed, my cable television was not connected until October, two months after I had arrived in Spain.

These are but a few of the political, economic, and cultural complications that cost me time as well as money. The residency process was burdensome. The legal fees put a significant dent in my budget. The daily hiccups, even the minor ones, caused frustration. In the end, the startup costs were much greater than anticipated and impeded my productivity—making progress with this book.

The costs detailed above might seem minor in the grand scheme of life, but they add up. And they are not all that unlike those that companies face when they expand globally. Political, economic, and cultural differences can create serious, often unanticipated obstacles, even in countries in which a company has some experience.

Building an Alternative Approach to Globalization

It is inordinately difficult to specify how risks in global markets will affect revenue and cost projections. So we must come up with an alternative approach that better approximates the risks. Unfortunately, managers continue to rely on the corporate finance techniques described above when evaluating global business opportunities. When asked, they readily admit that they adopt CAPM, WACC, and IRR discount rates that are oriented toward their home country and specific to their own company. In essence, they make the mistake of evaluating the profitability of their global businesses against domestic benchmarks. If a company typically earns returns of 8.5 percent domestically, then managers are likely to consider an 8.5 percent return in global markets to be adequate. Managers often recognize that global markets pose greater risks, but they turn to familiar models because they lack the tools to properly gauge those risks.

Managers have been relying on techniques their predecessors built for domestic business activities, and using those techniques to make decisions about globalization has led managers astray. The domestically oriented approaches described above are myopic at best and ruinous at worst. They simply do not attach an appropriate level of risk to the foreign market, which makes companies operating in foreign markets vulnerable to risk. This is the primary reason that global operations underperform and that global expansions have a much higher failure rate than domestic expansions. My task here is to provide managers with an alternative strategy.

We have established that we might not be able to estimate revenues or costs that reflect the true levels of uncertainty global markets impose. However, we can adjust the cost of capital we use for discounting purposes—that is, adjust our discount rate to reflect more accurately the risks we are undertaking. This would serve us well in the Newlandia example—and, frankly, in all cases.

We could follow an approach typically used in project finance for large-scale, capital-intensive infrastructure and public works projects (such as bridges or electricity plants) in developing countries. In evaluating the financial viability of these kinds of projects in developing countries, the discount rate applied typically reflects the institutional risks in the country in which the project is undertaken. I will follow that approach, incorporating underlying country-specific institutional risk factors into existing domestic discount rate techniques.

Bringing It All Together

Throughout this book I argue that managers can make successful, profitable globalization decisions on behalf of their company when they account for the institutional risks specific to the country (or countries) where they seek to expand. The few examples I have shown reflect that, when managers overlook the institutional—political, cultural, and economic—risks that go hand in hand with globalization, they set themselves up for failure. Accounting for the risks present in foreign markets makes it possible to adjust the cost of capital accordingly and to discount the company's cash flows more accurately. This results in more precise projections and better guidelines for managers seeking to decide where and how to globalize. Approaching globalization in this way represents a fundamental shift that will serve managers—and the shareholders they serve—very well.

The first step, of course, lies in understanding the institutions that underpin globalization's risks, and so in subsequent chapters I highlight the importance of institutions, institutional distance, and institutional risk. Essential to this discussion are the political, economic, and cultural elements of the global business environment that are at the root of institutional risk. Only then do I introduce my own approach to accounting for institutional risk: Global Acumen, a tool I developed to structure and streamline this process. We will revisit the Newlandia example using this more effective approach, and you will come to see the advantages of Global Acumen and how it plays out in several different globalization scenarios.

CHAPTER 3

The Impact of National Institutions on Globalization

Tthere are many factors that influence the likelihood of success in global markets, but a critical first step in successfully navigating the global landscape is to understand the unique factors that make globalization so complex and challenging. As I described in chapter 2, managers ordinarily make a case for globalization by building financial models: generating detailed projections for revenues, costs, and profitability. However, most globalization analyses lack a thorough evaluation of how the institutional environments in the host country and the home country differ, and managers often do not sufficiently consider the risks those differences are likely to present to profitability projections. This chapter starts to unpack the institutional factors that should inform that kind of risk analysis.

The preceding chapter touched on the many ways global business differs from domestic business. The two are so different that we cannot evaluate global projects merely on the basis of the financial techniques described in chapter 2 because they were designed for domestic business opportunities. We can only extend those techniques to global settings with significant modification to account for fundamental differences in institutional environments—political, cultural, and economic—in different countries.[1]

The most egregious mistakes managers make in global markets are not a result of misreading opportunities to increase revenues or decrease costs, but of applying domestic financial models without repurposing them to account for globalization's institutional risks. Managers must examine the role of institutions, institutional differences, and the institutional risks they generate to determine how all these are likely to influence financial projections.

Why National Institutions Matter

Fully appreciating globalization risks requires a sophisticated understanding of national institutions and will ultimately make it possible to account for their impact on profitability. Borrowing from Douglass North, I define institutions as "humanly devised constraints that structure political, economic, and social interaction... [and] provide the incentive structure of an economy."[2] This means that we can view any country as comprised of a unique collection of underlying institutions.

National institutions can be formal or informal. Formal institutions are those that govern behavior in a society. They typically shape behavior through laws, decrees, and edicts that demarcate boundaries separating permissible from impermissible activities. In addition to creating, amending, and abolishing explicit rules, formal institutions are also responsible for enforcing them. Structural entities that make up the formal institutional environment include governments, political parties, legal bodies, law enforcement and military organizations, and regulatory agencies.

Informal institutions, in contrast, do not shape or explicitly prescribe behavior and activity; instead, they sanction activity through a series of unwritten, tacit rules that evolve in a society. Informal institutions impose order through social conventions—by condoning and even rewarding certain behaviors and discouraging or ostracizing those who engage in others. Individuals in a society often internalize informal rules that embody its social norms, beliefs, and values, and they generally teach them to the next generation as a part of a broader socialization process. Academics typically refer to informal institutions of this sort as culture.

Whether members of a society create its institutions by design or they evolve historically without intention, they differ from country to country and sometimes markedly so. The United States and India, for example, have political institutions that resemble one another. Why? Because they share a common colonizer—England—that played a critical role in developing the institutions of both countries. And yet, although their political institutions are similar, their cultures are very different in religious makeup, philosophical leanings, familial structure, and demographic composition. Japan and China, by contrast, share cultural similarities that date back centuries, because Japan imported a system of philosophical and cultural ideals from China. However, culture is largely where the similarity ends; the two countries differ significantly in their political and economic institutions.

It should be obvious that institutional differences across countries can obstruct companies seeking to operate globally. Foreign companies are generally unfamiliar with the local institutional environment; they don't know the laws, the rules, or the customs; they cannot fully appreciate how the local economy works; they lack ties to powerful and well-connected local individuals and organizations that can act on their behalf; and they cannot rely on an established set of suppliers with which they have been working for years. Even the customers are new to foreign companies.

The institutional differences between countries are often so pronounced that one of the most celebrated findings in global strategy demonstrates that foreign companies face significant disadvantages compared to domestic companies. Typically, it takes foreign companies longer to set up their operations, and they often have a higher cost structure; they also generally experience more run-ins with the law. Ultimately, the profitability of global companies suffers. They perform worse and exhibit a higher rate of failure than similar domestic competitors. This disadvantage born out of institutional differences is known as the "liability of foreignness."[3]

China provides the setting for a classic cautionary tale about globalization. Given a population of more than 1.3 billion people and the market potential that goes hand in hand with a consumer base of that size, the prospect of expanding to China is enough to make any manager's eyes light up. The potential is seemingly limitless, but on further inspection, it becomes clear that China poses tremendous challenges for Western companies.

The first obstacle is economic. Though China has made tremendous strides and enjoyed incredible technological progress since opening its markets to global trade and investment in 1979, the development of its economic institutions and its infrastructure has lagged behind that in the West. Chinese financial markets are in their infancy, and physical infrastructure is not yet up to Western standards. The infrastructure cannot yet fully support a distribution system that encompasses all corners of China's vast territory, and the country remains a complicated place to conduct market-based transactions.

A second obstacle stems from cultural differences. Chinese consumers do not share many of the tastes and preferences of consumers from the West, which makes it difficult for Western companies to appeal to local consumers there. Moreover, in business, the Chinese rely more on interpersonal connections and relationships to get things done than their Western counterparts. Western managers are unaccustomed to such a relationship-based system, and the managers with whom I interact often complain that it takes much longer than expected to establish trusting business relationships in China. This lack of local connections can create serious impediments to business success.

A third obstacle grows out of China's political institutions. Western companies struggle to skillfully navigate China's political environment. It is often unclear to Western managers when and under what circumstances local governments and agencies have authority over business transactions as opposed to regional and/or national ones. This creates confusion that can result in delays and, in the extreme, costly run-ins with China's complex web of authorities. Moreover, as in most countries, China's rules and laws tend to favor the home team. China's government tends not to roll out the welcome mat for foreign companies but to treat foreign companies skeptically, as a potential threat to incumbent domestic companies or even to national security and sovereignty.

For many Western companies it has proven not only difficult but costly to capitalize on the seemingly vast opportunities and sell to China's consumer market effectively. In addition to the Walmart example I provide in chapter 1, large companies such as Amazon,

Apple, eBay, Google, GlaxoSmithKline, L'Oréal, and Tesco have found it difficult to gain a foothold in the market. Several, including Best Buy and Home Depot, have failed outright and have abandoned the Chinese market altogether.

We frequently hear that Chinese consumers have a particular affinity for Western luxury brands such as LVMH, Richemant, Kering, and Tiffany; however, even these companies have a rough time there. A high-level (C-suite) executive with one of the most respected luxury brands in the world told me not to believe the China hype. She said that most luxury brands have a presence in China merely because they feel they have to and not because it is profitable. To quote G.E's CEO Jeff Immelt: "China is big, but it is hard."[4]

It does not seem all that difficult for companies to increase their revenues by entering China. It is, after all, an enormous country, and all it really takes to increase revenues is one sale to a Chinese customer. But it is important to remember that increased revenues do not mean increased profits. And in China, as with any global market, the opportunities to increase revenues are fraught with risk—they come at a cost. To successfully navigate this challenging global terrain, managers need to get beyond seductive opportunities to increase revenues and come to understand the institutional risks that threaten to undermine the profitability of their business.

Keeping It Real: How Individuals Experience the Liability of Foreignness

The liability of foreignness afflicting foreign companies with little international experience is not unlike the challenges that immigrants face when they arrive in a new country. When they first arrive, they often find themselves at a loss, unfamiliar with the institutional features of their newly adopted country. Frequently, they do not speak the language or at least not well; they find it difficult to find their way around; they don't know the rules and the laws; they may not be familiar with the social customs; and they do not have ready access to a network of people to lean on for information and help when the going gets tough.

You may relate to this phenomenon on an individual level. When my father, who is originally from Spain and lived for some time in Cuba, first arrived in the United States in 1960, at age 32, he was, not surprisingly, overwhelmed. He spoke no English; he had little money; he knew practically nobody; and he had no place to live. Every day was a struggle for him. Although he is extremely well educated, it took him an inordinate amount of time to accomplish even the simplest of tasks, such as going shopping, that many of us take for granted. Once he was able to take care of his immediate needs and get settled into his new life, it still took him quite a bit of time to successfully navigate the culture, the laws, and the economy of the United States. His story, of course, has a happy ending, but it certainly was not smooth sailing, especially in the first few years.

These experiences should also resonate for anybody who has spent considerable time in another country, whether as a traveler or a resident. Those of us who have traveled to a country whose language we did not speak probably took a bit of time to figure out where to go and how to get there. Locals can figure it out much more quickly because they read the signs and can easily ask for help in the native language. They are also familiar with the local cultural, political, and economic environments.

Regardless of the specific situation, the cards are generally stacked against foreigners. As soon as they arrive, they discover that they are at a disadvantage compared to native inhabitants, precisely because they lack familiarity with the local political, cultural, and economic environments.

The Danger of "Seeing" Successful Globalization Everywhere

Just because companies are at a disadvantage in foreign markets does not mean that failure is inevitable. As you are doubtlessly aware, there are plenty of companies that do succeed in global markets in spite of the liability of foreignness: Apple, Coca-Cola, Goldman Sachs, IKEA, Microsoft, McDonald's, Samsung, Toyota, and Volkswagen, to name but a few. But don't be fooled by those global champions that readily come to mind. Just because it is fairly easy to think of companies, household names even, that globalization has served well does not mean that all or even most companies that have tried have been or can be successful globally. Rather, these companies listed above have specific qualities that are particularly well suited to globalization.

It would be dangerous to assume from a handful of ubiquitous global brands that profiting from globalization is fairly easy and straightforward or that all companies are or should be globalizing. Nonetheless, people easily make these assumptions when they fall prey to a bias social scientists refer to as an "availability heuristic." This mental shortcut causes us to overestimate the frequency of certain events because they come to mind more readily. For example, people tend to recall more easily certain causes of death—"newsworthy" events such as plane crashes and shark attacks—because the press tends to highlight and sensationalize these events more than deaths from natural causes. We therefore tend to believe they are more likely and overestimate their frequency relative to other causes of death, such as automobile accidents. It might be easy to generate a list of large and successful global companies based on what you hear and read, but the truth is that the Apples and Coca-Colas of the world are the exceptions, not the rule.

It Takes an Intangible (or Two or Three)

If foreign companies are generally at a disadvantage compared to domestic companies, then there must be specific factors that enable certain multinational companies to succeed where others fail. Research demonstrates that, indeed, successful global companies tend to have competitive advantages in the form of intangible assets: technological, marketing, and managerial capabilities that domestic competitors cannot match or easily imitate. These capabilities allow companies to overcome the liability of foreignness and earn profits in global markets.

Coca-Cola, for example, relies on its marketing prowess—its incredibly valuable and highly recognizable brand—to succeed in global markets. Companies such as Apple and Google rely on "killer" technologies that are far superior to those of their rivals. Even for companies seemingly as diverse as Goldman Sachs and IKEA, we can attribute their global success in large part to superior management capabilities and management systems. Goldman Sachs has learned to manage its investment banking business better than its competitors, hiring clever people and training them effectively in the "Goldman Sachs Way" so as to leverage valuable client relationships all over the world. Similarly, IKEA's management has organized the company in largely unparalleled ways, coupling simplicity and clever design with stores that have a consistent customer experience and layout. Each location may not offer the exact same selection of products, but customers who walk into any IKEA will find familiar offerings, a four-leaf clover layout, and the (now familiar) cash-and-carry concept.

The most successful global companies typically do not rely on only one valuable intangible asset—whether technology, marketing, or management—but exhibit strength in several of these areas. For example:

- Coca-Cola, widely recognized as one of the most valuable brands in the world, is not just about branding. It possesses other marketing strengths, including a deep understanding of sales channels, close relationships with customers, and a far-reaching distribution network. Coca-Cola even possesses valuable "technology" embodied in the secret formula that is critical to its flagship product.
- Apple's success stems not only from its stable of superior technologies—its phones, tablets, computers, operating systems, and other products—but also from a powerful brand and marketing skills. You have probably observed that it is one of the world's most valuable brands and a venerable marketing force.

- Powerful brand names and strong marketing have helped to complement and reinforce the management intangibles of IKEA and Goldman Sachs. In addition, IKEA boasts technological capabilities in furniture design, and Goldman develops and exploits proprietary technologies that its rivals struggle to match.

Keeping It Real: How Individuals Overcome the Liability of Foreignness

Just as with companies, individuals can use intangible assets—skills, capabilities, ingenuity—to help overcome the disadvantages they face in foreign countries. Immigrants can lean on specific skills to help soften the impact of the liability of foreignness. In the case of my father, he had a specific set of professional skills that were extremely valuable at the time he arrived in the United States.

My father is an agricultural and chemical engineer by training. He worked in the sugar industry for nearly 10 years before he left Cuba for the United States in 1960. Prior to 1959, and as a result of the Sugar Act of 1948, the United States regularly imported 700,000 tons of sugar per year from Cuba. After the Cuban revolution in which Fidel Castro became head of the Cuban government, relations between the United States and Cuba quickly soured. Beginning in 1960, the United States instituted an embargo on the trade of all goods and services with Cuba, jettisoning its agreement to import sugar. This created the prospect of sugar shortages in the United States.

Though my father spoke no English, and based purely on his skill set and experience, the US government deemed his expertise in sugar of "strategic" importance to the country's economic and political interests. He was therefore given the opportunity to legally remain in the United States, and he quickly found work in the US sugar industry.

This is not to say that the transition to the United States was easy for my father. He faced numerous challenges in adjusting to the institutional—political, cultural, and economic—environment. His intangibles, however, and the good fortune he had with the timing of his arrival certainly made the transition easier.

The Limits to Intangibles: Institutional Distance

Even for companies like those I describe above, which have painstakingly developed valuable technological, marketing, and management intangibles to overcome disadvantages in global markets, there are limits. Strong technological, marketing, and management intangibles neither guarantee a company's success in global markets nor imply that it will succeed in all countries. IKEA has performed well, generally, in global markets, but it has struggled in Russia. Although Apple and Google have done very well in many global markets, they both struggle for market share and profitability in China.

What matters critically to globalization success, and what most globalization analyses fail to address, is the so-called institutional distance between countries—the similarity (or dissimilarity) between the institutional environments of a company's home country and its intended host country. Success is not as simple as determining *if* a company possess valuable intangibles; it is important to know *whether* those intangibles are appropriate to the host country.

As you might expect, the greater the institutional distance between countries, the more inhospitable the host country is likely to be, and the more difficult it will be for companies to extend their intangibles there. Research demonstrates that

- greater levels of institutional distance present greater liabilities of foreignness and greater levels of globalization risk;
- the greater the institutional distance between a specific home country and a specific host country, the more challenging and more risky it is for companies to do business in a particular host country.

It is therefore paramount for managers to understand institutional distance in order to evaluate the viability of global expansion plans and appraise ongoing global operations.

Institutional Distance: A Primer

Think of institutional distance as a composite measure of the individual differences in political, economic, and cultural institutions between any pair of countries.[5] We measure this distance by:

1. quantifying institutions in the home country and in the host country,
2. creating country-specific institutional profiles,
3. comparing those institutional profiles across countries,
4. collapsing the profiles into one overarching measure of institutional distance by calculating a mathematical distance between them.[6]

Measures of institutional distance for a pair of countries indicate how far one country is from another in terms of its institutional makeup. For managers, institutional distance can be used as an indicator of the relative attractiveness of doing business in a particular country, the trade-offs among various strategies a company may use to enter a foreign market, how it should manage its foreign subsidiaries, and ultimately the likelihood that it will survive and thrive in foreign markets.

A company like IKEA, which has largely performed admirably in global markets, demonstrates an interesting phenomenon. IKEA first expanded globally in the 1960s and 1970s to European countries such as Norway, Denmark, Switzerland, and Germany, all of which are institutionally similar to Sweden. It was easier for IKEA to transfer its intangible assets to those markets and establish itself there. And yet, as I mentioned in chapter 1, IKEA has struggled to find its way in Russia.

IKEA was initially hesitant to enter the retail market in Russia because its managers felt there was a tremendous amount of risk involved in doing business there. There is a greater level of institutional distance between Russia and Sweden than between Sweden and its neighboring European countries. The higher levels of institutional distance between Russia and Sweden makes it more difficult for IKEA to conduct business in Russia the way it does in Sweden, Norway, Denmark, Switzerland, and Germany. For example, the company recently announced that it would no longer publish its promotional lifestyle magazine in Russia so as not to run afoul of Russia's gay propaganda laws.[7] And so in addition to struggling with corruption and graft as explained in chapter 1, IKEA encountered a host of obstacles in the Russian market that significantly hamper its ability to run a lean and efficient organization, effectively market to local customers, and ultimately earn acceptable levels of profitability.

More generally, and perhaps not surprisingly, IKEA performs better in global markets that are more institutionally similar to its native Sweden (such as Denmark, Norway, and Germany), and it performs worse in global markets that are more institutionally distant from Sweden (such as Russia). The lesson is simple: Companies typically have an easier time adjusting to foreign countries that are more institutionally similar to their own, and they are more likely to achieve profitability targets in those countries.

Understanding institutional distance is not exclusively the domain of large companies like IKEA. It is especially critical to small companies as well—perhaps even more so. Large, well-funded companies can often afford to shrug off global market failures. Global market failures may dent the egos of the managers who led the charge, as it is never fun to have to leave a market with your tail between your legs having risked—and squandered—the resources of your shareholders. But this kind of mistake often does not break the bank at a large firm. Small firms, by contrast, simply cannot afford to make these kinds of mistakes in global markets—a single one can be ruinous. It can therefore be instructive to examine the globalization approach adopted by a small company.

Logoplaste is a small, family-owned Portuguese company that manufactures plastic bottles and containers for the soft drink and consumer goods industries. As it began to grow and thrive in the domestic packaging industry, reaching the equivalent of €25 million in revenues in 1992, the company spotted opportunities to leverage technological advantages it had developed at home in foreign markets. As it sought to expand, it minimized its liability of foreignness at first by turning to markets that were institutionally similar to Portugal. Some of its earliest expansions were into Spain and Brazil, which share obvious cultural and political institutional similarities with Portugal.

As Logoplaste experienced early success with global expansion in institutionally similar markets, it began to expand into global markets that were a bit further afield, only to struggle in those institutionally distant global markets. Logoplaste entered the Malaysian market in 2009, following one of its longtime customers: Proctor & Gamble. Logoplaste's Malaysian operation immediately encountered difficulties. Logoplaste had a tough time with the startup phase, investing more than it had anticipated to identify, hire, and train local Malaysian employees to its exacting standards. In addition, senior executives in Portugal experienced difficulty interacting with and managing the company's local Malaysian workforce. These struggles hit the bottom line, as Logoplaste has yet to earn profits in Malaysia.[8]

Logoplaste discovered the hard way that business gets trickier as a company ventures farther from countries with more familiar institutional environments into those in which the institutional environment is significantly different from that in the company's home country. Moreover, given its size, Logoplaste must manage its Malaysian operations carefully, lest its troubles drag down its domestic operations. Of course, that's easier said than done.

Bringing It All Together

We are building a comprehensive list of factors to help managers understand globalization and the likelihood of success in global markets:

1. the *opportunities* to increase revenues and/or decrease costs;
2. the *capabilities* that companies bring to the table, relative to competitors, that will allow them to capitalize on the revenue-and/or cost-based opportunities; and
3. the *institutional distance* between the home market and a prospective host market.

The business literature provides a fairly straightforward understanding of the first two factors, and managers are accustomed to building them into their strategic and financial analyses. The third—institutional distance—is more challenging, and managers do not understand it as well as they should. However, if we understand and can measure the individual institutions of countries, we are in a position to calculate institutional distances between the home country and any potential host country. This is especially important because institutional distance underpins the liability of foreignness, and it therefore forms the basis for estimating the risks associated with globalization.

As I have mentioned before, institutional distance is not a new concept. Globalization scholars have long pointed to national institutions and institutional distance as fundamental to the understanding of global business. We scholars have devoted decades to understanding and measuring national institutions and institutional distance. We have identified the key institutions of a country, developed and validated measures, and used those measures to calculate institutional distances between countries. And still, we have yet to use this knowledge to create a measure or metric of risk that managers can incorporate into financial models. We have failed managers—a constituency that should be one of the main beneficiaries of our work. This book is an attempt to correct that deficiency.

The next several chapters address political, cultural, and economic institutions and discuss:

- how the academic literature measures them,
- which of those measures have proved particularly useful,
- where those measures are available, and
- how we can combine them to create a measure of institutional distance.

Subsequent chapters provide managers with the tools they need to convert measures of institutional distance into a meaningful institutional risk spread. Then, armed with a greater understanding of institutional risk and prepared to incorporate institutional risk spreads into standard financial models of globalization, we will revisit the Newlandia example I provided in chapter 2.

CHAPTER 4

Political Institutions and Globalization

Accounting for globalization's risks begins with an understanding of the institutions that are at the heart of those risks. Managers need a solid understanding of the political, economic, and cultural institutions in the countries where they wish to operate. These institutions affect the risks that companies face in global markets, and the levels of profitability they are likely to enjoy there. Managers hoping to expand globally, or those responsible for global operations, would be wise to examine them carefully.

The focus in this chapter is on political institutions, with a discussion of how managers can evaluate, measure, and account for political risks in a global environment. Subsequent chapters address economic institutions and cultural institutions.

Political Institutions 101: What Managers Should Know

Political institutions provide formal structure to a society, establish sets of relationships and interactions among societal actors, and govern the behavior of social and economic actors. They include all political, legal, and regulatory institutions at all levels of society.

Though research typically distinguishes between political, legal, and regulatory institutions that comprise a country's government, I treat them as a set because of the high degree of interdependence among them. They are inextricably linked and codetermined: a country's legal origins influence its political institutions; its political system influences the evolution of the legal system and legal institutions; its regulatory institutions are often a direct extension of its political and legal systems and structures. For this reason, I will discuss, evaluate, and measure these institutions as a group.[1]

It is critical that companies—a prominent set of economic actors— operate with a solid understanding of the political environment. Such an understanding can help generate important insights about a country's structure, organization, and risks. It helps provide context for the complex relationships in which companies are embedded and the sets of behaviors that it can engage in—the limits to organizational behavior and the rules of the game. It helps companies anticipate how institutions are likely to change in the future and therefore identify business opportunities that might arise in light of those changes.

The American companies Airbnb and Uber are excellent examples of firms using new business models whose success depends critically on the political environment—even within a company's home country. Airbnb and Uber both use web-based technology platforms to create online marketplaces that connect buyers and sellers. Online marketplaces are nothing new; companies such as Amazon, eBay, Yahoo!, and Google have long operated such marketplaces. But what sets Airbnb and Uber apart is that they are seeking to revolutionize what are traditionally heavily regulated industries: lodging and transportation, respectively.

Airbnb, which allows individuals (often travelers) seeking short-term lodging to rent space in private homes, makes a profit by collecting a fee on the transaction between the renter and lessor. Not surprisingly, in the United States traditional lodging establishments (hotels and motels) are crying foul. Trying to protect their business from outside competition, they maintain that private homes are not commercially sanctioned for tourism, and it is therefore illegal to charge people for staying there.

Uber provides a similar service in a different industry, acting as matchmaker between drivers and individuals looking for a ride. Its technology digitally connects drivers with fares. Although Uber has captured significant market share in the United States, its detractors claim it is simply an unregulated, unlicensed taxi service operating illegally, given that the appropriate authorities—that is, local US taxi commissions—have not sanctioned its activity. What is more, critics argue, Uber is putting riders at risk because it cannot ensure that drivers have met the rigorous qualifications for licensing or insurance that regulatory authorities require.

Uber and Airbnb have been able to get around some of these regulations by maintaining that they are technology companies; both claim that they simply provide a service to connect sellers of goods and services with interested buyers. By this logic, if Airbnb is not a lodging company and Uber is not a taxi company, they should not be subject to the regulations that govern those industries. Their position is that the onus should be on their independent contractors, who supply the goods and services—by providing rooms or rides—to comply with the laws that govern those activities.

Airbnb and Uber have been able to use this line of reasoning to some effect in the United States, defending the legality of their business models in court. In addition, they have been able to anticipate changes in the political environment and have lobbied institutional actors so as to influence the environment in their favor. In 2012 the city council of Washington, DC, for example, passed legislation legally allowing Uber the right to operate in the city.[2] Similarly, in 2014 the city of San Francisco changed its preexisting local laws to legalize short-term housing rentals, thereby benefiting technology-based housing rental companies like Airbnb.[3]

The Uber and Airbnb examples demonstrate the importance of understanding the political environment in one's home country. However, to be successful, managers need not be experts in the nuances of how political institutions function—in part because, as citizens educated in their home country, they generally already have a basic understanding of them. Should they find themselves in need of advice, help is often just one phone call away; lawyers and consultants who are experts and speak their language are ready to help.

In a global setting, however, the agility to navigate the political environment is even more crucial because institutions are so often very different from those in the home country. In global settings, managers are at a disadvantage in that they tend to struggle with even the very basics. They are less familiar with the kinds of business conduct and activities that are permissible there and therefore find themselves in trouble with the law far more frequently. The experiences of Airbnb and Uber in Europe again prove instructive.

Although Airbnb and Uber have largely been able to successfully navigate political hurdles in the United States, they have not enjoyed similar success in global markets. Operating globally has proved incredibly challenging, especially in Europe, where policymakers have responded unevenly to the upstart companies.[4] The taxi/lodging rules and regulations in European countries are much more complex and, in some cases, more onerous than in the United States. And under existing legislation it is not at all clear that Uber and Airbnb can even legally operate on the continent.

In Barcelona, for example, Airbnb was recently fined for acting as an accessory—allowing owners of homes to violate local laws that forbid the rental of private rooms for commercial purposes. In Germany, Uber is currently facing a host of serious legal challenges from the German Taxi Association, which has argued that Uber should be banned because the company lacks proper accreditation.

There is a potential for European regulatory agencies to ban Airbnb and Uber and companies that provide similar technology-aided marketplace services from operating in Europe. However, the bigger issue is that the differences in political environments between the United States and Europe make it more complicated and costly for these companies to operate there. The additional legal and regulatory compliance costs alone put them at a decided disadvantage compared to local companies.

Given that US municipalities have already demonstrated a willingness to adapt their laws and regulations to the business models of Uber and Airbnb (as in the case of Washington, DC, and San Francisco), it would be far simpler, far less costly, and much less risky for Airbnb and Uber to extend their operations to more cities in the United States than to extend them to some countries in Europe. Like any company that devises global expansion strategies, Airbnb and Uber should expand only once they account for the additional risks the political institutions pose in each potential market.

Navigating Political Institutions: The Broader Managerial Challenge

It is of course not only US companies, technology companies, or even large, well-funded companies that face challenges navigating the political environment in a foreign country. Studies demonstrate that foreign companies of all types run afoul of the law more frequently than domestic companies do. For instance, in 1995 a $100 million legal judgment in Mississippi nearly bankrupted the Loewen Corporation, a small Canadian funeral home operator.[5] Loewen later sued the US government, arguing that the legal system in the United States discriminated against the company by seizing its assets without due compensation, a violation, it argued, of investor protections under NAFTA.[6] Similarly, Japanese companies have had a notoriously difficult time navigating the political environment in the United States, resulting in costly, high-profile labor lawsuits for companies such as Mitsui and Toshiba.[7]

Just like domestic companies, foreign companies can hire local consultants and lawyers for guidance and advice, but they often end up making mistakes anyway, because of an inherently limited understanding of the local institutional environment. This, combined with the added expense of additional legal and advisory services, puts foreign companies at a decided cost disadvantage compared to domestic competitors.

To help managers understand and anticipate the risks that differences in political institutions between countries pose to their business, we need to explore a series of issues:

- What do I mean specifically by political institutions?
- What makes up political institutions?
- Are there reliable measures of political institutions?
- From what sources can we gather measurement data?

This chapter lays out answers to each of these questions and lays a foundation for a more detailed and essential examination of institutional risks in later chapters.

Analyzing a Country's Political Institutions

This section provides a framework for evaluating the political institutions of individual countries. Given that political institutions differ among countries, those differences can make it difficult for companies to conduct and manage business globally. No one set of political institutions is necessarily better or worse for globalization, and in the following analysis I do not make value judgments about which political systems and structures represent better or worse ways to govern. The aim is simply to shed some light on the different political systems and structures to which countries typically adhere.

The crucial insight is that when it comes to political institutions and globalization, everything is relative. It is not the set of political institutions within a country that makes it easier or harder to conduct business across borders; it is the differences in political institutions between countries that make coping difficult. However, to understand those differences and appreciate the risks they generate, managers must first understand the political institutions themselves.

The natural place to start to understand a country's political institutions—its structure, system, activities, and entities—is with its constitution. This set of organizing principles not only spells out a country's form of government, but also how it shall be governed, its law-making entities and activities, its legal procedures (the process of making and enforcing laws), and the boundaries of its law (fundamental rights of citizens and limits to the power of the entities and individuals that govern).

Next it is essential to dig deeper into the country's political and governmental bodies: the executive, legislative, and judicial branches; the roles and responsibilities of each branch; and the scope of power each one holds. Managers should consider the structure of each entity and the individuals who are empowered to lead them:

- how these leaders come to power (are they elected, appointed, or chosen in another way?);
- the roles and responsibilities of those who hold political positions of authority;
- the frequency of elections—if any—that determine who holds those positions of authority; and

- how long individuals in positions of authority can serve in those positions.

It is also important to examine more practical considerations, such as:

- the type and number of political parties;
- the extent to which the political system has built-in checks and balances (such as veto power);
- whether the judicial branch is independent of the executive and/or legislative branches;
- the relative balance of power within a country—whether the power lies with the central government or with the individual regions, provinces, or states.

Beyond the political institutions themselves, understanding their stability is essential to understanding their viability. It is crucial to know the extent to which the populace views the government as legitimate and the likelihood that the government is under threat from some sort of internal or external shock.

A common internal shock could be a protest intended to effect change or challenge the existing government. In the extreme, a civil war is an internal shock that threatens to overthrow the government and undermine its constitution. External shocks, by contrast, are extraterritorial; they involve other countries. For example, an external shock could arise from a public debate or disagreement that manifests itself in verbal conflict between countries. In the extreme, an external shock could take the form of an armed conflict or war between countries that threatens to unseat the existing government.

Political Institutions and Differences: China and the United States

The differences between China and the United States in political institutions and political systems are so pronounced that companies seeking to globalize from one to the other face great challenges. The main differences are the following:

- The United States is a federal republic in which the states and the federal government share power. China is a socialist republic in which the national Communist Party oversees and sanctions the operations of the regional and provincial governments.

- There are (technically) various political parties in both the United States and China, but in the United States only two (Republican and Democrat) dominate political activity and hold most of the power at both the state and the national level. In China one party—the Communist Party of China—dominates the political apparatus.

- Both countries hold elections to select individuals who will hold national, regional, and local office. However, in the United States, citizens typically elect legislative representatives as well as local and regional officials directly and elect the chief executive (the president) indirectly through the Electoral College. China, on the other hand, has a more hierarchical electoral system, whereby the National Communist Party typically nominates candidates to run for office at the local level. Individuals at the local level then directly elect representatives from among those candidates. Those representatives, in turn, elect the representatives at the national level, all the way up to the chief executive (the premier).

There are, of course, many and more nuanced differences between China's political institutions and those of the United States, but even these basic descriptions illuminate the challenges in global expansion from one country to the other. Knowing, for example, that the United States is organized as federal republic in which the states have substantial power means that a foreign company can often concentrate its efforts on receiving sanction to operate from individual states or even cities—as in the case of Uber and Airbnb. In China, local authorities might be able to sanction business activity, but given that the ultimate authority rests with the national government, it is more important that the central government regard a foreign company as legitimate. A failure to understand those subtleties can make entry into the Chinese market much more complicated for a US company and vice versa.

Analyzing a Country's Legal Institutions

The lines between legal institutions and political institutions are blurred. In fact, in some sense you can view a country's constitution as part of its legal structure. It is, after all, the most basic law of the land, detailing individual inalienable rights and the roles and responsibilities of the executive, legislative, and judicial branches of government.[8]

However, it is important to identify and distinguish between the legal system and the legal structure of a country. When I refer to a country's legal institutions, I mean the legislative and judicial system rather than the legal or judicial apparatus (the structure of the legislative and judicial branches of government—how the country elects or appoints those who serve in legislative and judicial roles). It is more helpful to view structural features of the judicial structure of government as part and parcel of the political institutions I describe above. Instead, I focus here on the balance between the roles of the legislative and judicial branches, and the law-making system itself: how lawmakers propose, ratify, amend, and abolish laws, how the judicial system interprets them, and how various agencies enforce them.

The best way to begin to understand legal institutions is to examine a country's legal origins and legal process. Currently, there are three main legal systems practiced widely in the world: civil law, common law, and religious law.[9]

Civil Law

The most widely adopted legal system throughout the world, civil law traces its roots to Roman tradition as set forth in the Law of the 12 Tables (ca. 449 BC). The Roman emperor Justinian later expanded it in the *Corpus Juris Civilis* (ca. AD 529). Civil law is built around a codified set of core principles: explicit statutes and codes developed to protect individual rights and prevent magistrates (judges or justices) from acting arbitrarily.

By design, civil law systems limit the power of the judicial branch of government, with the role of courts limited to the application of law. Judges do not interpret laws; they simply determine the facts and apply the appropriate legal code. Since the legislative branch develops and codifies laws that are specific enough for the courts to apply, it typically has a more central role than the judicial branch.

Though civil law is the most popular legal system throughout the world, not all countries practice civil law in the same way. Over the years several variants have evolved, including Napoleonic (in France, Italy, and Spain), Germanic (in Germany, Austria, and Switzerland), Scandinavian (in Sweden, Denmark, Finland, and Norway), and Socialist (in China and the former Soviet Union).

Common Law

Common law systems have a shorter history than civil law systems, but they still trace back to eleventh-century England. The courts play a particularly active role in common-law societies. Although legislatures propose, introduce, and enact laws, these laws tend to be more general than the ones in civil law systems. The former are primarily based on principles, with judges left to interpret how the laws ought to apply to specific circumstances.

Once judges have rendered decisions on how laws apply to a specific situation, their decisions become legal precedent—a de facto guide for future interpretations of the law as it might apply to other situations. In this way, common law renders lawmaking an evolving, cumulative process, and the judicial branch in common-law countries plays a more critical role than the legislative branch. Although scholars hold up the United Kingdom's common law system as the canonical example, many former British colonies, such as Australia, India, and the United States, practice a variant of common law.

Religious Legal Systems

In religious legal systems, the laws are based on religious documents, such as the Torah, the Bible, or the Quran. Countries with religious legal systems have an officially sanctioned national religion and adhere to its moral codes of conduct. For any specific activity that the religious document does not address, religious leaders adjudicate to determine whether it is consistent with the document's underlying moral code. In this way, religious leaders exert influence on government affairs.

Although countries with religious legal systems typically empower the legislative and judicial branches with traditional lawmaking functions—proposing, ratifying, amending, applying, enforcing, and dissolving laws—these branches are limited in their powers because they are subject to the oversight of religious leaders. The religious leaders ultimately determine whether the laws that the legislative and judicial bodies propose (as well as ratify, amend, apply, enforce, and/or dissolve) are consistent with the national religion's moral code. These religious leaders exert an outsize influence, with powers that are greater, in some circumstances, than those of executive, legislative, and judicial representatives. Iran and Saudi Arabia are examples of large countries that have largely adopted religious legal systems based on Islamic law—Sharia.

Combined Legal Systems

When you examine the legal systems of individual countries more closely, you start to realize that few adhere to one kind of legal system. Although we tend to distinguish among civil law, common law, and religious law countries, it would be an oversight to consider them as completely separate. Most countries lean toward one or another; however, few have adopted one system to the exclusion of the others.

The United States, for example, is considered a common law country, but the US system has traces of civil law. The state law of Louisiana, purchased from France in 1803, is based on French civil law. Similarly, Germany, whose system has a strong tradition in civil law, reflects common law leanings in its law of Industrial Action (*Arbeitskampfrecht*).[10] Several Middle Eastern countries have adopted a mix of religious law and some other kind of law. Morocco, for example, has adopted a mix of French civil law and Islamic law (mostly in the area of family law). Moreover, given that both civil law and common law were born out of the codification of early religious beliefs and tenets, religious law has certainly influenced their development.

Globalization and Legal Institutions

Legal institutions influence the kinds of activities companies can and cannot engage in. These institutions set boundaries and influence the rules of the game, and companies—as players in that game—must generally abide by those rules. This is not to say that companies are passive players. They try to influence the rules in their favor. However, for the most part there is no getting around the fact that legal institutions, and legal actors, play a central role in economies.

For managers of global companies, it is important to realize that differences in legal institutions can make it difficult to operate in other countries. Academic studies demonstrate that, when it comes to globalization, it is typically easier for companies to operate in countries that share the same legal system. It should therefore be easier for a US-based company like Airbnb to operate in the United Kingdom than in Spain—and not simply due to a common language, but because the legal systems of the United States and the United Kingdom are similar. Airbnb might be able to navigate a common law country like the United Kingdom more effectively because it is more accustomed to responding to legal challenges by arguing that its services are legitimate based on precedent. By contrast, it might be more difficult for Airbnb to justify its operations in a civil law country like Spain, which explicitly prohibits the commercial use of private property.

Analyzing a Country's Regulatory Institutions

Regulatory actors (agencies and individuals) and the regulations they propose, ratify, amend, abolish, and enforce comprise regulatory institutions. Regulatory bodies, created by legislative and political bodies through statutory law, share similarities with both legal and political institutions. Like political actors, the leaders of regulatory agencies can be appointed or elected or can simply inherit their positions. Like legislative bodies, regulatory agencies have the power to create explicit codes of behavior that carry the force of law. They propose, ratify, amend, and abolish rules and laws. Regulatory agencies can also serve as executive and judicial actors, adjudicating and enforcing rules and laws, monitoring economic actors subject to regulation and taking punitive action to enforce regulations when necessary.

In some sense, regulatory institutions fill gaps that legal and political institutions leave unaddressed and typically do so in the domain of industrial activity. Whereas political and legal institutions influence policy broadly in society, the roles and responsibilities of regulatory institutions are limited to specific areas of economic activity. In the United States, for example, the government charges bank regulators like the Federal Deposit Insurance Corporation, the Federal Reserve Board, and the Office of the Comptroller of the Currency with oversight of financial institutions in the banking industry. They enact rules of conduct, monitor banking institutes to ensure that those banks comply with the rules of conduct, and mete out penalties when banks violate established rules of conduct. This authority, however, is limited to the banking sector, and these regulators have very little, if any, power in other industries, such as telecommunications.

As with political and legal structures, countries differ in the kind, number, and practices of their regulatory structures. Banking tends to be heavily regulated in nearly all countries, whereas there is a less widespread tradition when it comes to the regulation of issues such as worker safety, health services, and the environment.[11] Some countries have multiple regulators for a given industry, as with banking in the United States. Other countries have only one, as with banking in China (the China Banking Regulatory Commission, CBRC). Similarly, regulators might be able to serve longer terms in some countries than in others.

Regulatory independence also varies; in some countries, regulatory bodies are run independently of other branches of government. In others, they may be independent in theory, but politicians meddle in practice. In yet others, regulatory agencies are not independent at all. Whatever the case, regulatory agencies are typically subject to oversight by political and legislative actors, who have the right to amend their scope or, in extreme cases, revoke their charters.

Finally, while regulators in some countries have almost exclusive power to enforce regulations, other countries limit these enforcement powers, relegating regulatory agencies to a mere advisory role. In general, regulatory bodies in Anglo countries, such as the

United States, have more autonomy and authority, and those in Asian countries like China tend to have less.[12]

It can be a challenge for a company to operate in a regulatory environment that is different from that of its home country—just as it is difficult to navigate a country with different political and legal institutions. In global markets, companies often have an inadequate understanding of local regulations, the regulatory agencies to which they are subject, and the roles and responsibilities of those agencies. This limited understanding means that firms are more likely to run into trouble with regulators.

For example, Uber is currently embroiled in a tremendous regulatory battle in Germany, and these kinds of battles are not limited to a particular company, country, or industry. They are common for companies operating overseas. Corroborating that point, the majority of respondents to a recent China survey conducted by the American Chamber of Commerce indicated that US companies feel that they are unfairly "targeted" by Chinese regulators, with local regulations biased in favor of local Chinese companies.[13]

A recent study in the banking sector demonstrates that foreign banks operating in the United States are significantly more likely to be the target of regulatory action—being flagged for more consumer protection, information disclosure, anti-money laundering, and anti-terrorism violations—than are comparable US banks.[14] As of this writing, foreign banks such as HSBC, Barclays, Standard Chartered, Royal Bank of Scotland, Credit Suisse, and Bank of Tokyo-Mitsubishi UFJ are either under investigation or have already been fined for doing business with Iran, a country the US government and US banking regulators have blacklisted.[15]

Russian media regulators passed legislation in 2014 limiting the broadcasting of commercials for cable and satellite TV channels. This severely hinders the ability of foreign cable companies to generate revenue, as commercials provide a critical source of revenue for television content providers. Similarly, media regulators in Russia passed regulations to take effect in 2016 that would limit the ownership foreign companies can take in local media companies. In response to these regulatory changes, the US-owned Cable News Network (CNN) announced it would reconsider offering its English-language news channel in Russia.[16] Other prominent foreign media companies like the BBC, Bloomberg TV, and the German Burda Media are also reevaluating their strategies in Russia.

These examples highlight how regulatory differences between countries pose challenges and create compliance burdens. Accordingly, managers face a complex set of decisions and trade-offs regarding these differences.

Measuring a Country's Political Institutions

Practically speaking, managers have neither time for nor do they need deep, detailed insight into how a country's political, legal, and regulatory institutions were designed, created, and structured, or how they function on a day-to-day basis. The aim here is merely to provide an overview, a framework for establishing a context for political considerations that relate to globalization.

If managers do not require a detailed and nuanced understanding of how political institutions function in specific countries, then when seeking to expand into a particular country, where can they turn for guidance to help them better understand the political environment? It is wise to turn to specialists—scholars, consultants, lawyers, and accountants—who have developed an expertise in dealing with political institutions. Some of those specialists have even developed ways to reliably measure and quantify important elements of political institutions, and managers can use these to evaluate relevant political differences between countries. Some measures are broad in scope, simultaneously evaluating various political, legal, and regulatory institutions—a kind of one-stop shopping—while other measures provide more detail on a particular set or subset of political institutions.

For all-inclusive data, managers can turn to the Worldwide Governance Indicators (WGI). Scholars developed the WGI in conjunction with the World Bank and the Brookings Institute to capture elements of a country's political, legal, and regulatory institutions. WGI's political measures evaluate four factors:

- voice and accountability, or the extent to which the populace elects its government;
- political stability, or the presence and level of social unrest, armed conflict, and terrorist threats;
- government effectiveness, or the extent to which the government is seen as credible and acts credibly;
- corruption, or the extent to which public officials use the power of their office for private gain.

WGI measures legal institutions through an assessment of the rule of law: the extent to which actors in a society respect and abide by the law and the consistency with which the government enforces the law, especially insofar as contracts and property rights are concerned. WGI also includes a measure of regulatory quality—the soundness of regulation.

In the realm of political institutions:

- The World Bank Database of Political Institutions (DPI) measures aspects of a country's political system, ideological leanings, electoral rules, level of electoral competitiveness, number and types of political parties, structural characteristics of the executive and legislative branches of government, and the level of checks and balances built into the political system.
- Witold Henisz, a professor at the Wharton School of the University of Pennsylvania, developed the Political Constraints (POLCON) Index to focus on checks and balances across the legislative, executive, and judicial branches of government. This database reflects the insight that the greater the checks and balances in a political system, the more political actors are constrained from acting unilaterally, and the greater the policy stability of a country.
- Like the POLCON measure, the Center for Systemic Peace captures indicators of stability; however, it focuses more on political

than policy stability. It publishes some particularly interesting measures on internal and external conflict, war, and the likely continuity of the government.

- Transparency International publishes an annual Corruption Perception Index that captures the level of corruption within a country's government sector.

For data on legal institutions managers can turn to sources highlighted in an influential study entitled "Law and Finance."[17] For example:

- The Foreign Law Guide publishes data on legal origins (such as whether a country uses a system based on civil law or common law).
- The Digest of Commercial Laws of the World compares countries based on 22 commercial legal factors.
- The World Justice Project collects and publishes data on the rule of law and the effectiveness of judicial systems.

Because regulation tends to be industry specific, there are generally fewer measures that focus exclusively on the regulatory institutions of nations rather than their political or legal institutions. But that does not make a country's national regulatory structure any less important. In fact, the Organization for Economic Cooperation and Development (OECD) recently highlighted the need for a more robust framework to measure and evaluate regulatory effectiveness and regulatory quality across countries.[18] That said, there are various sources we can turn to for measures of regulatory institutions at the national level, but they tend to be embedded within other measures of legal and political institutions. For example:

- As part of their focus on the rule of law, the World Justice Project also collects and publishes data on the regulatory effectiveness of countries.
- The World Economic Forum's Global Competitiveness Report includes a measure of regulatory quality as a part of its assessment of global economies.

- The Doing Business Index, supported by the International Finance Corporation and the World Bank, captures several features of national regulatory institutions.

These are a few high-quality measures of political institutions, but this is certainly not an exhaustive list. There are a number of alternative sources of data:

- For a solid qualitative understanding of a country's political institutions, the *CIA World Factbook* can be an excellent resource.
- Similar to the *CIA World Factbook*, the Economist Intelligence Unit publishes qualitative data on countries' political, legal, and regulatory systems.
- There are proprietary sources of data published by various consultancies—such as the Eurasia Group or the PRS Group— geared toward the measurement of geopolitical and legal risk. The Eurasia Group, founded by my colleague Ian Bremmer, specializes in the measurement of geopolitical risk. Similar to the Eurasia Group, the PRS Group specializes in geopolitical risks, but its data also includes measures related to a country's legal environment.
- Other sources of country-specific data include (but are not limited to) Nouriel Roubini's RGE Macro Analytics, Pankaj Ghemawat's CAGE Comparative Data, and NationMaster.

Table 4.1 lists sources for measures that can help guide managers in their quest to understand political, legal, and regulatory institutions. It is not an exhaustive list; however, it details a set of accurate and reliable sources for data on political institutions.

Bringing It All Together

Political institutions are incredibly interesting, but they are admittedly nuanced and complex. Managers need not understand and appreciate the full depth of their complexity and nuance, as the goal is not to achieve academic levels of enlightenment. Managers do, however, need to have a basic familiarity with political institutions

Table 4.1 Political Data Sources

Source	URL	Political	Legal	Regulatory
Worldwide Governance Indicators	http://info.worldbank.org/governance/wgi/index.aspx#home	X	X	X
Database of Political Institutions	http://www.worldbank.org/en/research	X		
POLCON	https://mgmt.wharton.upenn.edu/profile/1327	X		
Center for Systemic Peace	http://www.systemicpeace.org/	X		
Corruption Perception Index	http://www.transparency.org/research/cpi/overview	X		
Foreign Law Guide	http://referenceworks.brillonline.com/browse/foreign-law-guide		X	
Commercial Laws of the World	http://legalsolutions.thomsonreuters.com/law-products/		X	
World Justice Project	http://worldjusticeproject.org/		X	X
Global Competitiveness Report	http://reports.weforum.org/global-competitiveness-report-2014-2015/	X		X
Doing Business Index	http://www.doingbusiness.org/		X	X
CIA World Factbook	https://www.cia.gov/library/publications/the-world-factbook/	X		
Eurasia Group	http://www.eurasiagroup.net/	X		
PRS Group	https://www.prsgroup.com/	X	X	
RGE Macroanalytics	https://www.roubini.com/	X		
CAGE Comparative Data	http://www.ghemawat.com/cage/	X	X	
NationMaster	http://www.nationmaster.com/	X	X	

and understand the challenges that differences in political institutions can cause when conducting business overseas. In the context of globalization, it is especially important for managers to be able to accurately measure political institutions, to get one step closer to quantifying and accounting for the risks posed by differences in political institutions between countries in terms of dollars and cents.

How can measures of political institutions help account for globalization's risks? A preview of coming attractions: Let us assume we measure a particular political institution for which, on a certain scale, the United Kingdom receives a score of 1, the United States a 2, and China a 10.[19] For the purposes of assessing globalization risk, the significance lies not in the absolute numbers, but in the *relative difference* between the numbers. The greater the difference between countries, the greater the risk to a company wishing to globalize to that other country. Thus, based purely on the political institution differences between the United Kingdom, the United States, and China, we can safely assume that it will be easier for a US company to expand to the United Kingdom (given a political difference of 1) than to China (with a political difference of 8). Those differences can also help us begin to make inferences about the risks involved in operating in a certain country. However, before we get deeper into the specifics of how to convert raw measures of institutions into useful measures of global risk, it is essential to delve into the two other national institutions that impact global business: economics and culture.

CHAPTER 5

Economic Institutions and Globalization

I n an ideal world, managers would simply engage in the whole-
sale transfer of products, services, operations, and business
activities from the domestic market—where they are familiar
with the various institutions—to a foreign market. Adopting such
an approach is typically easier and more cost-effective—benefitting
from what we refer to as "economies of scale and scope" in global
markets—than recreating the business from scratch. In practice,
however, managers often discover that it is difficult to conduct business in global markets in precisely the same way as in the domestic
market. There are a host of impediments to transferring an existing
domestic business model abroad.

In the preceding chapter we explored political institutions and the
impediments—and risks—that differences in those institutions can
generate for multinational corporations. Now that we have an overview of political institutions, we are prepared to consider economic
institutions and the way they differ from one country to another.
Managers may not always have political institutions on their radar,
but most are keenly aware of economic institutions even if they do
not always think of them as institutions.

Managers are trained to think in terms of market opportunities:
opportunities to increase revenues, decrease costs, and increase profits. Yet despite the preoccupation with revenue, cost, and profitability factors, managers typically do not think about the complex set

of economic institutions that underpin those factors. This chapter builds on an existing familiarity with market opportunity to provide a more nuanced understanding of economic institutions, with a focus on how they relate to globalization and global risk.

Economic Institutions 101: What Managers Should Know

Managers intuitively recognize the importance of economic institutions to their bottom line, and yet they continue to make countless mistakes when they expand into global markets. Among these mistakes may be the following:

- overestimating a particular market's potential
- misjudging the quality of local employees or local inputs
- underestimating the likelihood that the market is vulnerable to a recession or other adverse developments
- overlooking the impact of currency fluctuations
- failing to realize how a country's physical and economic infrastructure will impact the company's business operations.

Misreading these factors in a foreign market can have costly consequences. Let us take a closer look.

Overestimating Market Potential

The most important—and often most obvious—economic institution any company must consider when expanding abroad is the size of the local market and the level of wealth of its consumers. Given that customers cannot buy products they cannot afford and do not buy products that do not meet their economic needs, managers often begin by assessing whether there is demand for their company's products, whether local customers can afford them, and whether their companies can be competitive in the local marketplace. Managers use those assessments to generate revenue estimates.

But generating accurate sales estimates requires more than simply estimating market size, consumer wealth, and competitive positioning. Foreign revenue estimates are much harder to generate—and much less precise—than domestic revenue estimates due to a simple reality: foreign companies are at an informational disadvantage compared to local competitors when it comes to understanding local consumers. Managers of foreign companies often lack the detailed information they need to accurately project revenues, and as a result, there is typically much more variability in their sales estimates. This can set up a company for failure.

Miscalculating Local Sales in India: Kellogg's and Daimler

An excellent example of economic miscalculations is the attempt by the Kellogg's company to expand into India in the mid 1990s with its flagship corn flakes brand.[1] The company took note of India's rapid economic growth and burgeoning middle class. What it did not understand, however, was the difference between the middle class in a developing country like India and that in an already developed country like the United States. The result of this oversight? Kellogg's overestimated the potential for its sales in India as well as the appeal that ready-to-eat cereal products would have there. Despite a $65 million initial investment in India and additional millions spent on marketing and promotion, Kellogg's failed to make much of dent in the Indian market. It simply priced many local consumers out of the market.

Similarly, in 1994 the German multinational automotive corporation Daimler miscalculated the Indian market when it introduced its Mercedes brand there in hopes of appealing to the growing wealthy market segment. It soon discovered, however, that its automobiles were priced too high even for this segment of the market. This was compounded by the fact that its manufacturing facility in India could not produce automobiles cost-effectively, and at a scale that would allow the company to lower prices. As a result, the company had year-over-year losses. Daimler still operates in the Indian luxury automobile market today, but it continues to struggle, having captured only around 0.4 percent of the country's automobile market—far less than its 5.4 percent market share in Europe or its 2.5 percent market share in the United States.[2]

Misjudging Quality

Managers are trained to pay acute attention to sales figures and also to costs, and they often look to globalization as a means to reduce those costs. You are probably familiar with the business practice of subcontracting production to developing countries, where the costs can often be orders of magnitude lower than in the domestic market. You are probably also familiar with the business practice of global sourcing, where companies acquire inputs from foreign markets at a fraction of the cost of producing or acquiring them at home. These decisions require managers to estimate the cost savings they can achieve by substituting foreign labor and inputs for domestic labor and inputs. They will normally take into account potential savings in labor costs, input costs, and operating costs, but—just as it is difficult to estimate sales accurately—it is difficult to accurately estimate cost savings. There are many hidden costs to globalization that are difficult to estimate. Lower costs can compromise quality and can mean substandard operating procedures.

Offshore Outsourcing and Labor Quality: A Cautionary Tale

In the 1980s and 1990s the trend among companies in the United States and United Kingdom was to outsource customer support and service—that is, IT support—to countries like India, where the costs were a fraction of those in the home country. Despite this lower sticker price, many companies soon discovered that the quality of the outsourced work did not meet the standards they had become accustomed to in the United States or the United Kingdom. This strategy also had an impact on India's labor market. As foreign companies followed the same strategy of piling into India to reduce costs, labor market conditions in India firmed up and wage inflation soon followed. In fact, outsourcing to Indian firms drove up wages so much that the practice ceased to provide benefit for the foreign firms.

As a result, the last decade or so has seen an increasing trend toward onshoring—companies bringing back to their home country activities that they had once sent offshore. The onshoring trend is not limited to IT services, either. The manufacturing industry has also undergone a wave of onshoring, as Western companies increasingly bring home manufacturing work they had subcontracted to India, China, and other low-wage countries.[3]

Anticipating Economic Shocks

Given how difficult it is for managers—or anyone—to anticipate shifts in their own country's economic environment, imagine trying to anticipate sudden economic swings, such as recessions, as an outsider. If we look back to the severe financial crisis and economic recession in the United States from 2007 to 2009, when GDP fell by more than 4 percent from peak to trough, we see that it did not spare American companies and banks, which were staffed with knowledgeable managers. Yet, however challenging it might have been for American companies to deal with the financial crisis, that challenge was amplified for foreign companies. Foreign companies were similarly caught off guard by the suddenness and severity of the crisis; lacking early warning systems and strong ties in the local market, they were impacted disproportionately.

The inability to accurately predict or prepare for sudden changes in the local economic environment certainly creates risks for domestic companies, but it can wreak havoc for foreign companies. Foreign companies are often ill-prepared to deal with local economic shocks because they are at an informational disadvantage relative to domestic companies, and often not as well prepared to deal with them. Because managers cannot prepare for what they cannot anticipate, there is greater uncertainty in their financial projections.

Caught Off Guard by an Economic Shock: Vitro in the United States
In response to the 2007–2009 financial crisis in the United States, Mexican companies—especially those whose fortunes were tied to the US market—experienced a particularly sharp deceleration in sales that took an extreme toll on their bottom lines. Vitro, a large Mexican multinational producer of high-quality glass products for the beverage, construction, and automotive industries, was caught off guard.

Vitro's problems were twofold. First, it had made big bets on the price of natural gas—a vital input used for firing silicon into glass—in anticipation of rising natural gas prices. Second, Vitro had a tremendous exposure to the US automotive and construction industries. In the wake of the financial crisis, US demand for housing and automobiles flagged and the price of natural gas cratered. Vitro lost more than $200 million just on natural gas contracts, and US sales and income declined so precipitously that Vitro was forced to file for bankruptcy in 2010.

The Impact of Currency

When the salient factor of foreign currencies is added into the mix of variables, the economic environment becomes even more complicated for a company trying to compete in global markets. As investors know too well, it is extremely challenging to estimate whether a foreign currency will rise or fall and by how much. Exchange rates can change suddenly and unexpectedly.[4] And regardless of their size, companies that operate globally must deal with currency risk.

Losing Money on Currency Exchange: Hypothetical Example
with Real Implications

How could a company lose money on foreign exchange? Using a simplified hypothetical example, let us assume that a US automobile company (we will call it US Autoco) sells cars in Brazil in the local currency (i.e., collects Brazilian reals from Brazilian consumers). Assuming that US$1 (USD) is worth R$2 (reals) today, a car that costs USD 10,000 should cost approximately R$20,000, which US Autoco would collect today in Brazil. If the company acts immediately, it can take those R$20,000 and exchange them for USD 10,000. However, the value of the Brazilian real could change tomorrow, due to unforeseen circumstances.

If US Autoco waits until tomorrow to exchange its Brazilian Reals into USD, and by that time the value of the R$ weakens against the USD such that USD 1 now yields R$2.5, that R$20,000 US Autoco collected would no longer be worth USD 10,000, but only USD 8,000— a 20 percent loss in revenue in just one day. And indeed, consistent with this hypothetical example, General Motors announced a drop in revenue and profitability in 2013 when the Brazilian real fell by 7.8 percent against the US dollar.

Similarly, as a result of the economic slump in the European Union and a weakening euro (EUR), large US companies, such as Proctor & Gamble, Caterpillar, and Microsoft, blamed a spate of disappointing earnings in part on the strengthening of the USD against the EUR.[5] Aside from a drop in demand that usually accompanies a recession, the sudden shift in the EUR/USD exchange rate had a dramatic effect on their bottom lines.

The dynamics driving down the earnings of Proctor & Gamble, Caterpillar, and Microsoft are similar to those I describe in the hypothetical example above. Let us assume that a US software company (we will call it US Softwareco) earned profits of €1,000,000 from the EU in 2014 and anticipates that it will likewise earn the same level of profits there in 2015. Even if only the exchange rate changes, US Softwareco's profitability will change. This is because the average exchange rate in 2014 for the EUR was USD 1.33, but in early 2015 it dropped into the range of USD 1.10. If that exchange rate remains constant for the remainder of 2015, and nothing else changes, US Softwareco's profitability will take a 17 percent hit, from USD 1,330,000 in 2014 to USD 1,100,000 in 2015.

Given how suddenly exchange rates can fluctuate—as in the cases of the Brazilian real and the Euro—it is clear from the examples that currency exchange should be a serious consideration for anyone managing global operations.

Gaining Money on Currency Exchange: Hypothetical Example
with Real Implications
Exchange rate shocks also happen in the opposite direction—in a foreign company's favor. If the Brazilian real were to strengthen against the USD, such that today USD 1 yields R$2 but tomorrow it yields only R$1.5, our hypothetical US Autoco would have benefitted from waiting that extra day to exchange its Brazilian reals. That is, the same R$20,000 it collected in the example above would be worth more than USD 10,000 in exchange today and instead would be worth USD 13,333 (R$20,000/1.5) tomorrow, for a foreign currency gain of 33 percent.

In the time I've been writing this book while on sabbatical in Spain, I myself have benefited from a drop in the value of the euro. When I came to Madrid, I rented an apartment from a local landlord who wanted to receive monthly rental payment in euros. However, as an employee of a US university (NYU's Stern School of Business), I get paid in US dollars. This mismatch between receipts and expenses creates currency risk for me.

But I got lucky. When paying my first month's rent and security deposit, the EUR/USD exchange rate stood at around USD 1.36 (i.e., 1 EUR yielded USD 1.36). As of this writing, it stands at around USD 1.10. My rent has therefore gone down some 19 percent in USD terms. So if I were paying (let us say) EUR 1,000 per month for my apartment, rather than having to convert the initial USD 1,360 into EUR each month, I now only have to convert USD 1,100 to pay my monthly rent. That is a savings of USD 230 per month. I definitely benefitted, but it would have been risky for me to count on that kind of reduction in cost. Likewise managers should not assume that they will be the beneficiary of foreign exchange movements.

Hedging Currency Risk

Large currency swings like those I describe in the examples above (in the 10–25% range) are more the exception than the norm, and yet these same dynamics play out for global companies on a smaller scale almost on a daily basis. Given that managers do not want to expose their companies to risk, you may ask how managers can minimize their exposure to this kind of foreign exchange risk. The answer, typically, is through managing—or "hedging"—currency risk. Hedging provides a means of locking in a certain exchange rate in advance, so as to protect a company from exchange rate fluctuations.

Returning to the hypothetical example of US Autoco operating in Brazil, if the company can predict it will make a R$20,000 sale next week, it can enter into a standard future or forward contract today with a bank (or any financial institution that specializes in currency exchange) in anticipation of that sale, locking in a particular exchange rate. For a fee, the company is likely to find a financial institution willing to guarantee the going rate of USD 1 in exchange for every R$2, regardless of the direction in which the currency moves. US Autoco therefore would lock in the exchange rate just before—or immediately upon realizing—the sale and thus does not have to worry about exchange rate fluctuations after the sale. And this is a smart strategy for many globalizing businesses to consider.[6]

Although hedging allows companies to minimize the currency risk that is inherent to doing business in a global marketplace, this means of mitigating risk is not free. Whether they hedge or not, global companies still bear additional costs, either in the form of currency risk (if they do not hedge) or by paying staff or outside advisors to manage their hedged positions (if they do hedge). This is yet another example of how differences in economic institutions add to a global company's overall liability of foreignness.

Economic Infrastructure

Differences across countries that impact global business activity go well beyond the straightforward issues of customer purchasing power, cost/quality considerations, macroeconomic fluctuations, and currency risk. They also include physical infrastructure—the basic building blocks of economic activity. A country's infrastructure embodies one set of institutions that managers tend to overlook when seeking to globalize. You might not immediately think of this as an economic institution, but infrastructure creates a basis for broader economic activity, and the following types of infrastructure matter especially to economic outcomes:

- transportation (bridges, tunnels, roads, airports, and seaports);
- services (water and sewer);
- energy (the availability of energy supplies, the establishment of electricity-generating facilities, and the development of reliable energy-distribution facilities);
- technology (hardware, software, and network resources);
- financial (a well-functioning banking sector and a sound financial system of exchange).

Without the appropriate infrastructure, it is difficult for companies to conduct business in a particular country, and differences in infrastructure development between countries can handicap global companies.

Infrastructure's Operational Challenges: Multinationals in China

It is no secret that Western companies have difficulty distributing their goods in China (I provided an example of this phenomenon with Walmart in chapter 1). China has made great strides in developing its economic infrastructure, but it still lags behind many developed markets. A recent report by the Boston Consulting Group (BCG) concluded that China's "logistics infrastructure is more fragile and disorganized than that of Western countries."[7] As a result, multinational companies generally carry higher levels of inventory in China than in other countries, and it is generally costlier and more time-consuming to manage logistics in China than elsewhere. According to the BCG study, "Western multinationals can expect about 20 percent of the costs of their Chinese operations to be logistics-related, compared with an average of about 10 percent in the West."

Logistical challenges have dogged Walmart throughout its tenure in China. It has been difficult for the company to maintain a large, nationwide retail footprint in China because the country's road, railway, and port transportation systems do not yet meet Walmart's demanding distribution standards. Moreover, China's information technology infrastructure lags behind in speed and connectivity, making supply chain management, inventory tracking, and automated order processing more challenging. It should therefore come as no surprise that China, the largest consumer market in the world, accounts for only 2 percent of Walmart's sales, while contributing very little, if any, profitability.

Defining Economic Institutions

Now that I have shared some stories about specific economic factors and why each one is important to global companies, I should formally define what I mean by economic institutions. Economic institutions certainly influence the development of the aforementioned factors—market potential, the quality of local inputs and local employees, the potential for macroeconomic shocks, the country's currency regime, and the country's economic infrastructure. Each is a measurable manifestation of economic institutions that, no doubt, influences revenues, costs, and profits. Moreover, each is a correlate of the condition of a country's economic institutions. However, each is not an economic institution in and of itself.

Economic institutions are more rudimentary than the factors I describe above. They are the basic units of an economy—comprised of economic actors, systems, and structures—and the essential building blocks to economic activity. I cannot overstate the importance of economic institutions to a country's economic environment and economic development, and it is critical for managers considering global expansion to take them into account.[8] It is therefore helpful to briefly examine each economic institutional unit separately.

Economic Actors

This term refers to any individual or group that:

- acts as a singular unit (individual, company, organization, government agency, financial institution, etc.);
- has the right to make economic decisions on behalf of the unit;
- directs factors of production (land, labor, capital, and/or knowledge).

Think of economic actors as parties engaged in business activity. They can be individuals or organizations that own, allocate, use, and direct factors of production and engage in transactions involving said factors in exchange for some consideration, either monetary or otherwise.

Economic Systems and Structures

Economic systems and structures refer to a country's market orientation—the well-established sets of arrangements that govern economic activity as well as the behavior of economic actors. These include:

- the allocation of resources among the various economic actors in society;

- the means of exchange of goods and services;
- the rules that govern ownership—who owns (or can legally own) the factors of production;
- the roles of economic actors that exchange economic inputs (i.e., the factors of production) or economic outputs (i.e., goods and services developed using the factors of production); and
- the rules that govern interaction among economic actors.

There are two primary economic systems/structures that currently dominate the global landscape: capitalist and command.[9]

Capitalist Economic Systems
These systems typically permit private economic actors to own factors of production, and they afford those actors wide latitude in deciding how to allocate those factors to productive ends. In a capitalist system, the market plays a central role in coordinating economic activity, and market-based considerations influence the allocation of resources and the decisions of economic actors. The United States, for example, is a country that likely comes to mind when one thinks of a capitalist economy.

Command Economic Systems
In command economic systems, the state (rather than private economic actors) typically owns the factors of production. The state generally acts as the economic coordinating mechanism, allocating and directing factors of production—determining how factors of production are put to use, by whom, and which goods and services are produced and in what quantities. As a result, the market plays a relatively small role. For example, to some extent China exhibits characteristics of a command economy.

Less Common Systems and Structures
Other economic structures and systems include:

- the feudal systems of medieval times, often characterized by lords that owned the land, while vassals managed the factors of production on the land, enjoying the fruits of the factors of production only in exchange for loyalty to the lord;

- gift economies, where markets play little role and individuals offer valuable items without any expectation of reciprocity;
- barter economies, which do not use currency to equilibrate trade; instead, economic actors exchange goods and services directly.[10]

Combined Economies

In practice, although pure capitalism and pure command systems are at opposite poles of the spectrum of economic systems, most countries are a hybrid of capitalist and command economies. We often characterize the US economy as capitalist, despite its many elements of central planning. The US government sometimes manages the provision of goods and services, especially in situations where markets do not function properly. Similarly, we could describe China's economy, which is largely state-driven, as a command economy, but in some cases—and increasingly in recent years—individual economic actors own private property and make decisions about how to use factors of production.

Managing Economic Institutional Differences: Henry Schein's Global Expansion

As you might expect, having to navigate different economic institutions is a key obstacle to a company seeking to expand globally. The more dissimilar the economic institutions of a pair of countries, the more difficult it is for a company from one country to conduct business in the other and the greater the risk connected with expansion into that country. Henry Schein, a US-based publicly traded company and one of the world's largest direct-to-office dental, medical, and veterinary sales, distribution, and service companies, has encountered some of these institutional challenges in its global operations.

Henry Schein predominantly sells products manufactured by health care equipment and device manufacturers directly to the offices of dental, medical, and veterinary practitioners. Its value added includes an extensive product catalog, a tremendous sales force, a far-reaching distribution footprint, and an attentive postsales service network. In recent years Schein has capitalized on its accumulated knowledge of the dental, medical, and veterinary businesses to offer practitioners a range of valuable consulting, financial, and technology services.

Henry Schein has successfully replicated much of its business model in global markets (the company currently operates in more than 30 countries) by taking a graduated roll out approach. It chooses countries carefully, looking for strategic fit between economic opportunity and institutional risk. Schein's expansion pattern reflects such an approach. It undertook a concerted global expansion campaign in the early 1990s to countries that were economically (and more broadly, institutionally) similar to the United States, like Canada, the United Kingdom, and Western Europe. From there it expanded further afield, with recent expansions into more institutionally distant countries like China and Brazil.

Once Schein chooses to enter a particular country, it manages risk by adopting business structures and tailoring operational strategies to the economic realities of that country. For example, in some European countries the economic system differs markedly from that in the United States, especially in those countries that lean more toward a socialist than a capitalist economic system. In those countries, medicine is largely socialized and potential customers are primarily large, state-run public health care systems rather than private health care practitioners

Governments are notoriously difficult customers. They tend to use their heft to squeeze suppliers for discounts, take longer to pay than private customers, and generally do not value after-sales service in the way private health care providers do. Therefore, when considering global expansion, Henry Schein has been careful to concentrate its efforts on countries that share similarities in economic institutions and structure to the

United States. In cases where the company enters countries with very different economic institutions, it tends to focus on segments of the market that are similar to those in the United States.

For example, in a country where the state runs the public health care system but social insurance does not cover dental and veterinary services, Henry Schein might concentrate on the private dental and veterinary markets rather than on medical ones. The company has learned how to deal with differing economic institutions effectively by tailoring its product and service offerings to the institutional realities of each market.

Measuring Economic Institutions

Measuring economic institutions is not nearly as challenging as measuring political or cultural institutions. Given that managers and policymakers have a keen interest in economic outcomes, there is already an abundance of country-level economic data. The challenge, however, is to sift through all the data to determine which will best help us accurately account for differences in these economic institutions between countries.

Using Macro-Level Data

One place to start is to examine a country's gross domestic product (GDP), GDP per capita, and GDP growth. These figures can give us a sense of the potential size of the market, the wealth of the consumers, and the likely growth of that market. These data are available from a number of sources, including the United Nations, the World Bank, the International Monetary Fund, the Penn World Table, and the *CIA World Factbook*.

To understand the impact of globalization on a company's costs, managers might look to data on the factors of production, such as labor, land, natural resources, and capital (e.g., machinery) costs. Organizations like the International Labor Organization, the US Bureau of Labor Statistics, the Organization for Economic Cooperation and Development (OECD), and the World Bank publish data sets on various factors of production costs, especially labor costs.

It would be shortsighted for managers, however, to solely or even predominantly rely on macro-level data—such as GDP, GDP per capita, GDP growth, labor costs—to generate revenue and cost projections for global markets. Although these data can help us develop estimates, they are not detailed enough to generate accurate projections. For this, managers typically prefer detailed industry-specific data. Industry associations and focused consulting and analysis organizations specialize in the collection and publication of such industry-specific metrics.

Luxury Goods in China: A Hypothetical Example

Assume that in 2013 China had a GDP per capita of approximately USD 7,000. This raw number is meaningful to a manager of a luxury goods business looking to expand to China; the number indicates that compared to the United States (with a GDP per capita of approximately USD 53,000 in 2013), Chinese consumers, on average, are not exceedingly wealthy. However, China is an extremely large country, and averages can be misleading. The average GDP per capita tells us very little about the distribution of wealth in China or where large concentrations of wealth might exist. For instance, cities like Shanghai and Beijing have a higher concentration of wealthy inhabitants, and average levels of GDP per capita in those cities are two to three times the national average.[11]

Though certainly informative, aggregate GDP data might not be as helpful to managers as more micro, industry-specific data. And we can go far beyond macroeconomic measures to devise more concrete estimates of market size and market potential for the Chinese luxury goods market. In fact, estimates suggest that Chinese consumers are likely to spend about 180 billion yuan (or USD 30 billion) on luxury goods in 2015.[12]

As a luxury goods retailer, we can use that as a starting point to estimate our slice of the luxury market pie rather than relying on blunt GDP per capita estimates. That is, if our market share of the luxury goods market stands at about 1 percent in the markets where we operate, we might reasonably estimate that we have the potential to generate USD 300 million in sales (1% of USD 3 billion) in China. Data like GDP, GDP per capita, GDP growth, and labor/land/capital costs can still inform our financial projections, but industry-specific data, when available, usually trump macroeconomic data.

From Macro Data to Detailed Risk Factors

We have established that managers can find fairly robust data to help project revenues and costs; however, market and cost data cannot help gauge the levels of risk present in global markets. Because managerial projections tend to be more imprecise for global markets, we need to go beyond macro-, or even industry-, level market and cost measures of economic activity to identify measures that can provide insight into the variability in economic institutions across countries. This will allow us to get a better sense for the confidence we can have in our projections.

Direct Measures of Institutions. We can dig a bit deeper to measure more fundamental characteristics of a country's economic institutions: its economic actors, systems, and structures. They can reveal useful information about the likely risks to operating in a particular country. Measures that begin to get at these issues include:

- indicators that capture the roles of economic actors in society— the extent of ownership rights; the balance between private consumption and government consumption; and the balance between private investment and government investment;
- indicators that capture the role of markets in society, that is, the extent and level of industrial competition; the existence and type of regulations limiting competition (e.g., price controls, trade barriers, foreign investment limits); and the state of capital markets.

A variety of sources measure fundamental aspects of economic institutions. The World Bank Country Policy and Institutional Assessment (CPIA) database contains information on a country's property rights, how property rights facilitate private economic activity, and how property and contract rights are enforced.

Individual components (consumption, investment, government expenditure) that make up a country's GDP, published at some of the same sources I list above, can shed some light on the balance of economic activity between private and public actors. The World Bank's World Development Indicators publishes data on the state of a country's capital markets: its stock market and its banking sector. There are also a variety of proprietary sources of data on property rights, private economic activity, the state of capital markets, economic regulation, and competition.[13]

Comparing Economic Institutions Using GDP Components. Examining the underlying components that make up a country's GDP can be useful to get a sense for fundamental differences between economic institutions in different countries. By construction, GDP is the sum of consumption, investment, government expenditure, and net exports. A simple comparison of consumption levels between countries can provide a quick, though rudimentary, indication of the relative balance between private and public economic activity in a country. For example, in the United States, personal consumption typically constitutes nearly 70 percent of total GDP, whereas in China it accounts for only around 35 percent. Those numbers alone would suggest that private actors are more involved in economic activity in the United States than they are in China. Companies based in the United States that are accustomed to selling goods to private entities (whether individuals or businesses) would therefore be wise to think carefully about how business models that are dependent upon private consumption will translate to a country where private consumption is less robust.

Comparing Economic Institutions Using Capital Market Structure. There are many sources to which companies seeking to raise capital in the United States can turn: venture capital firms, private equity firms, hedge funds, pension funds, insurance companies, banks, public equity/debt markets, and private individuals. In countries like Germany and Japan, although private investors and public markets exist, banks primarily dominate the market, which results in a more controlled flow and allocation of capital.

By comparing how capital markets are structured in different countries, managers can get a sense for whether the country's capital system is more banking-based or market-based. Companies from the United States (a more market-based system) might find it more complicated to raise capital in certain foreign markets especially in those where long-term relationships with local banks are particularly important.

Indirect Measures of Institutions. As a complement to or even a substitute for direct measures of economic institutions, we can look to country-based indicators of economic development. Although economic development indicators might not directly measure economic institutions, they are correlates of those institutions and are useful for gauging differences in economic institutions in different countries. Measures of economic development include the following:

- indicators of educational attainment (literacy rates and rates of tertiary education);
- indicators of infrastructure development: for transportation (air and sea ports, railways, and highways); for energy (access, reliability, and availability); and for information and communications (penetration rates for fixed telephone lines, mobile phones, personal computers, and broadband Internet access);
- indicators of knowledge development (e.g., research and development in science and technology, patents, and intellectual property).

These data are available from some of the sources described above.[14]

Volatility-Based Measures. If we are most interested in assessing risk, we might be better served to identify measures—either direct or indirect—that specifically capture the volatility in a country's economic institutions. That is, we can move beyond measures of raw economic institutions to those that measure the risk factors inherent in a country's institutions.

Research suggests that the economic growth of nations is typically characterized by a long-term growth trend coupled with short-term volatility around that trend. When short-term risk is extreme, the fundamental economic institutions of a country are particularly unstable and can be subject to radical change.

As a result, the confidence we can have in, and the precision with which we can estimate, the trend is compromised.

When managers make revenue and cost projections, they typically base their estimates on the trend. They tend to underestimate or ignore the role of volatility in the trend. When economic risk (volatility) in a market is great, we cannot be as confident in our revenue or cost estimates, and our projections are more likely to be off. It is therefore helpful to measure not just economic institutions themselves, but also their volatility so as to better understand how risk can upset business projections.

The Importance of Volatility: Revisiting China's Luxury Market. Returning to our previous example regarding the Chinese luxury goods market, we know estimates suggest that it is likely to reach USD 30 billion by 2015. However, that prediction is based on long-term growth trends, but real economic data fluctuate in response to unanticipated shocks. If we build our financial projections assuming USD 30 billion is a certainty, we run the risk of under- or over-estimating the USD 300 million revenue potential.

Therefore, business leaders considering expansion into China (or any country for that matter) should understand not only the *expected size* of the market and the company's potential slice of the market, but also the *risk* that the market estimate itself could be inaccurate. And to the extent that the market estimate turns out to be inaccurate, managers should also be prepared to assess by how much an inaccurate estimate is likely to impact projections. Understanding the underlying volatility in economic institutions can help generate expectations for inaccuracies in financial projections.

Accounting for Volatility. Fortunately, analysts have built macro-economic measures that can help capture the risk and volatility inherent in economic institutions. These measures include the following:

- sovereign credit ratings,
- sovereign bond spreads,
- sovereign bond insurance rates (credit default swaps),
- imputed volatility from GDP growth rates, currency rates, and inflation rates.

Calculating volatility metrics from published GDP, currency, and inflation data is relatively straightforward, and the base data necessary to make those calculations are widely available from some of the sources I list above.

In addition, we can access government bond yield data via Bloomberg or Thomson Reuters. Economists suggest that the rate of interest (yield) on publicly traded sovereign bonds reflects, in part, the market's collective view of a country's economic risks. Further, we can obtain government credit rating data from ratings agencies such as Fitch, Moody's, and Standard and Poor's (S&P). Independent credit ratings agencies rate governments by their creditworthiness and the likelihood that they will repay investors. These ratings can be used as a general indicator of a country's economic risk. Finance professor Aswath Damodaran uses these sovereign ratings to calculate country-specific economic risk spreads indicative of risk differentials across countries.[15] Finally, Markit, Thomson Reuters, and S&P Capital IQ publish credit default swap (CDS) data. Investors can buy CDS as a type of insurance to protect against default on government bonds. As with most forms of insurance, sovereign CDS are more expensive when risk is greater, and so increases in the price of CDS indicate greater levels of risk in a country's economic institutions.

Comparing Economic Institutions Using Sovereign Bond Spreads. As of this writing in early 2015, the US Treasury 10-year bond is trading at a yield of 2.36 percent (the rate at which investors are willing to buy or sell them). This implies that the US government can (more or less) borrow money today from investors for around 2.36 percent for up to 10 years. By contrast, the Greek sovereign 10-year bond is currently trading at 8.05 percent. Investors are demanding much higher interest rates on money they lend to Greece. From a comparison of bond yields (a 5.69% spread between Greek and US sovereign debt), we can conclude that investors see greater risks with lending money to the Greek government than to the US government—and they require higher compensation in exchange for taking the risk. The broader lesson is that differences in sovereign bond yields between countries offer important insights into the perceived economic risk in a country. Current bond prices suggest that Greece is economically more risky than the United States, and managers of US-based companies operating in or considering an expansion to Greece would be wise to take that additional risk into account.

Comparing Economic Institutions Using Credit Default Swaps. In contrast to sovereign bonds, which typically trade in terms of their yield (interest rate), CDS typically trade in terms of basis points. For example, as of this writing, US CDS trade at 17.50 basis points (0.175%). At this rate it would cost USD 1,750 per year to insure USD 1,000,000 of US government bonds against default. By contrast, Greek CDS trade at 752.88 basis points (7.5288%), which equates to USD 77,528.80 per year to insure the same amount—USD 1,000,000—of Greek government bonds against default. Participants in the sovereign debt insurance market therefore view the default risk of a country like Greece as significantly greater—nearly 45 times greater—than that of the United States. This is another means of expressing the additional levels of business risk present in Greece compared with the United States.

Table 5.1 lists a variety of sources that can help guide managers in their quest to measure economic institutions. It is not an exhaustive list, but it can be useful in identifying accurate and reliable economic data.

Table 5.1 Economic Data Sources

Source	URL
United Nations Data	http://unstats.un.org/unsd/databases.htm
World Bank Data	http://data.worldbank.org/
International Monetary Fund Data	http://www.imf.org/external/data.htm
Penn World Table	https://pwt.sas.upenn.edu/
CIA World Factbook	https://www.cia.gov/library/publications/the-world-factbook/
International Labor Organization	http://www.ilo.org/global/statistics-and-databases/lang--en/index.htm
U.S. Bureau of Labor Statistics	http://www.bls.gov/data/
WB Country Policy Institutional Assessment	http://data.worldbank.org/data-catalog/CPIA
WB World Development Indicators	http://data.worldbank.org/data-catalog/world-development-indicators
Index of Economic Freedom	http://www.heritage.org/index/

Continued

Table 5.1 Continued

Source	URL
Economic Freedom of the World Index	http://www.freetheworld.com/
Bloomberg Government Rates and Bonds	https://www.bloomberg.com/markets/rates-bonds
Thomson Reuters Datastream	http://financial.thomsonreuters.com/en.html
Fitch Ratings	https://www.fitchratings.com/
Moody's	https://www.moodys.com/
Standard and Poor's Rating Services	http://www.standardandpoors.com/ratings/sovereigns/ratings-list/en/us
Markit	http://www.markit.com/product/pricing-data-cds
Standard and Poor's Capital IQ	http://www.spcapitaliq.com/
Aswath Damodaran	http://people.stern.nyu.edu/adamodar/
U.S. Bureau of Economic Analysis	http://www.bea.gov/
Euromonitor International	http://www.euromonitor.com/
Economist Intelligence Unit	http://www.eiu.com/home.aspx
IHS Economics and Country Risk	https://www.ihs.com/industry/economics-country-risk.html
Global Competitiveness Report	http://reports.weforum.org/global-competitiveness-report-2014-2015/
Doing Business Index	http://www.doingbusiness.org/
CAGE Comparative Data	http://www.ghemawat.com/cage/
CAGE Comparative Data	http://www.ghemawat.com/cage/

Bringing It All Together

This chapter demonstrates that, just as with political institutions, managers seeking to globalize benefit from understanding the economic institutions in those countries where they plan to do business. This empowers them to better appraise and account for the risks they will face in those markets.

Operating in different countries with different economic institutional profiles is inherently risky, but a set of accurate and robust measures of economic institutions will help us compare them and express economic differences in a way that allows us to accurately account for the risks the economic institutions in each country present. However, before we get down to the detailed work of crunching those numbers, I turn to one last critical institutional factor: culture.

CHAPTER 6

Cultural Institutions and Globalization

This chapter addresses the final piece to the institutional puzzle: culture. We begin with examples that demonstrate the unique impact that culture can have on companies operating in global markets, followed by definitions of cultural institutions, a discussion of cultural difference, and ultimately, guidance for how to measure culture. Only once we have a means to measure cultural institutions can we comprehensively account for the business risks associated with all of the institutional challenges—political, economic, and cultural—that companies face in global markets.

Does Culture Really Matter?

Most of us probably have a particular notion of culture and why it is important, but you may not have fully considered how it can influence business activities. Of all the institutions that matter in a global context, culture is probably the least understood and least concrete of the institutions I discuss in this book. You may therefore not be surprised to learn that it has proven the most difficult for business researchers to conceptualize and measure.

Because cultural institutions are so difficult to define and measure in precise ways, some economists have questioned their relevance altogether. They object to the conceptualization and measurement of culture because they regard it as merely a catchall for social phenomena that we cannot fully, and precisely, explain. The benign view is that to the extent that cultural institutions are legitimate, they have little impact on business activity. The extreme view is that culture is not a legitimate social institution, and that more precise measures of other institutions—political and economic—would eliminate the need to consider culture at all.

I could not disagree more. Culture is indeed an important social institution in its own right, and research demonstrates quite convincingly that it has a great influence on business—especially global business. It is true that cultural institutions have proved a bit more difficult to measure than, for example, economic institutions, but our measures are getting better by the day. Anthropologists, psychologists, and sociologists have made great strides over the past 25 to 50 years in defining and measuring culture. Some measures of culture have even been devised specifically for business use. So yes, culture matters! Now let's see how.

Cultural Institutions 101: What Managers Should Know

We are all familiar with stories of foreigners committing cultural faux pas—a French expression that translates to "false step." Many are the mistakes tourists make when visiting other countries. Visitors to some Western European countries such as Spain or France, for example, may not know to kiss an acquaintance on the cheek, and those who do not do so risk being perceived as cold and unfriendly. In some countries like the United States, by contrast, people consider it a bit forward to kiss a casual acquaintance. Hosts in some parts of Asia expect guests to remove their shoes after crossing the threshold so as not to track dirt into the home, whereas in some Western countries like the United Kingdom, hosts would be more likely to consider this uncivilized and disrespectful. These faux pas by leisure travelers can certainly cause embarrassment, but locals tend to be forgiving of cultural slipups, especially when committed by otherwise well-meaning visitors.

The stakes are much higher, however, when it comes to business, where profits hang in the balance. Culture takes on heightened importance in global business settings, and business owners, managers, employees, customers, and suppliers expect—and require—greater cultural sensitivity. Interpersonal interactions matter a great deal when managing employees with different cultural backgrounds and negotiating transactions with foreign businesspersons. Mastering these cultural differences in business settings is challenging, and managers are often flummoxed by foreign cultural norms and expectations. As you would imagine, this can result in botched business deals, fractured partnerships, and lost opportunities.

Some Common Business Faux Pas

When Western managers visit Japan, they are often unsure whether to bow or extend a hand in greeting. Similarly, in Japan it is not always clear to Western managers whether it is appropriate to make eye contact when speaking with current or potential business partners. The Japanese can consider this rude, especially if the individual holds eye contact for any length of time. In Western countries, however, this signifies that you are being attentive and value what a person is saying.

Misunderstandings can also arise in terms of expressions of agreement and/or disagreement. In Western countries, it is perfectly acceptable to speak transparently and overtly express disagreement or refute someone's argument, while in Asia people consider it rude to openly disagree; it can cause embarrassment or public humiliation. In Asia, people believe that giving and exchanging gifts is a normal part of doing business, whereas in Western countries, as in the United States, this can be considered offensive—and potentially even tantamount to bribery.

Cultural traditions can even dictate business roles and procedures. For example, in Asian and Latin cultures, business hierarchies matter very much; managers at the highest level direct affairs and lead meetings, and junior managers typically remain quiet and follow directions. In contrast, in Western countries, such as Sweden, it is perfectly acceptable for junior employees to openly question their bosses, even in a public setting.

Keeping it Real: Learning Cultural Lessons the Hard Way

When I spent time working in Mexico City in the mid-1990s I learned—the hard way—an important cultural lesson about the different views on hierarchy in business. I was attending a meeting—a bidder's conference—as the most junior employee on the team. Our executive team and our CEO were in attendance, as were the CEOs of our large competitors. Upon arrival at the meeting, we were all seated at a large conference table. Normal chitchat ensued.

After a few minutes listening to the various CEOs and executives exchange niceties, I decided to break into the conversation. As soon as I opened my mouth, the conversation stopped, and all the people in the room turned and stared at me. I finished what I had to say, but the stares—not to mention the screeching halt the conversation had come to—made me incredibly uncomfortable. The message came through loud and clear: junior employees are expected to be like children; they should be seen but not heard.

On the ride back to the office, one of the vice presidents explained to me that in Mexico it was not my place to interject and speak to managers of that status; I should speak only once they had spoken directly to me. Although it is generally acceptable in the United States for a junior employee to engage in conversation with his or her superiors, in Mexico speaking out of turn in that manner was not just inconsiderate, but rude. This was a valuable lesson, and ever since I have been acutely aware of culture's influence on behavior in foreign business settings.

Culture affects not only the decisions a manager makes but, by extension, how the local market views a company. A seemingly minor cultural faux pas that a manager commits can hamstring a company and torpedo even the best-laid global business plans. David Ricks provides examples of several such costly mistakes in his book *Blunders in*

International Business.[1] They run the gamut from correctable gaffes—(inadvertently humorous) mistranslations and minor religious insensitivities—to major bungles that can bring down the house.

For example, attempting to introduce the Miller Lite slogan "Great taste, less filling" to Spanish-speaking markets, Miller mistranslated it as "Filling, less delicious." Schweppes marketed its tonic water in a promotional campaign in Italy as "Schweppes Toilet Water." Embarrassing? To be sure. But insurmountable? No. The ads were certainly easy enough to fix, which is not the case with so many other instances of cultural transgressions in business.

More serious cultural mistakes can take a big toll on companies and have measurable consequences. Offensive advertising campaigns that culturally misjudge local consumers, serious religious transgressions, and failing to account for culture in negotiations with business partners: These can all negatively impact profitability and, in the extreme, destroy businesses. The following examples reflect the wide array of cultural impacts that companies can experience in the global marketplace.

Cultural Insensitivity: Fiat and China

In 2008 the Italian automobile manufacturer Fiat apologized to China for what Chinese customers viewed as a profound cultural insensitivity. In an ad for Lancia (a Fiat-owned division), actor Richard Gere drives a Lancia Delta from Hollywood, CA, in the United States to the Potala Palace in Lhasa, China. This is significant because Lhasa was formerly part of Tibet, the Potala Palace was the residence of the Dalai Lama prior to the Dalai Lama's exile from Tibet, and the relationship between Tibet and China is complicated (to say the least), and it is a particularly sore topic for the Chinese. What is more, Richard Gere has been an outspoken supporter of the Dalai Lama and an independent Tibet.

The advertisement sparked outrage among Chinese consumers, some of whom vowed never to buy a Fiat. But a potential drop in sales was the least of the company's problems. The Chinese government considered the advertisement an affront to the People's Republic and attributed to Fiat the intent to incite conflict.

Fiat created the advertisement for the European market and never even meant to run it in China. However, the company's marketing team should have realized that due to global technology and worldwide communications, Chinese consumers were instantly able to see the ad on YouTube. Fiat quickly made a public statement to distance itself from Richard Gere and apologized for any miscommunication its messaging caused, but the damage had been done. To this day Fiat remains but a tiny player in China—the largest automobile market in the world.

In the modern global marketplace, companies are naïve to assume that strategies they design for one culture will not impact business in countries across the globe. It is hard to believe that Fiat was entirely unaware that it was choosing a controversial setting and spokesperson for the ad—perhaps managers even thought that was part of its appeal. Or maybe they trusted the judgment of an outside advertising agency to conceive the ad. Regardless, this example clearly demonstrates that managers are wise to think more comprehensively and integrate a more sophisticated understanding of cultural sensitivities when devising significant marketing initiatives—at home or abroad.

Erroneous Cultural Assumptions: Gerber in Japan

Some companies misjudge another culture, not just in terms of its attitudes but also in terms of its dietary customs and familial roles. Gerber, the baby food company, encountered cultural challenges in Japan that went well beyond just flawed marketing. Its products were literally lost in translation.

When Gerber first entered the Japanese market, it positioned its baby food as it had in the United States: as a wholesome, natural, healthy, and convenient product. However, its products did not go over so well in Japan. The typical diet of babies in the United States was then—as now—very different from that of Japanese babies, who are more likely to eat rice with sardines than rice with turkey.

Reflecting on Gerber's initial struggles in Japan, the firm's CEO at the time, Alfred Piergallini, admitted, "We were like all other companies initially and figured everyone would like what was American and buy American.... But it is evident that each country not only likes different foods, but also has different feeding habits and practices."[2]

It turned out that the Japanese frowned upon the practice of offering babies prepared food from a jar. This more traditional society viewed the preparation of baby food as the responsibility of the household's primary caregiver and matriarch: the mother or grandmother. Gerber was ultimately able to adapt its products and offerings for the Japanese market, but not without significant cost and years of trial and error. What is more, Gerber's missteps have resulted in a very small market share for the company in Japan. Gerber lags the market leader, a Japanese company named Meiji, by a significant margin.

Cultural Transgressions of Faith: Thom McAn in Bangladesh

Serious cultural mistakes can have far more dire repercussions than falling profit margins. Thom McAn, an American shoe company, learned about the unintended business consequences of religious insensitivity. The company has traditionally marked each pair of its shoes with its script logo. Unfortunately, a portion of its signature script looks like the Arabic word for Allah. So when Thom McAn attempted to sell sandals in Bangladesh, Muslims there took offense. These consumers perceived that the company was trying to desecrate Islam by having them—quite literally—tread on the name of God. This was especially problematic in Bangladesh, not only because insulting Allah is forbidden in Islam, but because people there consider the foot to be unclean and the least significant part of the body. Thom McAn's unintended mistake precipitated a riot in which 50 people were injured and one person was killed.

Was Thom McAn responsible for that collateral damage? You could argue that the company had almost no way to anticipate it was making such a provocative mistake, but had its managers done market research in advance, they might have been aware of the deep cultural sensitivity of the market and avoided offending prospective customers. They might have chosen to leave the traditional script logo off the product entirely or to replace it with block letters. This oversight was dangerous as well as costly.

Cross-Cultural Differences: Western Businesses in Asia

The sentence, "It's not personal; it's strictly business" from *The Godfather* movie exemplifies the fairly clear delineation in cultural expectations between personal and business dealings in the West.[3] When Western cultural expectations come into conflict with differing expectations in other countries, business relationships can sour quickly. This can be particularly damaging in dealings between Western and Asian companies. Relationships are extremely important in Asian countries, where individuals often blur the lines between business dealings and personal interactions.

In the early 1980s, the Dow Chemical Company, a US firm, was involved in a high-profile dispute with the Korean Pacific Chemical Corporation (KPCC), with which it had entered into a joint venture. Dow became so frustrated that its leadership publicly questioned the motives of its partner in the media, going so far as to suggest that KPCC was intentionally trying to sabotage the venture.[4] Taking public what KPCC viewed as a private conflict caused the Korean firm to take dramatic action and immediately withdraw from the partnership.

Even assuming Dow wanted an exit and was ultimately pleased with the outcome, it seems clear that Western cultural norms guided the decisions of its management, which did not count on its Korean partner's sudden, extreme response. In addition, publicly demonstrating its cultural insensitivity could have hurt Dow's relationships with other potential South Korean partners as well as with South Korean customers. Going about the dispute differently could have led to a more amicable outcome and opened the door for other prospective partners beyond KPCC.

Japanese-owned Honda and British-owned Rover had a similar misunderstanding in the 1990s that likewise ended with the dissolution of what had been a long and fruitful partnership.[5] In the mid-1970s the two companies formed a strong, profitable alliance for the joint manufacture of automobiles in Europe that lasted into the mid-1990s. In 1994, when British Aerospace (BAe)—Rover's parent company at the time—decided to exit the automobile business and sell off its Rover division, Honda was the natural candidate for buying Rover. BAe had been losing money on Rover and was looking for a quick exit. However, as a Japanese company that culturally places a particularly high premium on relationships, Honda wanted to approach the deal methodically so as to preserve its delicate balance of supplier and dealership relationships before moving forward with any Rover deal.

Honda expected that BAe would respect the relationship between the two companies and afford Honda the right to take time to consider the acquisition. At the very least, Honda expected that BAe would apprise Honda of any developments with the sale, even granting Honda the first right of refusal should the prospect of a deal with another firm arise. This was Honda's fundamental misunderstanding of its British partner—and of Western business culture, in which transactions tend to come first and relationships second.

BAe likewise misread the Japanese culture, in which business is personal; it inferred from Honda's delay in decision making that Honda was not interested in acquiring Rover. BAe therefore forged ahead and accepted an unexpected (and lucrative) offer from BMW without consulting Honda. Honda accused its former partner of betrayal. "How Could a Western Ally be So Unreliable?" read headlines in Japan.[6] Business reporters asked, "How could Rover—and especially its perfidious parent, British Aerospace—fail so blatantly to respect the Japanese commitment to long-term relationships?"[7] Ultimately, Honda concluded that "British firms do not attach much value to relationships built up over many years."[8]

BAe may have secured a perfectly lucrative deal with the buyer of Rover—Bavarian Motor Works (BMW)—that was a success in the short term, but this perceived gesture of disrespect may have cost the company future business possibilities with Honda—or other Asian companies—in the long term. If the company had handled the situation more delicately, it could have preserved the relationship with Honda, regardless of who bought Rover in the end, and could also have helped Honda save face and avoid public humiliation.

Coping with Culture

Though the examples above describe situations in which companies mismanage culture, many companies learn to span cultural divides with aplomb. They dedicate extra resources to understanding the local cultural environment and appropriately tailor and translate their business practices to that environment. They conduct in-depth market research to make sure they are culturally sensitive in their foreign dealings. They engage experts—managers with experience in a particular country, or consultants who specialize in cultural training—to help navigate foreign terrain. However, even those companies that successfully navigate cultural differences often do so at a significant cost. Coping effectively with culture—dedicating extra resources, conducting market research, enlisting the help of experts—is neither free nor easy.

When the Canadian company Four Seasons entered the Paris hotel market by acquiring the George V in 1998, it went to great lengths to present itself as sensitive to traditional French culture. It undertook a series of calculated moves: hiring famed French designer Pierre-Yves Rochon to redesign the property and refurbish it to its art deco glory and luring famed chef Philippe Legendre from Taillevent as executive chef of the hotel restaurant (Le Cinq). Four Seasons thereby not only appealed to its customer base of wealthy travelers, but also demonstrated respect, particularly for French artistry and design, and paid homage to the cultural significance of food in France.

This strategy seems to have worked, as the George V has been consistently ranked among the best hotels in the world. And yet the George V has one of the highest cost structures of any hotel in the Four Seasons family of hotels, and higher even than that of any other comparable Parisian palace hotels.[9] Star chefs and famous designers come at a price.

What We Mean by Cultural Institutions and Culture

The variety of examples in this chapter reflect how dealing with foreign cultures can, at best, result in additional costs for a firm, from translating and tweaking marketing campaigns, to modifying products to better meet local conditions, to changing management styles to accommodate the local culture. At worst, not accounting for culture can result in years of underperformance, lost profitability, or—in the extreme—outright failure.

Now that we have seen some of the cultural mistakes that managers should avoid as well as how managers can effectively deal with culture and avoid those mistakes, we should turn our attention to how to define culture and measure cultural institutions. Once we clarify these concepts, we can identify suitable measures that will allow us to estimate the impact of culture on global companies.

At their most basic level, cultural institutions are critical building blocks of culture, the unique and distinct identity of a collective. Of course, that begs the question: What does culture mean? Professor Phil Rosenzweig's definition, of "a shared system of meanings, ideas, and thought," yields a number of insights.[10] First, to the extent that a collective shares a culture, it has boundaries that distinguish its members from nonmembers. Second, the symbols, pictures, sound, speech, and writing that a collective uses to encode and transmit experiences embody its culture. Third, the process of encoding and transmitting experiences influences the interpretations, ideas, and thought of the collective. This process helps current and future members of the collective make sense of the world around them.

Other definitions of culture provide additional insights. The Dutch social psychologist Geert Hofstede, who is one of the most prominent cultural scholars in the management field, refers to culture as the "software of the mind."[11] I would take this analogy even one step further and describe culture as the operating system of the mind: an interface between our brains and our behavior. Culture is vital to the functioning of our "hardware" (brain and body) and provides a foundation for "operations" (behavior and actions) that the hardware will carry out. Culture influences how we perceive, interpret, process, and respond to stimuli, and as such its influence reaches beyond a shared system of meaning, ideas, and thoughts. Culture also shapes and influences behavior.

The Acquisition of Culture

Unlike instincts, which individuals gain from biological inheritance and need not learn, people typically learn their culture. Members of a collective deliberately pass on their culture from generation to generation. Scholars John van Maanen and Andre Laurent believe this cultural indoctrination begins at birth, with messages that people transmit through "gestures, words, tone of voice, noises, colors, smells, and body contact we experience; with the way we are raised, washed, rewarded, punished, held in check, toilet trained and fed; by the stories we are told, the games we play, the songs we sing or rhymes we recite; the schooling we receive... right down to the very way we sleep and dream."[12]

Because elders of the collective transmit cultural teachings to us so early in life, we tend to take these teachings for granted and fail to recognize just how deeply ingrained they are in our social structure, routines, and interactions. Learned social structures, routines, and interactions become second nature to us and underpin our entire system of assumptions and beliefs about how the world works. Culture therefore exerts a strong influence on how we view, experience, and engage with the world and colors our view of how the world is and how it should be.

The Development of Culture

Of course, this brief discussion should not oversimplify the highly complex nature of culture. Culture is incredibly nuanced, and research has taught us a great deal about its foundations, its development, and the ways in which it changes and evolves over time. We know that a combination of institutions and historical events influence the formation of a culture: political, legal, economic, geographic, educational, technological, social, linguistic, and religious. I will focus here on the social, linguistic, and religious aspects of culture because research suggests that these factors have a distinct and outsize influence on a nation's cultural development. The remaining political, legal, geographic, educational, and technological factors are better viewed, and more directly measured, as political and economic institutions.

Social Influences

We can begin to understand cultures by observing systematic patterns of behavior, interaction, and structure within a collective. We can look to social values such as the role of families, the role of individuals, the importance of friendships, and the way the collective views formal positions of power. India, for example, with its well-defined ancient caste system, has a fairly formal social structure. Although the Indian government has attempted to formally protect lower castes from discrimination and even suppress elements of the caste system, the caste system is so deeply rooted that the country continues to exhibit a high tolerance for inequality. The United States, by contrast, has a less formal social structure—at least compared to India; there is less social stratification based on class or position there.

Language Influences

Language is another lens through which we can view a particular culture. In Spanish, as in other Romance languages, nouns have gender; they are either masculine or feminine. Typically, nouns that end in "o" are masculine and those that end in "a" are feminine. (As you are probably aware, English does not distinguish gender for most nouns.) The "masculinity" or "femininity" of nouns can influence how people in Hispanic cultures view what words represent, and this can be quite distinct from how people from Anglo—or Asian or other—cultures view those same words.

Religious Influences

A fundamental aspect of religion—which some would maintain is a culture unto itself—is its theology, philosophy, morality, and beliefs about human existence and human interaction. A religion's most basic tenets, including the ways in which its tenets evolve, can influence cultural formation and evolution. In many ways, political tensions between Spain and Turkey, for example, result from their different interpretations of world events, interpretations that can be traced to how religions have shaped the two countries. While the Catholic Church has profoundly influenced the historical and cultural development of Spain, Islamic traditions have over centuries had a predominant influence in Turkey.

Who Shares a Culture?

In the discussion above I speak about culture in terms of a collective. But this begs the question: What is a collective? Basically, a collective refers to any group that shares common experiences and/or values. Any such group can develop a distinct culture. You may have heard of a certain "corporate culture," for example, the buttoned-up, professional culture of an investment firm like Goldman Sachs or the laid-back, thrifty culture of a design-focused retail outlet like IKEA. Educational institutions can also develop distinct cultures. The business schools at NYU and Michigan, for example, have quite different student bodies, faculties, and staff. They have developed systematically different sets of structures, routines, and interactions. They have developed strengths and specialties in different areas. I often hear prospective students describe such cultural differences between universities like NYU and Michigan in terms of a different "feel" they get when they visit the respective campuses.

Sports teams can also have particular cultures. People characterize the New York Yankees baseball team as professional and businesslike, probably in part because the organization requires more formal attire for official business travel and bans its players from wearing long hair or growing facial hair below the lip. By contrast, many describe the culture of the Boston Red Sox—the chief rival of the New York Yankees—as anti-Yankees, both on and off the field. Management permits—and at times has even encouraged—Red Sox players to grow out their hair and sport long, bushy beards. The players have embraced such an unkempt, unprofessional-looking identity that at one point, around 2004, they proclaimed themselves "The Idiots," in homage to the team's cast of goofy, eclectic characters.

Each of us also subscribes to smaller subcultures within our society that are differentiated from the main culture; the musical genres such as jazz, hip hop, punk, and alternative are some examples. An individual can also simultaneously be a part of a metaculture, a kind of broader collective that transcends his or her primary culture, such as that of MBA students, professional athletes, or business managers.

Surely you have experienced some of these differences yourself and are familiar with the unique cultural characteristics of your own company, school, religion, sports team, or other groups.

National Culture

Although a variety of groups develops distinct cultures, the principal cultural unit of interest with regard to globalization is the nation state. Research shows that countries, like other social collectives, have distinct cultures. As you might expect, cultures vary significantly from one country to the next, and people from the same country tend to have more in common with their compatriots than with people from other countries. That is to say, if we draw at random any two citizens from Canada and any two from the United States, it is likely that the two from the United States would share more culturally in common with one another than they would with either of the two Canadians, and the same would be true for the Canadians.[13]

Why National Culture Matters to Business

When it comes to globalization and cross-border business dealings, national culture matters a great deal. Because culture is familiar and habitual to those from a particular country, it can be hard for members of a collective from one country to understand how others from another country could possibly not share their worldview. However, as world history and current events around the globe have shown us, individuals from countries with distinct cultures sometimes make sense of the same events in entirely different ways. Differences in worldview are at the root of such cultural misunderstandings and become even more salient when one group interacts—as in business dealings—with another that does not share the same culture. An appreciation for differing cultures enables us not only to understand the motivations behind certain behaviors, but also—even more useful—to predict future behavior. Managers who understand the significance of culture are therefore well-positioned to devise strategies for effectively dealing with and managing the cultural complexities inherent in global business.

Measuring Culture

One way to improve our understanding of, and appreciation for, the way national culture impacts global business is to quantify how cultures differ from one country to another. Once we know whether and how two cultures differ, we can account for the ways in which those differences are likely to impact a company from one country that does business in another. As with the discussion above, the focus is on measures of language, religion, and social structure, because these best capture the impact of national culture on global business.

Measuring Language

To measure the impact linguistic differences are likely to have on a business, we first need to know which languages a country's population speaks. The work of Douglas Dow is particularly useful to that end; he uses data from Raymond Gordon's classification of 6,912 languages throughout the world to identify each country's three most widely spoken ("major") languages (those that at least 20% of the population speak).[14] This enables us to compare the primary languages of any two countries, to determine what percentage of one country's population speaks the language of another, and to get a sense for how difficult it will be for a company from one country to operate in another. The more the spoken languages of any two countries resemble each other, the easier it will be for companies from one country to conduct business in the other.

Measuring Religion

Following the same basic procedure, Dow measures the prevalence of major religions in each country. He accounts for the three most widely practiced religions in each country, down to the denomination or sect.[15] For a country where Islam is the predominant religion, these data would indicate the percentage of the population that is part of each denomination: Sunni, Shia, etc. For a country that is predominantly Christian, the data would likewise indicate the percentage that is Catholic, Protestant, Baptist, etc. Once we account for the dominant religions in any one country, we can devise a religious similarity index that compares its top religions to those of another country. This provides a sense of the relative religious makeup of two countries—information that can be highly valuable for global business purposes, because it is easier for companies to operate across countries that share common religious characteristics.

Measuring Social Structure

We can draw upon well-established research in the area of social structure to expand our understanding of national culture. Hofstede is probably best known for his work in this domain. Starting in the late 1960s and early 1970s, he attempted to capture the social dimensions of national culture that are of particular interest to business managers. He identified and measured four key social dimensions of culture: individualism/collectivism, power distance, uncertainty avoidance, and masculinity/femininity.[16] The primary characteristics of each dimension are as follows:

- Individualism/collectivism: The first dimension refers to the extent to which societies value individual self-reliance and individual achievement (individualism) as opposed to social cohesion and group welfare (collectivism). In countries with individualistic cultures, such as the United States, it is socially acceptable for individuals to put their own needs ahead of those of the group. By contrast, countries with collectivist cultures, such as Japan, expect individuals to subjugate their own needs in favor of those of the group.
- Power distance: This dimension measures the extent to which there is an unequal distribution of power (hierarchy) within a society and whether its members regard that unequal distribution of power as legitimate. Countries characterized as high in power distance, such as India, generally have more clearly defined class systems, more unequal distributions of power, and often a greater cultural acceptance of hierarchy. In countries characterized as low in power distance, such as the United States, people tend to strive to minimize inequalities and to view each other as equals, irrespective of social or professional position.
- Uncertainty avoidance: The third dimension captures the extent to which a society is, generally, comfortable with risk,

uncertainty, and ambiguity. Countries that are low in uncertainty avoidance are typically less rule-oriented and less rigid when it comes to applying rules. Accordingly, individuals from countries characterized as low in uncertainty avoidance are typically willing to take greater risks, whereas people in countries characterized as high in uncertainty avoidance tend to apply rules more literally and uniformly. Individuals from countries characterized as high in uncertainty avoidance also tend to avoid taking significant risks and to deliberate more in decision making.

- Masculinity/femininity: This cultural dimension so labeled by Geert Hofstede captures the extent to which societies stress values that anthropologists traditionally associate with gender-based roles. According to Hofstede, higher levels of achievement, assertiveness, and competition characterize countries that exhibit masculinity. Greater levels of compassion, cooperation, and consensus characterize countries that exhibit femininity.

Hofstede's research, while incredibly influential, is now quite dated. Of Hofstede's proposed cultural dimensions, researchers more recently have validated two of the four: individualism/collectivism and power distance. There is less empirical support for uncertainty avoidance and masculinity/femininity. I therefore concentrate my measurement efforts on his first two dimensions.

Sources of Cultural Data

In addition to the websites of Douglas Dow and Geert Hofstede, there are a number of excellent sources for national cultural data. The GLOBE project, a worldwide collaborative effort spearheaded by Robert House, seeks to develop measures of national culture. It has defined several more sociocultural dimensions than Hofstede did: performance orientation, uncertainty avoidance, humane orientation, institutional collectivism, in-group collectivism, assertiveness, gender egalitarianism, future orientation, and power distance.

The World Values Survey is a collaborative project social scientists created to study societal values. Although not specifically geared toward the study of national cultures, their data offer excellent

Table 6.1 Culture Data Sources

Source	URL
Douglas Dow	https://sites.google.com/site/ddowresearch/home/scales
Geert Hofstede	http://geert-hofstede.com/
GLOBE Project of Culture	http://www.uvic.ca/gustavson/globe/index.php
World Values Survey	http://www.worldvaluessurvey.org/wvs.jsp

measures of country-specific sociocultural attributes. The question-naire asks about societal views toward religion, authority, money, equality, and family.

Individual scholars, such as Shalom Schwartz, have also made tremendous contributions to our understanding of culture. Although his culture data are not publicly available, his work played a critical role in the development of the World Values Survey. He improved our understanding of basic sociocultural values—such as individualism and collectivism, egalitarianism and equality, and tradition and religion—and helped shape our understanding of how cultural values vary among countries.

Table 6.1 provides a list of sources from which one can collect measures of cultural institutions. It is not exhaustive; however, it is a good starting point to identify accurate and reliable sources of data on cultural institutions.

How Culture Relates to Other Institutions

For the purposes of understanding the full set of institutional risks associated with globalization, it is important to clarify how cultural institutions are related to, as well as distinct from, political and economic institutions. Broadly, cultural institutions are more informal than the other institutions, which are structural and formalized.

Political institutions are typically developed with a specific set of rules and with a web of detailed, established relationships between political organizations, agencies, and actors. In the United States, for example, citizens elect the leader (president) of the executive branch of government every four years via an electoral college. There are well-defined roles for the president as well as rules for how the president interacts with the legislative branch (Congress), which also has distinct and detailed roles and responsibilities. Cultural institutions, by contrast, tend to be embedded in complex social relationships that are often intangible and tacit. In many ways, culture encompasses the unwritten rules that govern social interaction.

Of course, we cannot consider any one institution—politics, economics, or culture—in a vacuum, given that they are all interrelated. We tend to observe that a set of political, economic, or cultural institutions follows a fairly systematic pattern. Researchers have discovered that certain cultural leanings tend to correlate with specific political and economic structures and vice versa. It would probably not surprise you that countries high in power distance tend to have more formal and rigid political institutions. Likewise, countries that are high in individualism generally have legal systems that are less rigid and rules-based (as in civil law) and more flexible and precedent-based (as in common law).

However, these institutional relationships go beyond a simple correlation; they are also causal: each institution influences the development of the others. The development and evolution of political and economic institutions influences how cultural institutions evolve. The reverse is also true.[17] A shifting economy can, for example, lead to a political regime change. Similarly, changes in the political landscape can spur or stunt economic development.

A final consideration that is important to our globalization discussion is how institutions change over time. We know that political, economic, and cultural institutions are not static, but how they change and at what rate remains an open question for experts in the field of institutional development. Thus far, research suggests that cultural institutions typically change at a much slower rate than political and economic institutions—over generations rather than in years. A culture that has been centuries in the making does not quickly dissolve, whereas political and economic institutions can change relatively quickly—sometimes rather suddenly. For example, in a coup d'état, political institutions change radically overnight, and yet a culture—with its shared systems of meanings, ideas, thought, values, and socially acceptable behaviors—tends to endure, regardless of sudden political institutional changes.

Our endeavor to measure institutions will reflect any underlying institutional changes as the measures change, but this broader discussion serves to highlight why it is so important to measure all country-based institutions. Basically, although political, economic, and cultural institutions tend to be related, they are not perfectly related. If they were perfectly related, measuring one would suffice to capture the effect of them all. But because they can and do change separately from one another, failing to measure one of them can lead to significant gaps in our understanding of all of them and to a flawed understanding of globalization.

The Importance of Understanding All Institutions: India and the United States

India and the United States share fundamental similarities in political institutions. They were both British colonies, and they inherited many political institutions from their former colonizer—democracy and common law. However, India and the United States tend to be extremely dissimilar in culture. The dominant religion in India is Hinduism. The dominant religion in the United States is Christianity. India considers Hindi an official language, but it is little spoken in the United States. India is much more collectivist than the United States, and it is much higher in power distance. India and the United States are also significantly different in economic institutions. The United States is economically more developed than India, and its economic institutions are historically less volatile than those of India.

Considering only India's political institutions might lull a US company considering entry into the Indian market into believing that, given the similarities, doing business there would be relatively easy. However, political similarity tells only a portion of the story. Many US companies struggle in India precisely because the economic and cultural environments are so dissimilar, and failing to consider economic and cultural institutions, in addition to political institutions, can lead to disastrous consequences.

Bringing It All Together

This chapter stresses the importance of understanding cultural institutions and illustrates the very real cultural costs that companies can bear in global markets. Managers are well prepared to make informed global decisions only if they understand the potential impact of culture and how to measure cultural differences, so as to account for the cultural risks their companies are likely to face in foreign markets.

More broadly, we now have all the raw material we need to begin thinking holistically and comprehensively about globalization risks. We know where to turn for accurate, robust measures of the various institutions that underpin the liability of foreignness: the political, economic, and cultural institutions that are at the heart of the risks to globalizing and global companies.

The obvious next step is to consider how to use these measures not only to account for those risks, but to create some kind of overarching risk measurement that allows us to express them in a financially meaningful way. The institutional measures empower us to compare countries and then to convert those differences into mathematical measures of risk. Ultimately, this enables us to create detailed cross-country risk spreads. Only then are we in a position to price the overall level of institutional risk for a pair of countries.

The next chapter provides a road map for how to use the individual measures of institutions you learned about in chapters 4, 5, and 6 to generate an overarching measure of institutional risk, bringing us one step closer to our goal of improving our global acumen. Undergoing this intensive analytical process will provide you with a distinct advantage: it will impart a unique understanding of global business that will enable you to deftly manage globalization's complexities.

CHAPTER 7

Using Global Acumen to Account
for Risk

This chapter builds upon the previous three to demonstrate how we can use measures of institutions to account for globalization risk. It is critical that managers of global companies understand not only political, economic, and cultural institutions, but also the ways those institutions differ across countries and the risks those differences can pose. To that end, it is important to briefly revisit the concept of institutional distance, which was formally defined in chapter 1 as the dissimilarity (or similarity) in institutional makeup between countries.

To summarize all that we have learned about institutions and institutional distance, we will begin with a simple exercise. Think about the following set of eight large and economically important countries: Australia, Canada, China, India, Japan, Russia, the United Kingdom, and the United States. Consider how they compare:

- Which countries strike you as similar? Which seem different? Why?
- If I told you that it was riskier for a US company to invest in some subset of these countries, which do you think would make up this subset?
- If I told you that it was riskier for a Chinese company to invest in some subset of these countries, which do you think would be in this subset?

- What assumptions did you make in coming up with your answers?

In chapters 4, 5, and 6 I discussed the political, economic, and cultural institutions of countries. Given that discussion, when you answer questions about similarities and differences between countries, you likely think in terms of those institutions. You probably immediately recognize that subsets of the eight countries are more similar to each other than to others, such as Australia, Canada, the United Kingdom, and the United States, because they have a similar institutional profile. By the same token, you may recognize that some of the countries—such as China and the United States—are very different because they share little in terms of institutional profile.

Differences in political, economic, and cultural institutions between countries can create impediments to globalization, and numerous examples from the previous chapters help drive home the point: Institutional distance underpins global business risk. Therefore, institutional distance most likely figured prominently in your answers to the questions about investment risk. The more similar the institutions in different countries, the lower the business risk to a company from one country that wishes to invest in the other. The more dissimilar the institutions in different countries, the greater the business risk to a company from one country that wishes to invest in the other.

But why stop simply with a qualitative understanding of institutions and the institutional challenges that companies face in specific global markets? We can go far beyond conventional understandings of institutions; we can measure and quantify the risks that institutional distance presents to global companies.

For nearly half a century, scholars have recognized the importance of measuring political, economic, and cultural institutions, and institutional distance is now a central topic of study in global strategy. Researchers have made great strides in identifying countries' key institutions, developing and validating measures of those institutions, and using those measures to calculate institutional distances between countries. Studies show a positive correlation between institutional distance and the level of risk in doing business across countries: the larger the institutional distance between one country and another, the higher the risk.

And yet, in spite of a variety of studies that tie institutional distance directly to globalization risk, the concept of institutional distance has not had a substantial impact on managerial practice. A central objective of this book is to overcome that knowledge gap. Companies have everything to gain from this added insight, and—as countless examples have shown—much to lose from disregarding it.

This discussion presumes, of course, that we can fruitfully convert measures of political, economic, and cultural institutions into meaningful measures of institutional risk. By the end of this chapter, you should have a much better understanding of how to do that and be able to generate institutional risk spreads from individual measures of institutions. You will also gain insight into Global Acumen, a global risk management tool that algorithmically converts measures of institutions into financially meaningful measures of risk. The path to get there might be a bit complex and technical, but the payoff is great.

Moving from Institutions to Institutional Distance

Any conversation about institutional distance should begin with individual measures of institutions. Once you have compiled measures for political, economic, and cultural institutions for a set of countries from the sources mentioned in chapters 4, 5, and 6 (or other sources), you can calculate the institutional distance between any two countries by comparing their underlying institutional dimensions. When the institutional measures of one country are mathematically close to those of another, there is little institutional distance between them; the countries are said to be "institutionally close." When the institutional measures of one country are mathematically far from those of another, the institutional distance between them is great; the countries are said to be "institutionally distant."

To illustrate the mathematical calculation of institutional distance let us extend the example of political institutions from chapter 4 and assume that we have a set of political, economic, and cultural scores for the United States of 1, 2, and 3, respectively; for the United Kingdom of 2, 3, and 4, respectively; and for China of 8, 9, and 10, respectively.[1] As before, we are not necessarily interested in the absolute scores or what those scores indicate about the country's institutional structure (though that might be interesting). We are interested in *relative* scores.

Comparatively, a cursory glance at the numbers indicates that the United States is *relatively* closer to the United Kingdom in its institutional makeup than to China. In fact, the numbers suggest that the United States is closer to the United Kingdom on every institutional dimension. Let us now express that mathematically, using a simple composite indicator. If we add up all of the institutional measures for each country, we get a total institutional score of 6 (1 + 2 + 3) for the United States; 9 (2 + 3 + 4) for the United Kingdom; and 27 for China (8 + 9 + 10). Mathematically, the United States is 3 institutional distance units away from the United Kingdom (an average distance of 1 unit per dimension) and 21 institutional distance units away from China (an average distance of 7 units per dimension). The individual political, economic, and cultural distances between the United States, United Kingdom, and China— along with the average institutional distances between them—are depicted in figure 7.1.

Even this rudimentary method for expressing institutional distance can yield important insights about risk (we will learn more

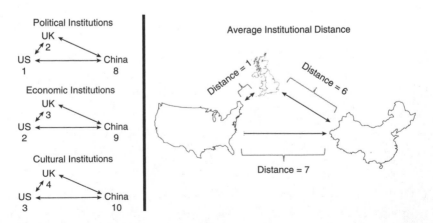

Figure 7.1   Institutional Distance Illustration.

about how academics calculate institutional distance later). As you might expect, when the institutional distance between one country and another is small, global expansion from one country to the other is relatively easy. When the institutional distance between a pair of countries is great, global expansion from one country to the other is relatively difficult. But the impact of distance does not stop there.

Research demonstrates that institutional distance correlates to a host of global business outcomes. Institutional distance negatively correlates to market entry, which simply means that a company is less likely to do business in markets that are institutionally distant than it is in those that are institutionally close. We also know that institutional distance negatively correlates to performance: foreign companies from an institutionally distant country typically perform worse and have a higher failure rate than those from a country that is institutionally close. In practice, this suggests—given that the United States is *relatively* closer institutionally to the United Kingdom than to China—that a US company is (on average) more likely to enter the United Kingdom than China and that a US company in the Chinese market is likely to experience greater difficulty than it would in the United Kingdom.

Research links institutional distance not only to globalization and global performance, but also to market-entry strategies in foreign markets (that is, the governance structures companies select in global markets) and global subsidiary management (how companies manage far-flung global operations). The greater the institutional distance, the more likely a company is to opt for shared forms of ownership and control, such as alliances and joint ventures. In addition, the greater the institutional distance, the more likely a company's product offerings are to vary from one country to another and the less likely a company is to centralize decision making at its domestic headquarters. In practice, this suggests that a US company is (on average) more likely to own its own operations in the United Kingdom than in China and more likely to use a joint venture in China than in the United Kingdom. Likewise, the company's product mix is likely to be more similar in the US and the UK markets than in the US and Chinese markets. Finally, US companies are likely to allow managers in the Chinese market greater latitude in making decisions for the Chinese market than they allow managers in the UK market.

What Managers Are Missing

Given these and other significant findings, it is time for institutional distance to make its way into the standard toolkit of managerial best practices. Managers should actively build institutional distance and institutional risk into their decision-making calculus. In my experience, most seasoned managers already recognize that global business is fraught with risk, but they have failed to develop the systematic tools—such as a detailed measure of institutional distance—to meaningfully express or account for that risk.

In conversations with managers from some of the largest and most sophisticated companies in the world, I found that most of them immediately recognize the importance of political, economic, and cultural institutions to globalization. They are also highly aware of the incredible challenges inherent in managing the many differences in institutions across borders. However, despite this awareness, many managers openly admit that in their global operations they do not explicitly account for these differences. For example, when reflecting on his business in India, a chief financial officer (CFO) at a Fortune 100 company told me, "We know India is different [from the United States]; we just don't know how to measure it." When one of my MBA students asked a chief strategy officer (CSO) of a Fortune 500 company, the executive acknowledged, "We do not approach global acquisitions any differently than domestic acquisitions . . . not because we do not want to, but because we are unsure how to."

There is clearly a knowledge gap here—even for experienced and well-informed global managers. Managers could avoid the most costly globalization mistakes and reduce overall risk if they knew how to integrate insights about institutions and institutional distance into their estimates of risk and their financial decision making tools. What we therefore need are some strategies to deal with global risk, strategies that convert measures of institutions into financial measures of risk.

The Nuts and Bolts of Institutional Distance

There are many ways to generate estimates of institutional distance. There are simple methods, using basic mathematical operations like subtraction and absolute values. There are more complex approaches, steeped in mathematical methods developed by Euclid or Mahalanobis. Whatever the approach, keep in mind the purpose: generating a meaningful measure of risk (and not an elegant mathematical theory of the world). Elegant mathematical approaches are certainly a noble intellectual pursuit, but remember: Complex does not always mean better. That existential discussion notwithstanding, there are several ways in which you can calculate institutional distance.

Using Simple Subtraction

The easiest way to think about distance is as a mathematical subtraction problem. If we have a particular institutional measure for two countries, we can express the distance between them by subtracting one number from the other. For example, if we were to measure economic institutions on scale of 0 to 10, and country x—let's say, the United States—has a value of 2, while country y—let's say, China—has a value of 9, we could express the distance between the two countries on the economic dimension as +7 (9 minus 2) or as -7 (2 minus 9), depending on the direction in which we perform the subtraction.

Using Absolute Value

An alternative is to use the absolute value of the difference between the two measures. Using the absolute value imposes a communicative property on the results, which means that changing the order of the operation (whether we subtract the value of country x from country y, or vice versa) does not change the answer. This is because the absolute value of x minus y is the same as the absolute value of y minus x (expressed mathematically: $|x - y| = |y - x|$). In the context of the example of the United States and China, that would be $|9 - 2| = 7$ and $|2 - 9| = 7$. In this case, the answer 7 (regardless of the direction of the operation) implies no distinction in the difference—country x is equally far from y as country y is from x.

Subtraction or Absolute Value: Does It Matter?

Most research on institutional distance favors the absolute value approach. The general assumption is that distance as a universal measure of length between two points in space is, by definition, the same in one direction as it is in the other. Think of the distance between Shanghai and New York. The distance between Shanghai and New York is the same as the distance between New York and Shanghai—more than 7,000 miles. It matters not in which direction you perform the operation; the answer remains the same.

The subtraction function, by contrast, is not communicative like the absolute value function. Simply changing the order of the operation changes the answer. Returning to the example of the United States and China, we could express the distance between the two countries on the economic dimension as +7 (9 minus 2) or –7 (2 minus 9). If you believe that the plus or minus value that results is meaningful, you would favor the subtraction approach.

That begs the question: Why might the direction of the difference matter? In our context, the direction of the difference could be significant if we believe that some kinds of institutional environments are more welcoming to business than others. If we have reason to believe that, when it comes to economic institutions, lower scores are better than higher ones, then positive differences will indicate lower risk. If it is qualitatively easier for businesses to navigate the economic institutions in the United States than Chinese economic institutions, then a difference of +7 bodes well for a Chinese company contemplating an expansion to the United States, while a difference of –7 suggests that a US company contemplating an expansion to China will have a more difficult time. Insofar as economic institutions are concerned, expanding from China to the United States is less risky than expanding from the United States to China.

In the New York-Shanghai example, the distance between them obviously does not change; however, the direction of the distance might matter very much to a business traveler. Due to the jet stream, winds travel across the earth continuously from west to east, which often makes flying east faster than flying west. Knowing, then, whether the flight is from New York to Shanghai or from Shanghai to New York can tell us a lot about how long a business traveler should expect the flight to take. Similarly, if we have reason to believe that moving in a certain institutional direction—from one country to another—provides an inherent advantage, we can assess which way the wind is blowing for business.

More Complex Approaches to Distance

There is a complicating factor when we rely on subtraction or absolute value techniques to generate measurements of institutional distances. By its very nature, institutional distance is not a singular measure we generate from a single institutional dimension—as in the simple example of the geographical distance between Shanghai and New York above—but an amalgam of interrelated institutional measures.

Each of the institutions discussed at length in this book—political, economic, and cultural—represents an individual dimension comprised of several subdimensions. And the individual subdimension measures listed in tables 4.1, 5.1, and 6.1 are not always measured on the same scale (from 0 to 10) across the board. Different data sources measure individual dimensions and subdimensions in different ways using a variety of scales. For this reason, it is often better to turn to mathematical techniques designed specifically to deal with such a situation. This is where Euclidean and Mahalanobis approaches can help.

Euclidean Approaches to Distance

Euclidean distance provides a means of calculating the shortest "ordinary" geometric distance between points in n-dimensional space (where n represents the number of different dimensions). For our purposes it can provide a simplified (collapsed and unitary) expression of institutional distance between a pair of countries from a set of political, economic, and cultural dimensions.

For example, using a standard Euclidian approach, we can express the institutional distance between two countries (let's call them x and y) mathematically as:

$$Institutional\ Distance_{x,y} = \sqrt{\sum_{i=1}^{n}(I_{ix} - I_{iy})^2}$$

- n is the total number of institutional measures you include in the calculation;
- I_{ix} is an individual observation for institution i from a set of institutions (I) in country x;
- I_{iy} is an individual observation for institution i from a set of institutions (I) in country y.

An institutional distance of 0 implies that the two countries share equivalent institutional profiles. An institutional score of greater than 0 implies institutional differences, and a larger value for institutional distance indicates a greater distance between two countries in their overall institutional makeup.[2]

Mahalanobis Approaches to Distance

Academics have used Euclidean approaches extensively to calculate institutional distance; however, some point out that Euclidean-based formulas do not take into account correlations among variables. This is problematic because, as mentioned in chapter 6, political, economic, and cultural institutions are highly correlated. In these situations, academics generally prefer Mahalanobis approaches to calculate distance. The advantage is that Mahalanobis distance takes into account covariances (correlations) across dimensions. We can formally express this approach as:

$$Institutional\ Distance_{x,y} = \sqrt{(I_x - I_y)^T S^{-1}(I_x - I_y)}$$

- I_x is a vector of institutional measures for country x;
- I_y is a vector of institutional measures for country y;

- S^{-1} is the inverse of the covariance (correlation) matrix between I_x and I_y;
- T indicates that we should transpose the resulting matrix.

As with institutional distances we calculate using Euclidean approaches, greater Mahalanobis distances imply greater institutional differences between countries, and smaller Mahalanobis distances imply greater institutional similarities between countries.[3]

An Application of Mahalanobis Distance

My colleague Zheying Wu and I calculated institutional distances using a Mahalanobis distance approach for a study recently published in the *Journal of International Business Studies*.[4] In that study we examine the entry of foreign banks into the US market. We found, generally, that foreign banks from institutionally distant countries face greater operational risks in the United States than banks that hail from institutionally close countries.

In our study, the Mahalanobis distance formula generates the following institutional distance outputs:

- 2.69 between Australia and the United States
- 4.99 between Japan and the United States
- 6.31 between South Korea and the United States.

Although the point values have no meaning in and of themselves, as a set they tell us about the *relative* challenges and risks to operating in the United States for companies expanding from Australia, Japan, and South Korea. The findings reinforce the idea that larger institutional distances imply greater risk, and smaller institutional distances indicate lesser risk. In that sense, the United States presents greater levels of risk to South Korean companies than to Japanese or Australian companies.

From Institutional Distance to Global Acumen

The overview of institutional distance estimation techniques—subtraction, absolute value, Euclidean, and Mahalanobis—serves to introduce standard approaches and highlight the connection between institutional distance and risk. And as we know, institutional distance relates to risk. Greater levels of institutional distance between countries are associated with higher business risk, and lower levels of institutional distance between countries are associated with lower business risk.

Another valuable takeaway from the introduction of institutional distance estimating techniques is that one should tailor the distance approach to the user's specific context. If we use many interrelated institutional measures and the direction of the difference does not matter, we want to skew toward Euclidean and Mahalanobis approaches. If the directional distances between institutions matter, we will want to find ways to incorporate elements of subtraction into our calculations.

To empower managers to take advantage of this learning in real time, we need to find a way apply these concepts so as to generate a simple, user-friendly measure of risk. It turns out that this is just a matter of taking the next logical step: translating institutional distances into meaningful risk measures that fit directly into managers' existing financial models.

This transformation is at the core of Global Acumen, an algorithmic approach to institutional distance developed after years of research and testing. The beauty of this approach is that the raw materials we need to compute the Global Acumen algorithm are the same ones we would use to calculate institutional distance between two countries. The procedures are similar to those we might use to calculate institutional distance, with only slight modifications.

Differences between Global Acumen and Institutional Distance

As with institutional distance, we start with measures of political, economic, and cultural institutions from two or more countries, and then we compare institutions across those countries. Unlike with the institutional distance calculations, however, we cannot simply rely on Euclidean or Mahalanobis approaches to generate accurate measures of business risk. This is for two reasons: one has to do with the range of output and the other with the symmetry in the output.

The Trouble with Range

By construction, the outputs that Euclidean and Mahalanobis distance approaches generate are bound by 0 at the low end of their range, as in the case where two countries share equivalent scores across institutions.[5] However, the upper end of the range for both Euclidean and Mahalanobis outputs is problematic because it is (theoretically) infinite. And unfortunately, managers cannot use infinite numbers in financial models.

To address issues related to the range of institutional distance output, we need to scale the output so that we can express it over a range that will be useful and meaningful to managers. This is easier than it might seem; it is just a matter of injecting the theory with a dose of reality.

The lower limit of the range is already fixed at 0. We can work with that. To define the maximum for the range, however, it is necessary to introduce some experience and know-how. I therefore considered what, from a financial perspective, might be a "reasonable" risk maximum and set the upper end of the Global Acumen risk range to 30 percent. This percentage represents the most extreme differences in institutions across countries. How did I arrive at 30 percent for the upper limit of the range of institutional risk? The percentage is based on insights derived from venture-capital practices and payback investment techniques. Whichever way you look at it, 30 percent is a reasonable maximum for the range of institutional risk.

Basing the 30 Percent Upper-Bound on Venture-Capital Practices. One way to arrive at an upper bound for the institutional distance range would be to liken global expansion to a risky venture such as a startup company. If we view global expansion in that way, we can derive some insight from venture capitalists (VCs), experts who evaluate the financial risk of investing in a start-up.

When evaluating a new venture, a VC applies a discount rate to project expected future cash flows and value the business, much as we did in the Newlandia example in chapter 2.[6] The greater the risk the VC sees in the venture, the higher the discount rate the VC will apply to cash flows. For pure start-ups, VCs typically employ discount rates in the range of 50 to 70 percent. For late-stage entrepreneurial ventures, they tend to use discount rates in the range of 30 to 50 percent.[7]

In undertaking global expansion for the first time, a company engages in the risky endeavor of expanding into unfamiliar markets. The risks are not quite analogous to those of pure start-ups because a company considering global expansion presumably has some experience before it ventures abroad. A company expanding globally is typically not starting from scratch. The risks for companies expanding globally are therefore more similar to those of late-stage entrepreneurial ventures than to those of start-ups.

In a preview of coming attractions, we will eventually add Global Acumen's risk output to our domestic discount rate (around 10%). If we take our overall desired maximum rate of return of around 40 percent (based on the average for late-stage entrepreneurial ventures), and subtract the required domestic rate of return of 10 percent, we know to set the Global Acumen maximum to 30 percent. This ensures that the highest overall discount rate (domestic plus global) will reach approximately 40 percent in the very riskiest ventures into the riskiest of markets.

Basing the 30 Percent Upper Bound on Payback Methods. Another way to think about the issue of the upper limit to the range is in more practical terms, using another frame of reference: If you were to make a risky investment—any risky investment—what would you consider a reasonable amount of time in which to be paid back? Would it depend on how risky the investment was?

When managers take on greater risks, they (reasonably) expect to be paid back more quickly than they would for a lesser risk. The payback period on an investment—the amount of time it takes to recoup your initial investment—is tied to the rate of return you expect to receive. Consider a specific example of an investment in a firm called Newcompany. If you were to make a $1,000 investment today in Newcompany, at 30 percent simple interest per year, you would receive $300 per year in interest payments. The amount of time it would take you to recoup your original investment (aka, the payback period) would be approximately 3.3 years ($1,000 divided by $300 per year equals about 3.3 years). Should you make that same investment in Newcompany at 10 percent simple interest per year? At 10 percent simple interest, your interest payments would be $100 per year, and the payback period would be 10 years ($1,000 divided by $100 per year equals 10 years).

All else being equal, the preferred investment is the former, the one with the shorter payback period. Of course, the decision depends on various cash flow assumptions, but investors typically like to receive their money back as soon as possible, and most managers would agree a payback period of 3.3 years constitutes a good investment.

Add in the requirements for the domestic cost of capital—that 10 percent figure I highlighted in the previous section—and the payback period gets even shorter. Let's say today you were to invest that same $1,000 into Newcompany at 40 percent simple interest per annum to expand into a new market (called, for this example, Farlandia). This derives from 30 percent for risks that are specific to Farlandia, plus 10 percent for those risks specific to Newcompany in its home country. The interest payments would be $400 per year, and the payback period on that $1,000 investment would go down to 2.5 years ($1,000 divided by $400 per year equals 2.5 years). Most managers would recognize that it is generally unrealistic, at least from a strategic perspective, to expect a return on investment of much more than 40 percent, even in the riskiest of environments.

The Trouble with Symmetry

A second concern with using Euclidean and Mahalanobis distances for the purpose of generating meaningful institutional risk metrics is that they presume, by mathematical construction, a symmetry that is unrealistic in the context of national institutions. As with absolute-value approaches, Euclidean and Mahalanobis distance formulas generate output whereby the distance from country x to country y is equal to the distance from country y to country x. This is problematic if we believe, for whatever reason, that the direction of the difference matters in some meaningful way—that it might be easier for a company from country x to do business in country y, or vice versa.

> ### *Symmetry: Revisiting What It Means, Using Real Data*
>
> When my colleague Zheying Wu and I calculated insti-tutional distances for our study published in the *Journal of International Business Studies*, we found an institutional dis-tance between Japan and the United States of 4.99.[8] Because we used a Mahalanobis distance method to calculate the insti-tutional distance, symmetry implies that the distance between the United States and Japan will also be 4.99, the same as the distance between Japan and the United States. Practically, that suggests that the risk to a US company expanding into Japan is the same as the risk to a Japanese company expanding into the United States. However, this is not a sound assump-tion; there would be different challenges for a Japanese and an American company attempting to make the transition into the institutional environment of the other country.

For the purposes of generating an accurate measure of institu-tional risk, it is less important to understand symmetry as a restrict-ing mathematical assumption and more important to know that it is not insurmountable. Global Acumen overcomes the symmetry constraint by incorporating elements of both distance (using a mod-ified/weighted Euclidean technique) and difference (using a subtrac-tion-based approach).

Incorporating Difference and Distance

Assume that it is easier for a Chinese company to deal with some institutions in the United States than for a US company to deal with those same institutions in China. This could be the case, for example, if the United States has a more stable economic environ-ment than China. If it is easier, and therefore less risky, to deal with economic institutions in the United States than in China, we need to consider not just the *distance* between the institutions in those countries, but perhaps also the inherent *differences* between those two sets of institutions. We need to supplement traditional *distance* approaches with *difference* approaches.

Obviously, we need to decide which sets of institutions require difference approaches (rather than distance approaches) and which sets require distance approaches (rather than difference approaches). Only then can we use an appropriate combination of distance and difference approaches to calculate our overarching risk metric.

Whether to calculate differences or distances hinges on the answer to one critical question: Are some kinds of national institutional structures inherently easier for businesses to manage than others? Addressing this complex issue is critical to devising appropriate risk metrics because it determines how to proceed with the analysis. The approach we adopt depends upon our beliefs about certain institutional dimensions or subset of dimensions as follows:

- If we believe it is hard for businesses to move in either direction (from a given starting point), we want to think more in terms of *distance* than *difference*.
- If we believe it is easier for businesses to move in one direction or the other (from a given starting point), we want to think more in terms of *difference* than *distance*.

With those considerations in mind, Global Acumen uses *distances* for political and cultural institutions and *differences* for economic institutions. The rationale is explained below.

Cultural Institutions
It is challenging for a company to go from one cultural environment to another, regardless of the direction. Consider Hofstede's individualism/collectivism cultural dimension; it stands to reason that expanding into a country with a culture that is more individualistic (and therefore less collectivistic) than one's home country is not necessarily any easier than expanding into a country whose culture is less individualistic (more collectivistic) than one's home country. This implies that—based purely on the basis of individualism/collectivism (IC) scores—it is not much riskier for a company from the Czech Republic (a borderline individualistic country, with an IC score of 58) to expand to China (a highly collectivistic country, with an IC score of 20) than to the United States (a highly individualistic country, with an IC score of 91). So, for culture, we likely want to think more in terms of distance than difference.

Economic Institutions

In this case, it is likely easier for a company to move in one direction (in terms of economic institution scores) than in another. It is easier for a company to transition from a country with unstable economic institutions to one with stable economic institutions than for a company to transition from a country with stable economic institutions into one with unstable economic institutions.[9] Therefore, for economic institutions, we likely want to think more in terms of difference than distance.

Political Institutions

Political institutions are a bit more complex and nuanced.[10] For example, I could certainly make the case that it is easier for a company to transition to a country where the political institutions are more stable than in its home country. This might lead us to treat political institutional measures as a difference rather than a distance. However, I have found instead that businesses and those who manage them are resilient and become accustomed to operating in particular political environments—usually those of their home country. If operations in a certain country call for close ties with political figures, then a successful company figures out which relationships will enable it to thrive. If "paying to play"—institutionalized gift-giving or monetary contributions—are an integral, accepted way of doing business in a particular country, then a successful company usually figures out how to work that system.

Challenges arise when a business accustomed to operating in a country with one set of political institutions transitions into a country with significantly different political institutions. The political strategies and practices a firm adopts in its home country are less valuable in countries that bear less of a political resemblance to that home country—irrespective of how those institutions are different from those in the home country. Regardless of the direction of the difference (again, in terms of political institution scores), it is difficult for a company to change the behaviors it has evolved to thrive in its home country. Coping mechanisms take years to establish and refine, and they have a tendency to ossify. I therefore treat political institutions as a distance instead of a difference.

The Nuts and Bolts of Global Acumen

Based on years of research and testing, Global Acumen generates globalization risk values between pairs of countries:

- over a *range* that extends from 0 to 30;
- using *mathematical distances* to account for differences in *cultural and political* institutions across countries;
- using *mathematical differences* to account for differences in *economic* institutions across countries.

Specifically, Global Acumen's algorithm generates output for any pair of countries by:

1. generating mathematical distances for the political and cultural institutional dimensions (based on a modified Euclidean approach, weighted to correct for the underlying covariance structure of the political and cultural institution data);
2. generating mathematical differences for the economic institutional dimensions (directionally calculated as home country economic institutions minus host country economic institutions, weighted and combined to correct for the underlying covariance structure of the economic institution data);
3. scaling all outputs from (1) and (2) so they are all on the same scale;
4. adding the economic difference scores to the political and cultural distance scores;
5. rescaling the resulting sum to generate observations that fall into the range from 0 to 30 percent.

That process results in risk output that we can interpret as a pairwise, country-specific globalization risk spread. The advantage of this approach is output in a form that is ready to be plugged straight into existing financial models tools. (More on that in chapter 8.)

Global Acumen: A Concrete Example

Global Acumen generates globalization risk spreads for pairs of countries.[11] To make this procedure more concrete and easier to

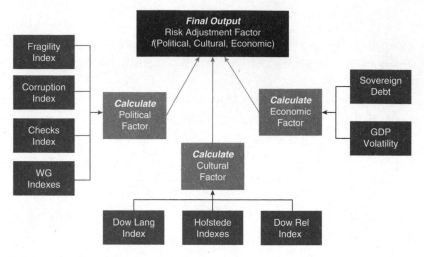

Figure 7.2 The Architecture of Global Acumen.

envision, let us see it in action. Figure 7.2 presents the overarching architecture for Global Acumen version 2.0.[12] This version includes the three overarching institutional factors—political, economic, and cultural—described in chapters 4, 5, and 6.

The institutional subdimension data for each country are drawn from the following sources:

- Political: the State Fragility Index (Center for Systemic Peace), Corruption Perceptions Index (Transparency International), Checks Index (World Database of Political Institutions), Rule of Law, Government Effectiveness, and Regulatory Quality (Worldwide Governance Indicators).
- Economic: Inflation-adjusted Sovereign Debt (Bloomberg and Damodaran), 5-year and 10-year GDP Volatility averages (imputed using data from the United Nations).
- Cultural: Individualism/Collectivism and Power Distance (Hofstede), Language Similarity and Religion Similarity (Douglas Dow).

The raw institutional data are run through Global Acumen's algorithmic procedures as described above: using a combination of mathematical distance (for the political and cultural factors) and mathematical difference (for the economic factor).

In chapter 8 I explore the details of how to apply the Global Acumen risk spread to financial models. As a foundation for that discussion, let us see what the Global Acumen output looks like for the eight countries mentioned at the beginning of this chapter (Australia, Canada, China, India, Japan, Russia, the United Kingdom, and the United States).[13] I present the data focusing on the United States as the home and/or host nation, and later present the full set of outputs across all eight countries.

Global Acumen Output

Table 7.1 reflects the risk output Global Acumen generates for US-owned companies expanding into Australia, Canada, China, India, Japan, Russia, or the United Kingdom (in descending order of risk).

You may not be surprised that the globalization risks are greater for US companies in countries that are more institutionally—politically, economically, and culturally—distant, such as Russia, China, India, and Japan, and that the risks are smaller in countries that are more institutionally similar, such as the United Kingdom, Canada, and Australia.

Table 7.1   Risk to US Companies Expanding Abroad

Country	Risk (%)
Russia	19
India	15.5
China	14.5
Japan	10.5
United Kingdom	4.5
Canada	4
Australia	3

Looks Can Be Deceiving: Institutional Versus Geographical Distance

At first glance, you might assume that the globalization risk to a US company would be higher in Australia than in Canada. After all, Canada is a geographic neighbor to the United States, while Australia is more than 9,000 miles away. What is more,

Canada and the United States have long been party to the North American Free Trade Agreement (NAFTA), which lowers cross-border trade and investment costs between the two countries.

However, the Global Acumen calculations reveal that the risks to a US company are slightly lower in Australia (3%) than in Canada (4%). A closer look at the underlying data reveals that the United States has more in common culturally with Australia than with Canada. Consider: One of Canada's largest provinces by population, Quebec—which is French-speaking—has a strong influence on Canadian culture. This means that, at least in part, Canada's cultural institutions in some ways are more similar to those of France (and other French-speaking countries) than to those of the United States.

Furthermore, be careful not to confuse geographic factors with economic institutions. While the extreme geographic distance and time-zone difference create high costs for US companies in Australia, those geographic factors do not say anything about the economic opportunities in each country. Managers can easily estimate the fairly straightforward freight costs between Australia and the United States (or Canada and the United States) and include them in standard financial projections as operating costs. It is much harder to quantify economic opportunity—especially the confidence that one can have in those economic opportunities—for financial models.

The lesson here is that it is a smart business move to use the Global Acumen calculations to challenge our assumptions—even informed ones—about what factors are most important when it comes to globalization risk. In many—if not all—cases, this should inspire us to look deeper at all of our assumptions about globalization.

Do Not Assume Symmetry in Output

You most likely noticed that the Global Acumen figures in table 7.1 express risk spread for companies expanding in one direction only:

Table 7.2   Risk to Foreign Companies Expanding to the United States

Country	Risk (%)
China	14.5
India	11
Japan	8.5
Russia	8
Australia	5.5
Canada	4.5
United Kingdom	3

originating in the United States and expanding outward to each of those seven global destinations. As I mentioned above, these risk spreads are not symmetric—not the same for expansions in both directions. What would happen if we look at risks to companies seeking to expand to the United States? Let us revisit the countries I cited in my previous example. Table 7.2 reflects risk spreads generated with Global Acumen for companies expanding into the United States from Australia, Canada, China, India, Japan, Russia, and the United Kingdom (in descending order of risk).

The risk spreads are largely as you might expect, but—surprise! China is the only country that *appears* to have symmetry—that is, for which the risks of operating in the United States are equivalent to those of a US company operating in China. Is that the answer you expected?

It Looks Like Symmetry, But Is It?

You will have noticed that there are (practically) equivalent risk spreads for businesses expanding from China to the United States and for those expanding from the United States to China (~14.5%). Many consider the United States to have a business-friendly environment, due to its relatively stable economy, robust capital markets, and the ease with which companies can do business there.[14] This might lead you to expect levels of economic risk that are higher for US companies operating in China than for Chinese companies operating in the United States. And yet that is only part of the story.

Figure 7.2 lays out the two components that makeup Global Acumen's economic factor (at right): sovereign debt and GDP volatility. These measures relate to fundamental economic risks in a given country. Given that Global Acumen calculates the economic factor as a difference rather than as a distance, the economic factor effectively captures the economic risk a company from a specific home country is likely to face in a specific host country. In essence, it accounts for whether there is a greater likelihood of experiencing a macroeconomic shock that will upset a company's financial projections in the home country or the host country. It is here that nonsymmetry enters the equation.

Let's break these factors down for the United States and China. The United States has a higher sovereign debt rating and a lower borrowing rate than China. Its lower sovereign debt rates would indicate lower levels of economic risk in the United States than in China. However, that is just the short-term sovereign debt picture; over the last 5-year and 10-year periods—the periods over which Global Acumen considers GDP volatility—the United States experienced a financial crisis and severe economic recession, which was more severe than the economic slowdown China experienced during that same period. The United States has therefore experienced greater economic volatility—more severe swings in its GDP—over the past 5 to 10 years than has China.

At this moment in history, and in this specific case, these two economic factors happen to roughly balance each other out, so that the overall levels of economic risk are now practically equivalent between the United States and China. This could certainly change in the days, months, and years to come. (And now you know where to look to anticipate those changes!)

This example underscores the value of understanding Global Acumen and the institutions that are critical to risk. Honing your understanding of the institutions that are critical to global risk and of the dynamics that shape how those institutions change over time will expand your knowledge of the complex, shifting global business landscape. This will set you apart from the crowd and give you an advantage when determining or assessing your company's global strategy.

Beyond the United States

I present only bilateral risk spreads for the United States and seven other countries in tables 7.1 and 7.2, but Global Acumen can do much more than simply generate risk spreads for US companies expanding abroad or for foreign companies entering the United States. The Global Acumen algorithm, developed nearly a decade ago, is meant to be equally useful for managers throughout the globe who seek to expand into almost any international market. It was designed to generate bilateral risk spreads for any pair of potential home and host countries for which there exist accurate political, economic, and cultural data. As of early 2015, the Global Acumen database includes 55 countries and calculates risk spreads for 2,970 unique pairs of countries.

As an example of Global Acumen's general appeal, table 7.3 provides bilateral cross-country risk spreads for each of the eight countries I mentioned at the start of this chapter—for each of the 56 distinct country-pair combinations (in both directions).

The best way to read this table is to focus first on a specific home country (on the left-hand side), and then analyze host

Table 7.3 Bilateral Risk Spreads for a Set of Eight Countries

	USA (%)	Russia (%)	India (%)	China (%)	Japan (%)	UK (%)	Canada (%)	Australia (%)
USA	0.00	19.00	15.50	14.50	10.50	4.50	4.00	3.00
Russia	8.00	0.00	7.00	4.50	9.50	9.00	8.50	7.50
India	11.00	12.00	0.00	6.00	12.00	13.00	12.00	11.00
China	14.50	14.00	11.50	0.00	14.50	17.00	16.00	15.00
Japan	8.50	17.00	15.00	12.00	0.00	8.50	7.50	7.50
UK	3.00	18.00	16.00	15.00	9.00	0.00	3.00	2.00
Canada	4.50	19.50	16.50	15.50	10.00	4.50	0.00	3.00
Australia	5.50	20.00	18.00	17.00	12.00	5.50	5.00	0.00

country suitors (scrolling from left to right). For example, if we select Australia—the last country in the first column—as our home country, simply scroll across the bottom row from left to right to see that for an Australian company, the expansion risk is 5.5 percent to the United States, 20 percent to Russia, 18 percent to India, and so on. Insofar as general host-country risk is concerned (reading the table from top to bottom), it probably comes as no surprise that Russia, which as of early 2015 is wallowing in economic malaise, presents the greatest levels of risk to foreign companies. Australia presents the lowest levels of risk. Japan presents intermediate levels of risk.

Bringing It All Together

Tackling globalization risk pricing is no easy task. It takes a bit of creativity and effort to convert raw measures of institutions into useful measures of risk using mathematical distance and difference formulas. This chapter explained how to do that in a step-by-step fashion. It detailed Global Acumen's basic schematic structure, highlighted the institutional raw materials used as inputs to the algorithm, and described how the algorithm uses established mathematical techniques to generate institutional risk spreads. The practical examples reinforced and justified the overarching approach and methodology and helped clarify how to make sense of Global Acumen's output.

Global Acumen is a great place to start when it comes to assessing global risk, especially for the far too many companies that have no system in place to evaluate these risks. Whether managers adopt Global Acumen's approach, seek out some alternative system, build their own algorithm, or simply use this book to understand the rationale behind accounting for institutional risk in global markets, the result will be more successful global strategies.

Still, knowing the institutional risk spread between two countries is only half the battle; the real value is in knowing how to *use* risk spreads to improve decision making. Meaningful risk spreads can complement existing strategic and financial decision-making models—if we apply them effectively. The next chapter walks you through how to incorporate cross-country global risk spreads into existing financial models—the next step in our journey toward improved global management practices.

CHAPTER 8

Global Acumen in Practice

With Global Acumen, we now have an accurate tool to account for the risks that companies face in global markets. We constructed it by comparing measures of political, economic, and cultural institutions across countries, relying on a combination of institutional distance and difference approaches to generate country-specific institutional risk spreads.[1] The question now becomes: How can we apply those risk spreads to real-world problems so as to enhance managers' toolkits and improve global management practices?

In this chapter I explain how to incorporate cross-country risk spreads into existing strategic and financial analyses. The process is quite simple, really. Recall that Global Acumen generates risk spreads that indicate the additional political, economic, and cultural risks that a company faces when it does business in another country. The Global Acumen tool reports risk spreads in a way that reflects the additional compensation—expressed in interest rate terms—that a company ought to expect in exchange for bearing the political, economic, and cultural risks of doing business in that country.

Armed with that knowledge, we can revisit the Newlandia example from chapter 2 to demonstrate how to add Global Acumen's risk spreads to a company's domestic discount rate to generate a country-specific discount rate that better accounts for political, economic, and cultural risks. By varying the levels of institutional risk present in a fictitious country like Newlandia, we can readily observe the impact of globalization risk on a company's bottom line.

This leads to a number of realizations. First, with the appropriate risk measures, it is relatively easy and straightforward to account for the financial impact of country-specific political, economic, and cultural risks. It is simply a matter of incorporating Global Acumen's risk spreads into familiar financial techniques that managers use regularly. Second, there is no longer any excuse to ignore institutional risk, and managers who continue to ignore such risks do so at their financial peril.

Revisiting the Newlandia Example

To get a sense of how Global Acumen's risk spreads work in practice, it is helpful to revisit the financial and strategic analyses presented in chapter 2. There I suggested that managers typically evaluate globalization opportunities by generating pro forma financial projections to gain insight into how globalization is likely to impact revenues, costs, and ultimately profitability. Managers try to detail and quantify every possible revenue and cost associated with the expansion and then use those estimates to assess whether they can profitably globalize. I use a simple hypothetical example to illustrate the process in which a US-based company considers expanding to an invented foreign country ("Newlandia").[2]

Refreshing Your Memory

The Newlandia example in table 2.3 assumes a five-year business opportunity that would generate $1,000 in revenues per year at a cost of $800 per year and thus at an annual profit of $200. Next, I assume a required initial investment of $550 to enter Newlandia (see table 2.2).[3] I then ask whether given this scenario it makes sense—in terms of overall profitability—to invest in Newlandia.

Managers typically rely on discounted cash flow techniques to determine whether business opportunities generate sufficient profitability to justify the investment. They discount future profits by an opportunity cost of capital—an interest rate that they could

Table 8.1   Business Projections for Newlandia: Assuming an 8.5% Discount Rate

	Year 0	Year 1	Year 2	Year 3	Year 4	Year 5
Revenues		$1,000	$1,000	$1,000	$1,000	$1,000
Costs		$800	$800	$800	$800	$800
Initial Costs	$550					
Profit	–$550	$200	$200	$200	$200	$200
Present Value	–$550	$184	$170	$157	$144	$133
Overall NPV	$238					

reasonably expect to earn if they had invested the initial capital in another way.[4] Once discounted, the cash inflows (profits) are added to the cash outflows (the initial investment) to generate a net present value (NPV) for the project. A positive NPV indicates that the business opportunity generates sufficient returns—and therefore that the manager should go forward with the investment. A negative NPV value suggests that the business opportunity fails to generate sufficient returns—and, accordingly, the manager should pass on the business opportunity. When the NPV is negative, the manager would be better served dedicating the initial investment capital to some other purpose.

Table 8.1 applies this technique to the Newlandia opportunity, mirroring the NPV analysis from chapter 2 (see table 2.3). I use a discount rate of 8.5 percent to convert future cash flows into present values, cash flows expressed in today's dollar equivalents. I then add each of the present value cash flows to the initial investment to arrive at the NPV. We can see that the Newlandia opportunity generates a NPV of $238 (see the "Present Value" line of the table, which is where we get the figures to calculate the NPV: $184 + $170 + $157 + $144 + $133 – $550). The positive NPV for the Newlandia opportunity suggests that an investment in Newlandia yields profits that are greater than the alternative of investing the $550 elsewhere. The investment into Newlandia therefore makes business sense; the manager would be wise to move forward with it on behalf of the company.

Of course, the analysis above is just a baseline. However, this baseline serves us well as we start to introduce various institutional risk factors into our Newlandia scenario.

Bringing Global Acumen to Newlandia

Using a NPV approach to think about globalization opportunities can be extremely valuable; however, a discount rate of 8.5 percent might not be as appropriate for global business opportunities (like those in Newlandia) as for domestic business opportunities. The 8.5 percent discount rate reflects a domestic discount rate, designed for use by a US company in the US market. It fails to take into account the political, economic, and cultural institutions of foreign markets and the risks they are likely to present to foreign investors.

Newlandia's political institutions are likely to be different from the political institutions in the United States; its economic institutions and cultural institutions are also likely to be different from those in the United States. In short, Newlandia's institutional profile is likely to be different from that of the United States, and the 8.5 percent discount rate does not reflect the additional risks those differences present.[5]

Our task, therefore, is to determine how to incorporate Global Acumen's risk spreads into existing financial models—like those in table 8.1—to improve financial analyses and strategic decision making.

Recall that by design Global Acumen uses political, economic, and cultural inputs to generate institutional risk spreads between pairs of countries and expresses them as interest rates falling in the range between 0 and 30 percent. I deliberately constructed its risk spreads in this way to complement existing financial modeling techniques, which are limited due to their heavy reliance on discount rates that are oriented to the domestic market.

Generically, the process works as follows:

1. Add the Global Acumen risk spread to the domestic discount rate.
2. Generate a country-specific risk-adjusted discount rate.
3. Replace the domestic discount rate with this new, country-specific risk-adjusted discount rate.

Now that we have step-by-step instructions for how to use Global Acumen spreads to adjust a company's domestic discount rate to account for cross-country institutional risk, let us see this process in action. Below we will apply Global Acumen to the Newlandia example. Because Newlandia is a fictitious country, I can vary its riskiness to see how sensitive the financials from table 8.1 are to changing levels of institutional risk. The expanded hypotheticals in this section demonstrate the real—even severe—consequences that can befall a company when its managers fail to account for institutional risk.

Global Acumen: Complement Instead of Substitute?

You will note that step 1 (above) retains the domestic discount rate: adding the Global Acumen risk spread to the domestic discount rate, rather than replacing the domestic discount rate with the Global Acumen risk spread. This is because it is more appropriate to view institutional risk as a supplement to, rather than as a substitute for, the discount-rate requirements that are specific to a particular firm. Risks in global markets are risks added to a company's existing operations—risks that a company takes on over and above those it already faces in the domestic market. Therefore, were we to simply replace the domestic discount rate with the Global Acumen risk spread, we would sacrifice important information about a company's general risk profile.

The opportunity cost of capital reflected in a company's domestic discount rate serves as an important signal about a company's health and well-being: its underlying "quality" and risk characteristics. Typically, a strong company that is managerially sound and operates in a less risky market has a lower discount rate and a lower opportunity cost of capital because it presents fewer risks to potential investors; there is a greater likelihood that the company will deliver results for investors. Apple Inc., for example, has an opportunity cost of capital of around 6 percent, whereas Cisco Systems Inc. has an opportunity cost of capital of around 7 percent.[6] Market participants currently view Apple as having lower levels of risk, better future prospects, better products, and a better overall management team.

When companies such as Apple or Cisco expand abroad, their idiosyncratic features—management, product, and industry characteristics—do not change. Investors still expect rates of return that are at least commensurate with the risk factors specific to the company.[7] However, in addition, investors also expect compensation for the country-specific institutional risk companies will take on by operating abroad. And, as I point out in the previous chapter, the greater the levels of risk that companies face in foreign markets, the greater those country-specific returns should be. This is why Global Acumen risk spreads were designed to be conjunctive with (rather than disjunctive to) the discount rate.

Varying Newlandia's Risks

In the context of our Newlandia example, if managers of the firm in question want to accurately reflect the risks Newlandia poses, they should adjust the discount rate (to generate more realistic present values from the future cash flows) by following steps 1–3 above. Of course, we cannot know the precise level of risk Newlandia poses to US companies, since no actual data or institutional measures exist for Newlandia. But let's assign it a hypothetical risk profile and Global Acumen spread to analyze how the financials in table 8.1 change under various alternative risk scenarios.

From chapter 7 we know the range of institutional risks that US-based companies face in several countries, with Russia posing high levels of risk, Japan posing moderate levels of risk, and Australia posing low levels of risk.[8] Let us assume for our purposes that Newlandia presents a moderate—rather than extreme—level of political, economic, and cultural risk to US companies. This would mean that Global Acumen might generate a risk premium for Newlandia that is similar to that of Japan, with a value of around 10 percent.

Whereas table 8.1 assumes that the risk of a US company expanding to Newlandia is equivalent to the risk of a domestic expansion

(8.5%), table 8.2 assumes that the expansion presents a greater risk (by an additional 10%, to be exact). We can return to the numbers in table 8.1 and use these hypothetical risk values to adjust the calculations. We simply follow the three steps outlined above:

1. Add the 10 percent Newlandia risk spread to the 8.5 percent domestic discount rate.
2. Generate a Newlandia-adjusted discount rate of 18.5 percent.
3. Replace the original discount rate (in the projections in table 8.1) with the new Newlandia-specific discount rate of 18.5 percent.

Notice in table 8.2 that applying a discount rate of 18.5 percent instead of 8.5 percent to the projections from table 8.1 significantly changes the calculus (compare the "New Present Value" row of the table to the "Table 8.1 Present Value" row). When we discount the $200 profit from year 1 by 18.5 percent, the present value amounts to only $169 ($200/1.185).[9] That is $15 less than the present value in table 8.1, discounted at 8.5 percent ($184 or $200/1.085). The present value of the profits for years 2 through 5 likewise decreases if we use this same 18.5 percent present value discount rate. The overall NPV of the Newlandia expansion therefore decreases from $238 in table 8.1 to $68 ($169 + $142 + $120 + $101 + $86 − $550).

Despite the added 10 percent risk premium and the corresponding increase in the discount rate to 18.5 percent, the NPV of the Newlandia project remains positive. A shrewd manager would still be inclined to enter the Newlandia market, even though the

Table 8.2 Business Projections for Newlandia: Assuming an 18.5% Discount Rate

		Year 0	Year 1	Year 2	Year 3	Year 4	Year 5
Revenues			$1,000	$1,000	$1,000	$1,000	$1,000
Costs			$800	$800	$800	$800	$800
Initial Costs		$550					
Profit		−$550	$200	$200	$200	$200	$200
New Present Value		−$550	$169	$142	$120	$101	$86
New Overall NPV		$68					
Table 8.1 Present Value		−$550	$184	$170	$157	$144	$133
Table 8.1 NPV		$238					

expansion would not generate quite as much of a return as the scenario table 8.1 describes ($68 versus $238). Moreover, managers can be more confident that their financial projections are sound and not grossly inaccurate as in table 8.1. The projections now faithfully reflect the risks of doing business in a country with moderate levels of risk such as Newlandia.

Upping the Ante in Newlandia

To see the impact of a higher risk spread on financial projections, let's consider an alternative scenario in which Newlandia is an even riskier country. Instead of assuming it presents moderate levels of institutional risk (10%) for a US company as in table 8.2, let's assume that Newlandia's Global Acumen risk spread with the United States is much higher: closer to what we found for Russia (19%) in chapter 7.

Assuming a 20 percent Global Acumen risk spread (a more straightforward, round number to work with versus 19%) for Newlandia, let's follow the three steps outlined above:

1. Add the 20 percent Newlandia risk spread to the 8.5 percent domestic discount rate.
2. Generate a Newlandia-adjusted discount rate of 28.5 percent.
3. Replace the original discount rate (in the projections from table 8.1) with the new Newlandia-specific discount rate of 28.5 percent (see table 8.3).

Table 8.3 Business Projections for Newlandia: Assuming a 28.5% Discount Rate

	Year 0	Year 1	Year 2	Year 3	Year 4	Year 5
Revenues		$1,000	$1,000	$1,000	$1,000	$1,000
Costs		$800	$800	$800	$800	$800
Initial Costs	$550					
Profit	–$550	$200	$200	$200	$200	$200
New Present Value	–$550	$156	$121	$94	$73	$57
New Overall NPV	–$49					
Table 8.2 Present Value	–$550	$169	$142	$120	$101	$86
Table 8.2 NPV	$68					
Table 8.1 Present Value	–$550	$184	$170	$157	$144	$133
Table 8.1 NPV	$238					

A 28.5 percent discount rate for the Newlandia opportunity yields a vastly different NPV than the 18.5 percent discount rate from table 8.2 or the 8.5 percent discount rate from table 8.1. The $200 cash flow in year 1, discounted at 28.5 percent, now only yields a present value of $156 ($200/1.285) rather than $169 (200/1.185) in table 8.2 (with an 18.5% discount rate) and $184 ($200/1.085) in table 8.1 (with an 8.5% discount rate). The 28.5 percent rate discounts future profits more harshly than the discount rates in either table 8.2 or table 8.1, and the result is a NPV of -$49 ($156 + $121 + $94 + $73 + $57 − $550). Under this scenario a manager would be better served to pass on the opportunity to expand to Newlandia.

The differences in NPV projections between table 8.3 (-$49), table 8.2 ($68), and table 8.1 ($238) are stark. They go from a set of projections suggesting that a firm can make money in Newlandia ($238, as per table 8.1) to a set suggesting that the same firm is likely to lose money (-$49, as per table 8.3). The difference, of course, is in the institutional—political, economic, and cultural—risks we assume in each scenario.

General Lessons from Newlandia

It is important to remember that the models presented in tables 8.1, 8.2, and 8.3 are simplified and incredibly nuanced. These are examples of how managers can use Global Acumen's risk spreads to improve global expansion decisions. As you are aware, the results you achieve from any application of the Global Acumen technique described above depend critically upon the revenue, cost, and domestic discount rate specific to your situation and on the Global Acumen risk spread between your company's home country and its intended target county. However, the examples highlight the following general lessons:

1. Managers should not regard specific institutional risk levels as indicative of any steadfast rule. A low level of institutional risk (low Global Acumen risk spreads) does not necessarily yield a positive NPV and does not mean that it is always profitable to expand to a particular country. By the same token, a high level of institutional risk (high Global Acumen risk spreads) does

not necessarily yield a negative NPV and does not mean that it is always unprofitable to expand to a particular country.[10] Companies should consider doing business in a country when profitability there is sufficient to offset the risk, irrespective of the risk level.

2. Although there is no steadfast rule associated with a given level of institutional risk, managers should understand how institutional risk generally affects financial models. For countries that pose greater levels of institutional risk, managers should expect greater revenues, lower costs, or both to compensate for the heightened levels of risk. From a payback perspective, these managers should expect shorter payback periods in countries that pose greater institutional risks. By contrast, for countries that pose lower levels of institutional risk, managers can make do with lower revenues, higher costs, and longer payback periods.

3. The Global Acumen discount-rate adjustment works best when you couple it with accurate domestic discount rates and precise revenue and cost projections. Inaccuracies in the domestic discount rate and in revenue or cost projections can result in misspecified models and erroneous NPV outcomes that yield poor recommendations. As with any financial model, accurate data increase the likelihood that managers will make sound global business decisions.

Most important, the Newlandia examples demonstrate how adjusting the domestic discount rate (adding the Global Acumen risk spread to the domestic discount rate) yields a more accurate picture of the true risks companies face in global markets. This simple approach empowers managers of companies large and small to accurately price globalization risk so they can make fully informed globalization decisions with reasonable expectations for the outcomes.

Dealing with Uncertainty: When Institutional Data Are Scarce

As previously mentioned, Global Acumen's database currently includes institutional data for 55 countries, yielding a total of

2,970 possible country risk pairs. These 55 countries account for more than 90 percent of the world's share of outward and inward foreign direct investment flows.[11] However, there are more than 180 officially recognized countries in the world, and Global Acumen thus lacks institutional data for more than 70 percent of the world's nations. This is in part because not all countries report reliable institutional data and also because some data services do not collect institutional data for certain countries. In practical terms, this means that in some cases managers might not be able to determine precise global risk spreads. The question therefore remains what managers should do when there are no adequate institutional measures for a particular country and a global risk spread for a pair of countries cannot be calculated precisely.

One alternative is to impute underlying institution data from observations in similar countries. For example, institutional data from Greece might, in certain instances, apply to Cyprus. Similarly, one might use institutional data from Algeria or Morocco to estimate elements of Tunisia's institutions. Although certainly not ideal, imputing institutional data by using a similar country proxy is one way to get around a lack of data and generate risk spreads for a country without individual institutional measures.

Another alternative is to group countries into categories. When we lack institutional measures for a specific country, we can often cobble together enough information to group countries into four risk categories (relative to the home country): low, medium, high, and extreme. Once we assign a country to a particular category, we can apply an institutional risk spread based on the data from chapter 7.

Chapter 7 introduced risk spreads for US-based companies expanding into the following countries: Russia (19%), India (15%), China (14.5%), Japan (10.5%), United Kingdom (4.5%), Canada (4%), and Australia (3%). Within this sample we observe risk spreads for low-risk countries (Australia, Canada, and the United Kingdom) that fall into the range between 3 and 5 percent, moderate-risk countries (Japan) that fall into the range of 8–12 percent, and high-risk (China, India, and Russia) countries that fall into the range between 15 and 20 percent. Any risk spread between 20 and 30 percent falls into the category of extreme risk.

Armed with that information, we can extrapolate and apply a risk spread to a country for which we lack certain institutional data. For example, we might lack institutional data for Belarus; however, to the extent that Belarus shares similarities with Russia—due to their common membership in the former Soviet Union and their close economic ties—we might apply a risk spread similar to that of Russia for a US-based company considering expansion to Belarus.[12] In a country like Sudan, for which we lack accurate cultural and economic institutional data but which the Fund for Peace considers a fragile (nearly failed) state, the institutional risks for a US-based company are likely to be extreme.[13] That would imply a risk spread approaching 30 percent for a US-based company considering expansion to Sudan.

Global Acumen versus Existing Alternatives

We have known for some time that globalization raises costs; the liability of foreignness that institutional distance creates makes it more challenging to operate in global markets. Yet it is difficult to specify precisely how those additional costs manifest in financial analyses like those in tables 8.1, 8.2, and 8.3. If we could detail each and every political, economic, and cultural cost associated with the liability of foreignness, we could simply add them into the "costs" line of our financial analyses and not have to worry about adjusting our discount rate. Since we cannot detail those costs with precision, Global Acumen provides the best current alternative: a tool that accurately estimates liability of foreignness costs via an institutional risk spread and adjusts a company's domestic discount rate based on that risk spread. This is not to say, however, that Global Acumen is the only option for addressing the institutional risks associated with globalization. Two other approaches are discussed below.

Option 1: Devise a Cost Contingency

If we know that globalization raises costs for firms, we might address the problem more directly by adjusting upward the anticipated costs in our financial analysis. That is, instead of adding a country-specific risk spread to the domestic discount rate and discounting the future profits by that country-specific risk-adjusted rate, managers can simply apply a cost contingency to their financial projections.

Many managers—especially in service industries such as consulting, banking, accounting, and law—have told me they use this strategy in the absence of specific measures to account for risk. For a consulting firm bidding on work in a foreign country, this would equate to adjusting the "costs" line estimates it uses to price the engagement. The firm would apply a larger cost contingency to an opportunity in a riskier country and a smaller cost contingency to one in a less risky country.

In the context of our Newlandia example this would mean that rather than adjusting the discount rate based on Newlandia's risk profile, we would do the following:

- add a separate cost line item estimating the liability of foreignness cost contingency;
- use the company's standard domestic discount rate to discount future profits.

Table 8.4 provides an example of how this might work out in practice. Specifically, we can assume a "Liability of Foreignness Contingency" cost of $20 based on the level of institutional risks we believe are present in Newlandia. All else remains the same as in table 8.1, including the company's 8.5 percent domestic discount rate.

The question remains, however, what contingency is appropriate. Why $20? When I ask managers about the contingency approaches they typically adopt, they readily admit they cannot be sure their

Table 8.4 Business Projections for Newlandia: Estimating Liability of Foreignness Costs

	Year 0	Year 1	Year 2	Year 3	Year 4	Year 5
Revenues		$1,000	$1,000	$1,000	$1,000	$1,000
Costs		$800	$800	$800	$800	$800
Liability of Foreignness Contingency		$20	$20	$20	$20	$20
Initial Costs	$550					
Profit	−$550	$180	$180	$180	$180	$180
Time Value	−$550	$166	$153	$141	$130	$120
Overall NPV	$159					

contingency is exact; they simply hope it is adequate to cover any potential risk. But hope is not a strategy, and guessing contingency costs is dangerous.

It could be viable to estimate the liability of foreignness using cost contingencies, and though I did not build Global Acumen expressly to estimate contingency costs, we can certainly tailor it to that purpose with some adjustments to its range. You may recall from chapter 7 that Global Acumen's country-specific risk spreads range from 0 to 30 percent. The same underlying risk premise is true for a cost contingency as for Global Acumen: the riskier the country, the greater the cost contingency. However, neither my conversations with managers nor research findings provide sufficient guidance for determining an effective cost-contingency range. Should we base the contingency on some percentage of revenues, on some percentage of costs, or make it independent of both? Questions such as these limit efforts to design accurate estimates of the liability of foreignness cost contingency, and Global Acumen is therefore currently the more precise and thus preferred approach.

Option 2: Market Risk Premiums and Risk-Adjusted Discount Rates

Another alternative comes directly from the field of finance, where research generally recognizes that global expansion presents additional risk, and where academics generally recommend adopting a discount rate adjusted by some market risk premium.[14] These techniques typically adjust the domestic discount rate (upward or downward) by cross-country risk spreads based on differences in the performance of stock markets and bond markets between countries. These approaches are similar, in some respects, to Global Acumen. For example, Aswath Damodaran, a finance professor at NYU Stern School of Business, bases his risk adjustments on sovereign debt ratings, sovereign default spreads, or relative differences in stock market performance.[15] He then adds the country-specific market risk premium to the company's domestic discount rate to create a country-specific risk-adjusted discount rate.

What makes market risk premium approaches like the ones described above challenging, however, is that there is little agreement in the field on how precisely to calculate the risk premiums.[16] Moreover, these approaches are based solely on measures of economic institutions. They do not include differences between political and cultural institutions and therefore generate imprecise estimates of the risks companies face in global markets. Global Acumen provides a more robust approach that integrates the full gamut of political, economic, and cultural risks a company faces and generates more accurate cross-country institutional risk spreads.

Bringing It All Together

We are now able to see in greater detail how globalization risk spreads can improve strategic decision making. When we incorporate Global Acumen's cross-country institutional risk spreads into financial analyses, we can account for liability of foreignness costs. With a remarkably simple and straightforward method, we can use Global Acumen's risk spreads to complement traditional financial modeling techniques, and for the purposes of cash flow analysis, we can calculate more accurate discount rates and NPVs for global companies.

Building on the risk "naïve" global expansion model for Newlandia presented in chapter 2—which generates biased financial results based on the misapplication of domestic discount rates to global expansion—we now see how financial projections change depending on country-specific institutional risk. A shift from markets with lower levels of institutional risk to ones with higher levels of institutional risk can swing financial results from profitable to unprofitable. The Newlandia example, therefore, serves to highlight the importance of pricing global risk accurately and incorporating those risks into financial analyses. Managers can avoid the mistakes that plague all too many global ventures if they simply use these techniques to account for country-specific institutional risk.

We can now use the Global Acumen technique illustrated in the more complex Newlandia examples as a foundation for applying the technique to more nuanced global-management problems. Multinational companies face a host of challenges in foreign markets, and foreign market entry is only one of them. Companies entrust managers with all kinds of strategic responsibilities that are global in scope, such as market entry, ownership structure, and the management of day-to-day operations. Moreover, these same managers have varying levels of international experience from which to draw. I therefore dedicate much of the next chapter to alternative applications of the Global Acumen institutional risk tool.

Global Acumen's utility extends far beyond the Newlandia market-entry application I present here. In chapter 9 I explain how Global Acumen can address a variety of complex problems that global and globalizing companies commonly face. To that end, we can:

- tailor how we weight various institutions in the algorithm to address characteristics that are specific to certain industries;
- modify the base algorithm to account for international experience;
- adjust the risk spreads to reflect differences in ownership structures that companies use in foreign markets;
- use the risk spreads as a performance benchmark to evaluate ongoing foreign operations and to stay abreast of institutional developments in current and potential host countries.

The context and content of this chapter serves us well as we enter into this new discussion of one of Global Acumen's greatest assets: its flexibility.

CHAPTER 9

Using Global Acumen in Other Contexts

Accounting for country-specific institutional risk is important in global business dealings. And applying Global Acumen's risk spreads to real-world business problems can help managers avoid common globalization mistakes, thereby improving our ability to make sound strategic decisions.

The Newlandia examples from chapter 8 demonstrate how Global Acumen can help managers make decisions about which country (or countries) to select for global expansion. This is a common, foundational concern for global and globalizing companies. However, it is but one among many issues that companies face in global markets and not the only application of the Global Acumen risk management tool. This chapter demonstrates how managers can apply Global Acumen to a range of globalization problems beyond those that deal with global expansion and market selection.

As described in chapter 7, Global Acumen generates generic risk spreads for a given pair of countries. The risk spreads tell us, broadly, about the level of institutional risks companies face in a particular country. Because it is generic, the baseline risk spread applies to the average company from a nondescript industry that is expanding to a particular country for the first time, and on its own. Though certainly helpful in thinking about institutional risk, the baseline risk spread might be of limited use to certain companies and/or to specific applications.

One advantage of the Global Acumen tool is that it is designed to be flexible. Managers can tailor the baseline risk spreads to an expansive set of global strategy problems and a wide variety of company-specific situations. With only slight adjustments, Global Acumen can help managers to do the following:

- assess different foreign market entry modes and ownership structures,
- accommodate for different industry characteristics,
- account for a company's prior international experience,
- benchmark the performance of existing foreign operations,
- monitor institutional developments in a particular country.

Application 1: Factoring in Foreign Entry and Ownership Structure

The Newlandia examples in chapters 2 and 8 assume a specific scenario, namely, that a company invests in a foreign subsidiary and establishes a physical presence in the foreign market to sell products or services there. But clearly a company need not take that step; it can expand globally in a variety of ways to meet a variety of objectives.

On the Sell Side

On the so-called sell side—when a firm looks to extend its own goods and services to a foreign market—global expansion can take several forms, for example:

- *exporting* finished products from its home market directly to customers in the foreign market;
- *licensing* its technologies out to other companies for use in the production of finished goods in the foreign market;
- *franchising* its business model to independent foreign entities that, in turn, use the business model to sell finished goods to consumers in the foreign market;
- forming an *alliance* with a local partner via business agreements, cross-equity holdings, or joint ventures to jointly develop and/ or sell products in the foreign market;

- making a controlling investment in a *subsidiary* in the foreign market to establish a base to sell products in that market or to manufacture goods for export to other markets.

On the Buy Side

The equivalent global expansion on the buy side—where a firm seeks to access goods and services that other firms create—could mean the company engages in any of the following:

- *importing* goods and/or services from foreign markets (perhaps via outsourcing);
- *licensing* technologies from foreign companies for use in its own domestic operations;
- *franchising* a business model from a foreign entity for use in its own domestic market;
- forming an *alliance* with a foreign partner via business agreements, cross-equity holdings, or joint ventures to jointly develop and/or sell products in its own domestic market;
- making a controlling investment in a *subsidiary* to gain access to foreign inputs that are critical to the company's domestic business operations and/or to establish a base to import goods from the foreign market to the company's domestic market.

Deeper Foreign-Market Involvement Entails Greater Risks

Irrespective of how a company decides to globalize, there is one constant: The level of institutional risk a company bears in a particular country varies with how it expands into that market. The more physical and capital assets a company commits to the local market, the more exposed these assets are to the risks in the local environment. Export and import modes of globalization entail much less risk, for example, than subsidiary investments in which a company ties up capital in a long-term investment. This insight holds important implications for Global Acumen as well as for the risk spreads that companies should apply to their particular mode of global expansion. Let us review a few specific cases and then circle back to discuss the implications for Global Acumen's risk spreads.

Lower Risk Entry Modes: Exporting and Importing

To limit its exposure to global risk, a company might opt to export goods to the foreign market or import goods from the foreign market. Each of these is a relatively hands-off means of globalization and can help companies avoid many of the potential pitfalls of institutional distance. A company can export products from its home market with little change, whereby foreign customers purchase the product on an "as is" basis. Similarly, a company can import products from a foreign supplier without having to spend much time (if any) in the foreign market.

Recent advances in information technology have made it possible to purchase foreign-made inputs or sell domestically made outputs directly over the Internet without ever having to set foot in a foreign country. And so compared to foreign market entry modes that require a physical presence, export and import strategies can minimize the institutional disruption globalization can cause to a company's operations. Exporting and importing do not require considerable additional cost; it is relatively easy for a company to get into these arrangements and, if need be, to get out again.

For example, since arriving in Spain for my sabbatical, I have become interested in the brands available at my local supermarket. I did not find many of the brands on the shelves at Spanish supermarkets that are common in the United States, and conversely many brands I buy at home in the United States are not available in Spain. (Sometimes the products on the supermarket shelves are the same but are sold under different brand names. For example, Tide laundry detergent is sold in Spain under the brand name Ariel.)

On one outing to the supermarket in Madrid, I was surprised to discover Stonewall Kitchen pancake mix. Based in York, Maine, Stonewall Kitchen is a relatively small producer of fresh and natural foods with estimated annual sales of $50 million.[1] Compared to a competitor such as Kellogg's with its annual revenues of around $14.5 billion, Stonewall is a tiny company with a limited global footprint, and it depends largely on exports to generate global sales. In Spain, several supermarkets carry Stonewall Kitchen products, which are imported by a company called Taste of America. Taste of America does not alter the products in any way; it simply purchases and distributes them; the company merely adds a label on each product that—in keeping with European Union regulations—details ingredients and provides directions for use in Spanish. This export practice exposes Stonewall Kitchen to very little risk in Spain. If its products sell there, the company gets additional revenue and, hopefully, profit. If not, it will not have made a great sacrifice for this small foray into globalization.

Although exporters like Stonewall Kitchen bear little risk in foreign markets, this is not to say that Stonewall Kitchen bears no risk. Among the company's risks are the following:

- Economic risk: The market may not be large enough to support an adequate sales volume and sufficient profitability. Competition may be fierce in the company's product category, which could prevent the company from pricing the products at a level that would generate a sufficient return.
- Cultural risk: The product itself may not be well-suited to the local consumer market (e.g., its flavor may not appeal to local tastes).
- Political risk: The company might have to deal with some regulatory hurdles, such as compliance with EU packaging regulations.[2] However, without a physical presence, there is limited opportunity for the company to become entangled in disputes with local companies or governmental agencies. It is often up to the import agent and distributor—Taste of America—to ensure that the labeling complies with local regulations.

Exporting, however, enables companies like Stonewall Kitchen to lower their overall institutional risk exposure by shifting many of those risks to a local import/distribution partner: in this case, Taste of America. As the local expert, Taste of America is presumably more familiar with the local political, economic, and cultural environments in Spain and can therefore help Stonewall Kitchen successfully navigate the institutional pitfalls that might otherwise thwart the company if it attempted to enter the Spanish market on its own.

Higher Risk Entry Modes: Investing in Subsidiaries

The stakes are much higher for a company that gets more deeply involved in foreign markets by making equity investments in subsidiaries. A company that invests in local subsidiaries often commits substantial sums to the foreign market and becomes ensconced in the local environment. This typically means that the company:

- maintains offices in that country, frequently with production facilities (sometimes even owning land);
- staffs its operations with local employees;
- deals with local suppliers, customers, and competitors on an almost daily basis;
- may have dealings with government officials and regulators.

These activities expose the company to a wider set of institutional risks in the foreign market: political, economic, and cultural.

The German firm Bayer AG, for example, is one of the largest pharmaceutical and chemical companies in the world and controls a network of subsidiaries throughout the globe. To give you a sense of its massive size and scope, in 2013 Bayer North America, the division of Bayer AG that runs the Canadian and US businesses, had sales of approximately $12 or 13 billion on its own.[3] And in 2014, one of Bayer North America's business divisions, Bayer CropScience, announced a $1 billion investment earmarked for R&D and production facilities in the United States.[4]

When Bayer makes commitments of this size to subsidiaries in a global market, it not only risks a tremendous amount of capital in the host country, but it also commits to physical assets that are hard to reverse later if the investment fails. These commitments expose Bayer to the full set of institutional liabilities in that country.

Since Bayer AG fully controls Bayer North America's operations in the United States, the parent company ultimately bears the risks associated with its US-owned subsidiary, and any negative institutional development can have a direct and substantial impact on its overall profitability. Unanticipated changes to policies regarding genetically modified organisms (GMO), for instance, could negatively impact

Bayer CropScience's profitability in the United States. Similarly, changes in government policy toward foreign investors might make portions of Bayer's North American business untenable.

When companies like Bayer AG make substantial, long-term, and irreversible commitments of this sort, the company is left to its own devices to manage the full slate of political, economic, and cultural risks. Bayer AG must therefore make careful decisions about the institutional risks the company is willing to bear.

Moderate Risk Entry Modes: Alliances

Of the various modes of entry, global alliances occupy a middle ground in terms of institutional risk. Global alliances are business arrangements in which a foreign company works jointly and cooperatively with a local company to offer products or services that mutually serve the interests of the partners. Because alliance partners typically share the risk as well as the reward, alliances tend to pose more institutional risk than exporting, importing, licensing, and franchising, and less institutional risk than owning a foreign subsidiary.

Companies use a spectrum of alliance arrangements, from simple contractual (nonequity) agreements, to more formal arrangements that include equity cross-shareholdings or the formation of an entirely new legal entity, as in the case of a joint venture.[5] When a company forms a global alliance with a local partner in the host country, that local partner can help the foreign company manage country-specific institutional risks, given its familiarity with the local political, economic, and cultural environments. It can help its foreign alliance partner avoid common institutional pitfalls.

For example, Shanghai GM is an alliance between the American company General Motors and the Chinese firm SAIC Motor. The two established a fifty-fifty joint venture in 1997 to manufacture and sell GM's Buick label in the Chinese market.[6] For SAIC, the joint venture brought much-needed technological insight into automobile engineering, assembly, and design. For GM, the venture provided access to the Chinese market. In addition, SAIC brought its local expertise. As a state-owned, well-connected Chinese company, SAIC helped GM to:

- reach consumers with marketing and distribution support throughout China;
- gain detailed knowledge about the local market, given SAIC's familiarity with Chinese culture and consumer tastes;
- navigate complex political, legal, and regulatory relationships that often flummox American companies in China.

Like Bayer AG (see pages 164 and 165), GM exposed assets to institutional risk and invested a substantial sum—nearly $1.6 billion in cash and in kind—in its Chinese joint venture. In contrast to Bayer AG, and much like Stonewall Kitchen (see pages 162 and 163), GM benefited from the aid of a local partner with local political, economic, and cultural expertise to help mitigate those risks. However, GM made a much larger commitment in China in terms of physical and capital assets than Stonewall Kitchen did in Spain. Institutional risks therefore have the potential to take a greater toll on GM than on Stonewall Kitchen.

In this way, alliances present moderate levels of risk to companies like GM. Of course, a company that engages in an alliance often trades one kind of risk (institutional) for another (partner). In the case of the GM-SAIC joint venture, GM was able to tap into SAIC's vast knowledge of China and piggyback on its existing relationships. And yet there was always the risk that the two corporate cultures would be at odds—as with the Dow-KPCC joint venture (see page 100)—which would create tension between the partners. Owning the majority of the equity in a foreign subsidiary, as Bayer AG did, avoids those partnership-related conflicts; however, in a country that poses high levels of institutional risk, an alliance with an experienced local company might just be worth the risks of partner conflict. So far, that has proved to be the case for GM; the alliance with SAIC has been profitable, and GM and SAIC have worked together on additional deals since 1997.

Modes of Foreign Entry: Weighing the Risks with Global Acumen

As you can see in the cases of Stonewall Kitchen, Bayer AG, and GM, trade-offs in institutional risk go along with global companies' decisions regarding foreign market entry modes and ownership structures. Academic studies detail those various trade-offs, but we do not need to rehash the trade-offs here. For our purposes, the important lesson for managers is that they must conduct careful financial analyses for the various modes of entry to determine the mode best suited to their specific situation.[7] This could mean comparing the cash flows associated with investing in a subsidiary, as in the Newlandia example, to the cash flows associated with an alternative scenario, for example, one in which a company invests in a joint venture with a Newlandian partner. And toward that end, Global Acumen can help.

I originally designed the Global Acumen algorithm with the baseline assumption that a company bears the full costs of institutional risk in the host market. That is, Global Acumen assumes a company that owns 100 percent of the equity in a foreign subsidiary also bears 100 percent of the costs related to institutional risk. However, we can adapt the baseline institutional risk spreads to consider the overall profitability of various entry modes and ownership options.

Adjusting for a Joint Venture
If an alternative option, such as a joint venture, can ameliorate institutional risk, then by how much should we adjust the risk exposure? Quite simply, the answer is that the amount is likely to be proportional to the company's equity ownership in the venture. So a company that owns a 50 percent equity interest in a joint venture should be able to lower its institutional risk exposure to 50 percent of the full risk amount. The local knowledge and experience of the foreign partner help offset the remaining risk.

Global Acumen is equipped to handle joint ventures because it has the ability to vary the percentage of institutional risk a globalizing company bears. The Global Acumen software tool has a function that allows users to generate modified risk spreads that are contingent on ownership structure. Users can vary the ownership risk spread from 0 to 100 percent based on the level of equity the investing company holds in the foreign venture.

For a company considering a fifty-fifty joint venture in Newlandia, for example, the institutional risk spread (which we would ultimately add to the domestic cost of capital, for discounting purposes) would be 50 percent of the initial institutional risk estimate for Newlandia. In the context of the original example from table 8.2 in chapter 8, where we assumed that Newlandia presented a 10 percent institutional risk, we would simply alter the steps to generate the Newlandia-specific discount rate. The process would be as follows:

1. Scale the Newlandia institutional risk spread of 10 percent by the 50 percent joint-venture ownership interest (50%of 10%= 5%).
2. Add the 5 percent (joint venture–scaled) Newlandia risk spread to the 8.5 percent domestic discount rate.
3. Generate a Newlandia adjusted joint-venture discount rate of 13.5 percent.
4. Replace the original domestic discount rate of 8.5 percent with the new, 13.5 percent discount rate.

Table 9.1 Business Projections for Newlandia: Assuming Shared Profit for Joint Venture (JV) and a 13.5% Discount Rate

	Year 0	Year 1	Year 2	Year 3	Year 4	Year 5
Revenues		$1,000	$1,000	$1,000	$1,000	$1,000
Costs		$800	$800	$800	$800	$800
Initial Costs	$550					
Profit	–$550	$200	$200	$200	$200	$200
New Present Value	–$550	$176	$155	$137	$121	$106
Shared JV Present Value	–$275	$88	$78	$68	$60	$53
New Overall NPV	$72					
Table 8.2 Present Value	–$550	$169	$142	$120	$101	$86
Table 8.2 NPV	$68					

Assuming a fifty-fifty joint venture, the discount rate drops from 18.5 percent in table 8.2 to 13.5 percent in table 9.1. This is because we are now adding only half of Newlandia's institutional risk to the domestic discount rate for discounting purposes (50% multiplied by 10%= 5%; 5% plus 8.5%= 13.5%). We should keep in mind, of course, that profitability estimates are also likely to vary in the joint-venture scenario. When we share an equity interest with a partner, we also typically share the investment costs and the profitability, and the line item "Shared JV Present Value" reflects that the company also shares half (50%) of the initial investment costs and half (50%) of the profits.[8]

Adjusting for Exporting

Let us now turn to what percentage of the institutional risk spread to apply when a company opts to export. In such a situation, the company likely holds no equity in a foreign entity, and its risks in the foreign market are limited. As illustrated in the Stonewall Kitchen example (see pages 162 and 163), exporting helps companies mitigate much of their institutional risk exposure, but it cannot completely eliminate risk.

It therefore makes sense to set Global Acumen's equity correction to a very low level, in the range of 5–15 percent, depending on how involved the company becomes in the export market.[9] In the context of the Newlandia example, this would imply that a company considering exporting to Newlandia might only bear 5–15 percent of the country-specific risk that Global Acumen's base algorithm projects. Assuming the company considering exporting to Newlandia bears 10 percent (the midpoint of the export range) of the original institutional risk spread of 10 percent from table 8.2, the appropriate discount rate steps are as follows:

1. Scale the Newlandia institutional risk spread of 10 percent by the export factor of 10 percent (10% of 10% = 1%).
2. Add the 1 percent export-adjusted Newlandia risk spread to the 8.5 percent domestic discount rate.
3. Generate a Newlandia-adjusted discount rate of 9.5 percent.

Table 9.2 Business Projections for Newlandia: Assuming Partial Profit for Export and a 9.5% Discount Rate

	Year 0	Year 1	Year 2	Year 3	Year 4	Year 5
Revenues		$1,000	$1,000	$1,000	$1,000	$1,000
Costs		$800	$800	$800	$800	$800
Initial Costs	$550					
Profit	−$550	$200	$200	$200	$200	$200
New Present Value	−$550	$183	$167	$152	$139	$127
Export Present Value	−$55	$18	$17	$15	$14	$13
New Overall NPV	$22					
Table 8.2 Present Value	−$550	$169	$142	$120	$101	$86
Table 8.2 NPV	$68					

4. Replace the original domestic discount rate of 8.5 percent with the new discount rate of 9.5 percent.

As table 9.2 illustrates, the new discount rate is 9.5 percent (10% multiplied by 10% = 1%; and 1% plus 8.5% = 9.5%). But again, keep in mind that profitability estimates are also likely to change under the export scenario. This is because the import and distribution company needs to make a profit as well, and therefore the full $200 in profit associated with a wholly owned subsidiary will not accrue to a company that exports. For the sake of simplicity, assume that 10 percent of the present values (both in investment costs and profit) accrue to the exporter.[10]

The simplified examples in tables 9.1 and 9.2 notwithstanding, it should be increasingly clear that Global Acumen is not limited to wholly owned subsidiary scenarios presented in previous chapters. The tool accommodates a variety of entry approaches to globalization beyond 100 percent of equity ownership in a newly created foreign subsidiary. In fact, we can tailor Global Acumen's institutional risk spreads to fit a company's specific needs, regardless how it seeks to enter a foreign market.[11]

Application 2: Factoring Industry Differences into Global Acumen

As mentioned above, the baseline Global Acumen institutional risk spreads were generated under the assumption that a company bears

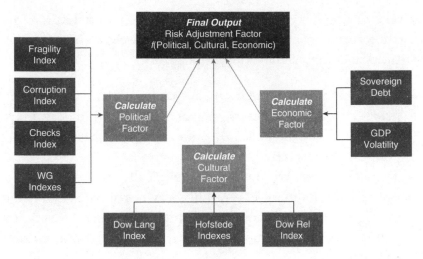

Figure 9.1 The Architecture of Global Acumen.

the full price of the institutional risks in the country in which it intends to operate. However, to generate that risk spread, we must assign weights to each of the political, economic, and cultural institutional pillars that comprise Global Acumen.

You may recall from chapter 7, where Global Acumen's architecture and construction are laid out (as depicted in figure 9.1), that the baseline risk spread is built on a prespecified set of weights for each of the underlying political, economic, and cultural components. Assuming we begin with equal weights for each institutional component—at approximately 33.3 percent for each of the three elements—the algorithm generates one set of risk spreads.[12] However, if we weight the institutional components differently—say at 40 percent for politics, 20 percent for economics, and 40 percent for culture—the algorithm generates a different institutional risk spread. For most applications the baseline weights will work just fine and the manager will not need to adjust them, but users have the option to change the prespecified baseline weights if they wish. The question then becomes: Under what circumstances should we should we consider altering the baseline weights?

One situation in which it might be appropriate to alter baseline weights is for industries with unique characteristics. Although in chapter 8 cross-country industry differences are assumed away (for the sake of simplicity), the truth is that some industries have distinctive features that might change how we weight the individual institutional components. For example:

- The fashion industry: Given that cultural tastes matter more here than political factors, managers in this industry might want to weight the cultural component more heavily and the political one less heavily.
- The energy industry: Energy is a politically sensitive commodity, and the industry is typically heavily regulated; therefore, managers of energy companies might choose to weight the political component more than the economic and/or cultural components.
- The financial industry: Banking is heavily regulated as well as extremely sensitive to economic volatility, and therefore bank managers might prefer to weight the economic and political components more than the cultural component.

This is obviously not an exhaustive list of industries for which it might make sense to modify Global Acumen's baseline weights, and managers in other industries might be justified in altering the baseline weights. For managers who decide that it is appropriate to alter Global Acumen's baseline weights, there is a built-in function that allows interested users to override the baseline weights and modify the weights of each of the individual institutional criteria. Users can vary each institutional component between 0 and 100 percent, with the only constraint that the sum of the political, economic, and cultural weights must equal 100 percent.

Application 3: Factoring Experience into Global Acumen

Global Acumen was designed for companies large and small and those with and without global experience. However, the baseline Global Acumen algorithm generates risk premiums assuming that a company has zero global experience in the country in question. For many companies, such as large multinational corporations, this is likely an inaccurate assumption. In fact, some companies have a wealth of experience operating in the same foreign country for years, and they make multiple follow-on investments along the way, learning from each one as they go.

Generally, experience affords a company the opportunity to learn about the markets in which it operates. It learns the intricacies of a country's political, economic, and cultural environments; it gains familiarity with local rules and norms; it develops relationships with local customers and suppliers; it becomes more comfortable operating in the local market; and it begins to look and behave increasingly like a domestic company. This experience helps companies overcome the costs related to institutional distance they faced in a once-unfamiliar market.

Revisiting the Bayer AG case can prove instructive in this respect. Bayer North America has operated continuously since the late nineteenth century, and it now employs some 15,200 people in the United States.[13] It has made a number of investments in the United States over the years. To evaluate the investment that Bayer CropScience announced in 2014—a $1 billion commitment in the United States—it would be unwise to use the "raw" (baseline) Global Acumen risk spread between Germany (Bayer AG's home country) and the United States (the host country), which is currently around 7 percent.[14] This is because Global Acumen assumes a German company investing in the United States with no prior US experience, whereas Bayer in fact has a wealth of experience there. Therefore, when calculating the appropriate institutional risk spread for Bayer North America to apply to its financial calculations for the CropScience investment, we need to take into account its experience and adjust the baseline risk spread between Germany and the United States accordingly.

Of course, we must now ask what the appropriate institutional risk premium should be for a company with significant experience in the local market (as with Bayer North America). Were we to set the experience correction to zero percent, it would treat Bayer North America the same as a domestic company making a similar investment, which is not entirely appropriate.

Research does suggest that experience can reduce a company's liability of foreignness costs—helping to avoid common globalization mistakes and lowering its institutional risk through an improved understanding of the local market—and yet institutional risk cannot be eliminated completely. A foreign company can glean a lot from experience, and it can learn to cope with and even lessen the burden of foreignness. However, it cannot eliminate all differences. Once foreign, always foreign, and even after many years the company remains a bit different in significant ways from its domestic peers in the host market.

Keeping It Real: Minimizing Foreignness through Personal Experience

The following vignette might help you relate to how the burden of foreignness persists despite years of experience in a foreign country or culture. My father—born in Spain, lived in Cuba, settled in the United States at age 32—is now a US citizen and has resided in the United States for more than 50 years. Despite all this time in the United States and even though he arrived with extremely marketable intangible business skills that helped cushion the blow of foreignness, he still feels he is at a disadvantage compared to native US citizens (like me).

The culture, for example, remains a bit tricky for him, as it is for any nonnative person. He continues to speak English with a thick Spanish accent that immediately identifies him as "foreign," and he sometimes struggles to understand American humor or people who speak quickly and use slang. Though he has made countless friends, he lacks a profound network of friendships in the United States that trace back to one's school days, and he simply does not have the option to lean on his oldest friends from childhood for help with serious issues in the United States, should he need it. He also struggles at times to discuss political and economic issues, not because he does not understand them, but because they are incredibly nuanced and complex.

My father has largely assimilated, and he feels at home in the United States; however, 50 years has proved insufficient to completely erase his liability of foreignness. It is simply harder and takes longer for him to cope with political, economic, and cultural complications in the United States than it is for me, a US citizen who was born and raised in the United States.

The Learning Curve of Experience

Research demonstrates that the costs associated with the liability of foreignness tend to approximate a learning curve. The more experience a company gains in the foreign market, the lower the risk it faces. A completely inexperienced company bears the full brunt of institutional risk. However, with experience, those costs go down—at first, exponentially. At some point, however, experience brings diminishing returns, in which each additional unit of experience fails to generate the same benefit as the preceding one. As I mentioned above, the liability of foreignness never reaches zero; a company can reduce its liability of foreignness only so much. It takes a company about 10 years for costs to reach their institutional nadir. After that, the benefits of experience begin to wane significantly, and ultimately they flatten out.

Figure 9.2 shows how a simple (approximated) learning curve applies to globalization risk spreads. The left side reflects that risk is the greatest for a globally inexperienced company, but as a company gains experience in the local market, any future investments in that country benefit from accumulated experience. By year 10, a company bears only a fraction of the risk it originally faced in the host market.

Learning curve effects were built into the Global Acumen algorithm using a variation of an exponential decay function. This allows Global Acumen to capture the significant benefits of early learning

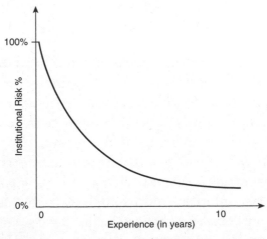

Figure 9.2   Learning Curves and Institutional Risk Premiums.

that a company generates in a specific country, with decreasing marginal returns in proportion to its increasing level of experience.

The Global Acumen baseline generates a global risk spread value based on zero years of experience in the local market, but the user has the option to adjust this value to reflect the number of years of experience a company has been operating in that market. Global Acumen then recalculates the risk premium, expressing it as a proportion of the original baseline risk.[15]

Application 4: Using Global Acumen as an Evaluation and Monitoring Tool

There is still another set of applications for Global Acumen's institutional risk spreads: they can serve as tools for benchmarking and evaluating global operations or as a means for monitoring political, economic, and cultural developments in a country.

A company with an existing global footprint needs an objective way to evaluate the performance of its various businesses. High-ranking executives with strategic responsibilities must make decisions such as whether to:

- commit additional resources to the businesses and divisions they oversee;
- continue to invest in, or expand, in certain countries;
- limit investment in some countries, exit certain businesses from a particular market, or shut down operations entirely in a particular country.

These are not easy decisions to make, but Global Acumen's risk spreads can help managers with them. One useful benchmark is to use the risk spreads Global Acumen generates to evaluate the profitability of a company's operations in a given country and to determine whether profitability expectations are met.

In addition to evaluating ongoing foreign operations, shrewd managers must remain vigilant to changing risks in global markets. They should stay informed and regularly scan the global environment to anticipate sudden changes in institutions and the impact those changes are likely to have on their ongoing foreign operations.

They should also be aware of how changes in institutional risk can influence the prospects of doing business in new markets. Managers must be ready to pounce when new opportunities present themselves, and they must be prepared to act swiftly and decisively when the institutional environment takes a turn for the worse. Global Acumen's risk spreads can help managers stay on top of institutional developments and keep tabs on the levels of risk in global markets.

Global Acumen as a Performance Benchmark

The Target Corporation recently announced it would abandon the Canadian market after only two years. Target opened stores in Canada in 2013, and before long its Canadian subsidiary was severely underperforming, generating operating losses that reached nearly $1 billion in the first year alone. A turnaround for Target Canada was uncertain, years away at best, and the company made the difficult decision to shutter its Canadian business entirely.[16]

Losses as large as Target's make performance benchmarking relatively straightforward; losses are an obvious symptom of a struggling business. However, even in the face of losses, shutting down a business is never easy, because managers often internalize the commitment they have made to a particular country and feel personally responsible for generating positive outcomes. I therefore applaud Target for making the tough, though necessary, decision to close the business rather than throwing good money after bad trying to resuscitate it.

Hefty losses made it a bit easier for Target's managers to make the tough decision to shut down its Canadian business, but this type of decision is not always as clear-cut in other situations. In many instances, a company that expands globally finds that the business is profitable, but only marginally so. Managers must periodically strategically evaluate global subsidiaries to determine whether to shore up their investment or exit altogether, and Global Acumen can help them with this.

As we saw in the Newlandia example, a global investment should generate a return that is at least equal to the domestic discount rate plus the country-specific risk spread. Assuming a company has an

8.5 percent domestic discount rate (as we have assumed throughout this book), then for an expansion to Canada, which has a 4 percent risk premium to the United States, the performance benchmark would be 12.5 percent. A 12.5 percent Canada-specific discount rate equips the manager to make a decision about ongoing Canadian operations based on one of the following four scenarios:

- If the business generates a return that is equal to or greater than 12.5 percent, the manager is likely to determine that things are going as planned, that the current strategy is working, and that strategic changes are not warranted.
- If the business generates a return that is less than 12.5 percent, but higher than the greater of the Global Acumen risk spread or the domestic discount rate (in this case 8.5%), the manager would want to take a closer look at the operation but might conclude that drastic action is not necessary.
- If the business generates a return that is between the domestic discount rate and the Global Acumen risk spread (in this case, between 4%and 8.5%), some strategic intervention might be appropriate to help prop up returns.
- If the business generates a return that is less than both the domestic discount rate and the risk premium (in this case, a return lower than 8.5% and also lower than 4%), it might be time to consider restructuring the business: culling product lines, delaying or suspending investment in the country, and/or selling portions of the business—especially if prospects for future profitability do not look promising.
- If the business continually generates negative returns, all strategic options—including selling or shutting down the business—should be on the table.

Global Acumen as a Risk Monitoring Tool

Managers can use Global Acumen's risk spreads to monitor developments in a particular country. We know from chapters 4 and 5 how geopolitical and economic developments can (suddenly or over time) significantly change a country's risk profile, impacting not only current operations but also future investment opportunities. As you might expect:

- with negative political and/or economic developments in a country, Global Acumen's spreads increase to reflect those new risks;
- with positive political and/or economic developments in a country, Global Acumen's spreads decrease to reflect those new risks.

Given these dynamics, managers would be wise to do the following:

1. Check Global Acumen's spreads on a regular basis to assess the level of risk in those counties where they have a business interest.
2. Update Global Acumen performance benchmark rates, given the updated levels of risk.
3. Conduct a strategic review using the updated performance benchmark rates to assess whether current levels of profitability meet expectations in those countries where they have current operations.
4. Consider how changes to a country's institutional risk-adjusted discount rate affects the company's stance toward that market—whether changes in risk profiles change the outlook for, and prospects of, doing business in that country.

The Bottom Line for Performance Evaluation and Monitoring

Repurposing Global Acumen for use as a performance benchmark or for monitoring country risk does not require any modification to the base algorithms. This is in contrast to the alternative uses I highlighted above: applying different weightings to particular entry modes, industries, or levels of company experience. We can add Global Acumen's risk spreads directly to a company's domestic cost of capital (as in the Newlandia example in chapter 8) at any time, to evaluate the performance of ongoing global operations.[17] Managers can also monitor Global Acumen's raw risk spreads at any time to gain a sense of the current levels of institutional risk in a particular country. But regardless of the specific performance evaluation or monitoring purpose, managers can use Global Acumen's risk spreads as a tool for strategic evaluation or simply to stay abreast of institutional developments in particular countries.

Bringing It All Together

This chapter shows how we can use Global Acumen with only slight modifications for the following purposes:

1. assessing different entry strategies and foreign ownership structures,
2. accommodating institutional differences across industries,
3. accounting for a company's levels of international experience,
4. setting a performance benchmark for evaluating ongoing global performance,
5. monitoring ongoing institutional developments in a particular country.

Some of these modifications—entry mode, industry differences, and experience levels—require adjustments to Global Acumen's baseline weights, and those options have been built directly into an accompanying Global Acumen software tool. Some applications—evaluating ongoing performance and monitoring institutional developments—are even simpler and do not require any adjustments.

The utility of Global Acumen is vast and certainly not limited to the four applications described in this chapter. Given its many possible applications and extensions, managers might also consider using Global Acumen to help them determine:

- the most appropriate staffing mix for a foreign subsidiary: whether to staff the local operation with more expatriate employees or local employees; and
- the best way to manage the local operation: in a more uniform, integrated fashion or a more flexible fashion tailored to the local market.

In a country that presents lower levels of institutional risk, staffing is not as pressing an issue, and managers have greater latitude when it comes to determining the staffing mix. It might also be easier for managers to extend products and strategies from the home market to the foreign market. Alternatively, in a country that presents higher levels of institutional risk, managers must exercise great care in staffing and should look for local employees with experience who can help fill gaps in institutional knowledge. In addition, managers might prefer to tailor products and strategies to the local environment, allowing the local subsidiary greater flexibility to determine how it runs the day-to-day operations.

In all of these cases, and more, utilizing Global Acumen's risk spreads leads to better globalization decisions and outcomes, making it an essential part of every global manager's toolkit.

CHAPTER 10

The End of the Beginning for Global Acumen

I have covered a lot of ground in making a case for why it is essential for managers to account for institutional risk in global markets. Because I wrote this book primarily with the busy manager in mind, I tried to keep the technical material relatively brief and light, yet relevant. I have explained why institutions are critical to globalization, introduced Global Acumen as a tool to account for institutional risk, broken down the Global Acumen algorithm into its simplest elements, and provided step-by-step instructions for its use—all while using real-world examples that resonate with managers.

Of course, I hope that academic readers—students and scholars—will find the general content of interest as well, given that Global Acumen is firmly rooted in research. It translates, extends, and converts research findings on institutional distance into a practical, powerful set of tools that can help companies address some of globalization's most vexing challenges.

This chapter, however, is not about debating the relative merits of this book for academic or managerial audiences. It is about setting the stage for what comes next for Global Acumen and what that means for our understanding of institutional risk. I therefore first take the opportunity to circle back and, with the benefit of all we have covered, fuse together various elements of the story, in hopes of making a lasting impression and planting some seeds for future work in the area of global risk management. Integrating all we have done and reviewing why it matters enables us to get a better sense for where we should go next.

Global Acumen really is only a beginning—a launching point. It helps foster a better understanding of globalization; it represents a novel approach to institutional risk; and it provides a powerful set of global risk management tools. However, there is much work still to do on Global Acumen, and I fully intend to keep refining it (with versions 2.2, 2.3., 3.0, 3.1, etc.). I can only hope my work thus far has sparked greater interest in the study of globalization and that others will follow suit with similar tools that refine and extend Global Acumen.

A Summary of Lessons Learned

Let's briefly review the key points of my argument:

1. There are harsh realities to globalization.
   - Globalization is incredibly complex and challenging for managers to accomplish profitably and effectively.
   - Managers tend to overestimate the benefits of globalization and underestimate its costs.
   - As a result, companies struggle with globalization far more often than they should.
2. Institutional differences matter in globalization.
   - At the root of globalization's challenges (the liability of foreignness) are differences in institutions—political, economic, and cultural—between one country and another.[1]
   - Political, economic, and cultural differences create risks for global and globalizing companies.
   - Managers make smart globalization decisions when they take institutional differences into account.
3. We can use institutional differences to estimate the effects of institutional risk.
   - We can measure individual institutions—political, economic, and cultural—and use those measures to compare two countries.
   - We can convert the comparisons mathematically into "risk spreads" that capture and accurately reflect institutional differences.

4. Global Acumen is a mathematical algorithm that estimates institutional risk spreads between countries in an effective, useful, and flexible way.
   - Global Acumen expresses risk spreads in terms of interest rates—over a range from 0 to 30 percent.
   - Global Acumen's risk spreads yield insight into the risks that companies are likely to face when they do business in a particular country.
   - Global Acumen's risk spreads are suited to a variety of strategic analyses, including those that rely on financial modeling techniques.
   - We can apply and tailor Global Acumen's risk spreads to a wide variety of situations. In this way Global Acumen can help managers:
     - make global expansion and market entry decisions,
     - appraise foreign entry modes and ownership structures,
     - account for industry-specific differences,
     - account for foreign experience,
     - generate performance benchmarks against which to evaluate ongoing global operations,
     - monitor political, economic, and cultural developments across countries,
     - address staffing and subsidiary management problems.
5. Global Acumen is a vital part of any manager's strategic toolkit. It can help managers:
   - avoid common globalization mistakes,
   - make smarter, better globalization decisions,
   - improve global management practice,
   - successfully navigate globalization's risks and complexities,
   - improve overall profitability.

Where We Have Been and Why It Matters

From the outset I have argued that companies often get their globalization strategies spectacularly wrong and that this tendency is not limited to small, inexperienced companies that are expanding globally for the first time. Unfortunately, failure is all too common, even among some of the largest and most sophisticated global corporations—even those with household names. In chapter 1 I discuss the examples of Tesco, Walmart, and IKEA, but the list goes on. These problems are stubborn; they dog companies again and again.

It Starts with the Manager

I identify a common theme among the failures: a fundamental misunderstanding and mispricing of the political, economic, and cultural risks companies face in global markets. Managers are generally smart and well-intentioned, and they do recognize that operating globally involves risks. However, they are woefully misinformed about the true nature of those risks. The problem, therefore, is the lack of adequate tools at a manager's disposal. Up to now, solutions that allow managers to quantify and accurately account for globalization's risks have been elusive. As a result, managers tend to:

- not realize or not accurately account for the impact of global risk on the bottom line,
- overestimate the benefits associated with globalization,
- underestimate the crucial role of the political, economic, and cultural differences between their home country and the host country to which they seek to expand or in which they already operate,
- learn the hard way—only once it is too late—that institutional differences can unravel even the best-laid business plans.

Understanding Institutions

The first step to a solution lies in recognizing the problem. And in this case, improving global strategic decision making requires improving our understanding of national institutions—our own as well as those of the countries to which we seek to expand. Since these institutions form the basis of the differences between countries, and because they are at the root of globalization's risks, it is crucial for managers to understand how they are likely to impact a company's global operations. Gaining an appreciation for these underlying institutions—political, economic, and cultural—makes it possible to see how differences between two countries make it difficult to conduct business across them, as I have shown with a range of examples

Measuring Institutions

Yet, it is not enough to simply understand, appreciate, and recognize that institutions create obstacles to globalization; we can do more. That starts with measurement. Measuring institutions can help us understand *how* institutional differences matter. Advances in various academic fields have yielded excellent measures of political, economic, and cultural institutions, which are available for a large number of countries.

A Means to Compare Those Measures

Once armed with measures of institutions, we need a procedure or formula, that allows us to fruitfully compare institutional measures for several countries. We can turn to existing institutional distance formulas from the academic literature to guide us. These formulas express institutional differences—and therefore globalization's difficulties as well—in mathematical terms. But this is only a half step, as institutional distance formulas, by their very construction, are limited in that they cannot generate measures of institutional difference in ways that are useful for managers.

Global Acumen: A Measurement Managers Can Use

However, we can compensate for these limitations. We can tweak institutional distance approaches to suit the needs of practicing managers. This is precisely what Global Acumen does. It expresses distance over a meaningful range and in a way that does not generate symmetric risks for pairs of countries.[2] It modifies institutional distance approaches to generate more precise institutional risk spreads for pairs of countries. What is more, Global Acumen expresses those risk spreads in a financially meaningful way that managers can use.

Global Acumen can help companies build in safeguards that protect against globalization's risks. Managers can:

- incorporate Global Acumen's risk spreads into existing financial analysis techniques—by adding the risk spreads to the domestic discount rates for NPV analyses, breakeven analyses, or internal rate of return (IRR) analyses;
- apply Global Acumen's risk spreads to determine:
  - which countries to enter or avoid,
  - which foreign entry modes and ownership structures to use,
  - which foreign initiatives and subsidiaries are meeting performance targets,
  - how to manage ongoing foreign operations—perhaps even as a strategic aid for staffing decisions.

Global Acumen also empowers managers to:

- tailor risk spreads to industry-specific conditions,
- modify risk spreads to a company's specific level of international experience,
- monitor ongoing political, economic, and cultural developments in specific countries.

Irrespective of the precise application, Global Acumen can help astute managers deal with the complexities inherent to an organization with geographically far-flung operations. It should therefore be a part of every manager's toolkit—whether for a company that is considering expanding for the first time or an internationally experienced company with a vast, existing global footprint.

Where We Go from Here: From Global Acumen's Infancy to Its Maturity

Though quite powerful, Global Acumen is still in its infancy. It would therefore be naïve of me to proclaim it is a panacea that will protect a firm from all of globalization's risks. Global Acumen, like any algorithmic approach to risk, has its flaws. This is an honest assessment and not an indictment, and does not undermine the usefulness of Global Acumen in helping managers solve some of globalization's most challenging problems.

Global Acumen is more advanced and more precise than other risk management approaches currently available. What is more, it is certainly better than "risk-naïve" approaches that fail to account for institutional differences between countries across political, economic, and cultural dimensions. However, the range of applications and the precision with which one can apply Global Acumen will no doubt improve with time, experience, and more robust measures of institutions. I would therefore exhort others to not only join me but to carry the torch and help refine and advance Global Acumen, in a collaborative effort to continually improve global management practice.

This book features version 2.0 of the Global Acumen architecture and tool, but it is my sincere hope that its evolution does not end with version 2 or with the conclusion of this chapter.[3] I believe we can find solutions to society's most pressing problems only through joint effort and cooperation, and I envision improved versions of Global Acumen that are yet to come will be the product of a collective enterprise.

With that in mind, I have attempted to explain the purpose, the design, and the construction of Global Acumen as clearly as possible and in considerable detail. I want readers not only to be able to follow the philosophy behind Global Acumen, but to understand it enough to contribute to its improvement. In that way, managers and interested researchers can build upon and extend Global Acumen or create institutional risk algorithms of their own. I encourage others to pursue every avenue and seek every opportunity, as I will, to improve upon not only Global Acumen, but more broadly to increase our understanding of globalization and institutional risk.

Improving Institutional Measures

One area where there is likely to be significant progress is with new and improved measures of institutions as inputs to the risk algorithm. Better institutional measures are bound to come along in the years to come. Some will be completely new; others will refine existing measures or update those measures more frequently. I am always on the lookout for better inputs, and there is progress every day in generating more accurate measures of political, economic, and cultural institutions. Better institutional measures will result in more accurate results, as better inputs yield better outputs.

Improvements to the Algorithm

There are certainly opportunities to refine Global Acumen's base algorithm. Although a strong theoretical justification underlies my approach, there is room for healthy debate as to the best way to construct institutional risk spreads.[4] Continued theory development, testing, backtesting, and experimentation will no doubt help refine Global Acumen going forward.

There is also room to improve how we apply Global Acumen to address globalization's challenges. As I mentioned above, I designed Global Acumen to be flexible—for companies large and small, experienced or inexperienced, to use in a variety of situations, and as a complement to existing strategic analyses and financial modeling techniques. But there are vastly more potential applications. Surely there are other ways managers can apply Global Acumen's risk spreads to improve their company's global operations, and I would encourage others to explore possible additional uses and alternative applications.[5]

Limits to the Application of Global Acumen

We should, of course, exercise caution in applying (or relying too much on) algorithmic procedures to solve complex globalization problems that, at their root, are a product of social interaction. Algorithmic approaches can certainly help us simplify and make sense of complex globalization problems, but we should always view them as a complement to managerial intuition and as a decision-making aid. With respect to Global Acumen, that means that there is no substitute for a deep qualitative and intuitive understanding of globalization's risks to help guide, inform, and improve Global Acumen's quantitative, algorithmic nature.

A manager should temper any application of Global Acumen with a healthy dose of realism. Given that globalization poses nuanced and dynamic problems, its risks are continuously evolving—and they sometimes change in ways that Global Acumen may not immediately capture and reflect in its output. A manager should seek to understand how and why institutions will change and how those changes are likely to impact risk. Sometimes understanding *why* institutions change and anticipating *how* they are likely to change in the future is more important than knowing a specific number attached to that change.

It is therefore essential that managers not only know how to apply algorithmic approaches like Global Acumen to account for institutional risk, but they must also know why and in what situations such approaches are most appropriate. Rather than merely taking output from Global Acumen and blindly plugging it into a financial model, a manager would be wise to carefully consider whether the output

- suits the intended application,
- makes sense given any recent or sudden changes to the institutional environment—either in the firm's home country or in the intended host country.

These considerations will only enhance the tool's value and utility.

Understanding Global Acumen's Limits: Institutional Change in Ukraine

One way to explain the current limits to Global Acumen is to consider how its risk spreads have changed in the case of Ukraine. Ukraine experienced a rather tumultuous political and economic transformation in 2014, and the country is now involved in an ongoing conflict with Russia over Crimea and disputed territory on its eastern border with Russia. In response, Global Acumen's risk spread between the United States and Ukraine suddenly jumped from 19.6 percent in early 2014 to nearly 23 percent in March 2014. By late 2014 it had reached 24 percent. This clearly places Ukraine in the extreme risk category, and the message is clear for companies based in the United States: Global Acumen suggests that Ukraine is a riskier prospect for expansion today than it was in early 2014.

Global Acumen can help detect institutional changes like those in Ukraine. It reflects those changes in its risk spreads. However, Global Acumen cannot predict how events in Ukraine are likely to unfold. Will the Ukrainian economy continue to spiral downward? Will it continue to be politically destabilized? Will it fall back into the Russian sphere of influence, or will it continue to politically integrate with the European Union?

This is where human experts can help. Experts with a deep qualitative understanding of Ukrainian institutions—as well as institutions in other interested protagonists like Russia, Europe, and the United States—can generate more accurate projections about future institutional trajectories and outcomes there. This is precisely the type of situation in which human intelligence can complement algorithmic approaches to institutional risk such as Global Acumen. Though Global Acumen can tell us the level of risk that might be present in a country today, human experts can help us anticipate what that level of risk might be tomorrow. When it comes to understanding future changes to any institutional environment, human intelligence can improve upon artificial intelligence.

Until better approaches, tools, and methodologies emerge, Global Acumen stands as a viable and robust institutional risk management solution. Certainly, as our collective understanding of globalization's institutional risks evolve, Global Acumen will evolve as well. I look forward to seeing and participating in Global Acumen's evolution. More generally, I look forward to being part of a broader institutional risk movement, as it blossoms from infancy into maturity, with risk approaches and algorithms that become increasingly sophisticated and accurate.

Finally Bringing It All Together

Managers see unbridled opportunity the world over, making globalization an exciting proposition for businesses everywhere. And they are right; there are tremendous opportunities in global markets. Tapping into global markets, especially fast-growing and developing ones, not only promises riches beyond our wildest imagination, but also empowers people the world over to work toward creating a better economic future. But as we have seen, there can be trouble when two opposing forces collide: the optimistic nature of managers and the fact that global markets, especially developing ones, can be precarious. There are missed opportunities at both ends of the spectrum; many companies have yet to realize the full potential of global markets, and simultaneously too many companies stumble in their attempts to globalize profitably.

Obviously, the answer to globalization's well-documented failures is not for companies to avoid global risks altogether, to stand on the sidelines and refuse to do business in foreign markets. But the stories of frustrating global outcomes I outline in this book certainly cry out for a new approach to risk. To play the complicated and high-stakes game of global strategy and reap the potentially high rewards, a manager who has read this book now understands the risks and is also empowered to accurately take them into account. This is the key to skillfully outmaneuvering those risks. Global Acumen can help managers do much more than avoid catastrophic globalization mistakes—it is a tool to help managers win at the globalization game.

Notes

1 Globalization: A Cautionary Tale

1. Trade data from the World Trade Organization, "Statistics: Trade and Tariff Data," https://www.wto.org/english/res_e/statis_e/statis_e.htm (accessed May 11, 2015). Investment data from United Nations Conference on Trade and Development "FDI Flows and Stocks," http://unctad.org/en/Pages/DIAE/FDI%20Statistics/FDI-Statistics.aspx (accessed May 11, 2015).
2. The World Bank http://www.worldbank.org/en/topic/poverty (accessed May 11, 2015).
3. See the case study, W. J. Henisz and B. A. Zelner, "AES-Telasi: Power Trip or Power Play?" (The Wharton School, 2006); or Paul Devlin's film *Power Trip* (2003), for more in-depth coverage of AES and its failed entry to Georgia.
4. I explain some of the specific issues that IKEA faced in Russia, along with more general issues that similar companies face in emerging markets, in a blog post. See R. Salomon, "So You Want to Do Business In a Developing Country?" September 15, 2009, http://www.robertsalomon.com/so-you-want-to-do-business-in-a-developing-country/ (accessed May 11, 2015).
5. See "Tesco Plans Foray into US Market," *BBC News*, February 9, 2006, http://news.bbc.co.uk/2/hi/business/4695890.stm (accessed June 24, 2015).
6. In June 2007 I wrote a blog post forecasting that, given its strategy, Tesco would have trouble entering the US market. See R. Salomon, "Tesco's American Foray," June 27, 2007, http://www.robertsalomon.com/2007/06/ (accessed May 11, 2015). In March 2008, it was clear that many of those predictions had come true; Tesco failed to make a profit in the US market and exited a short time later. See R. Salomon, "Update: Tesco's Venture into the U.S.," March 4, 2008, http://www.robertsalomon.com/update-tescos-venture-into-the-us/ (accessed May 11, 2015).
7. For an in-depth review of China's infrastructure development, see Y. Chen, S. Matzinger, and J. Woetzel, "Chinese Infrastructure: The Big Picture," *McKinsey Quarterly*, June 2013, http://www.mckinsey.com/insights/winning_in_emerging_markets/chinese_infrastructure_the_big_picture (accessed May 11, 2015).
8. See U. Galani, "No Froth in Starbucks' Buyout in Japan," *New York Times*, September 14, 2014, http://dealbook.nytimes.com/2014/09/24/no-froth-in-starbucks-buyout-in-japan (accessed May 11, 2015).
9. See J. I. Siegel, "Lincoln Electric," Harvard Business School Case 707–445, November 2006 (revised August 2008), http://www.hbs.edu/faculty/Pages/item.aspx?num=33844 (accessed May 11, 2015).

10. See "A World of Pain: The Giants of Global Finance are in Trouble," *The Economist*, March 7, 2015, http://www.economist.com/news/finance-and-economics/21645807 -giants-global-finance-are-trouble-world-pain (accessed May 11, 2015).

11. Another way to think about the increase in the pace of globalization is by looking at the growth of the World Trade Organization (WTO), whose member states commit to broadly liberalizing cross-border trade. In 1995, its founding year, there were 128 WTO members; there are currently 160. China became a member in 2001 and Russia in 2011. As of this writing, WTO members account for approximately 96 percent of all global trade and 97 percent of the world's GDP.

12. See T. L. Friedman, *The World is Flat: A Brief History of the Twenty-First Century* (New York: Farrar, Straus and Giroux, 2015). See also T. L. Friedman, *Hot, Flat, and Crowded: Why We Need a Green Revolution and How It Can Renew America* (New York: Farrar, Straus and Giroux, 2008). T. Levitt was among the first to make flat-world arguments in "The Globalization of Markets," *Harvard Business Review* (May 1983).

13. For the purposes of this book, political institutions also refer to legal and regulatory institutions. For more, see chapter 4.

14. See R. Florida, "The World Is Spiky," *Atlantic Monthly*, October 2005; or P. Ghemawat, "Distance Still Matters," *Harvard Business Review* 79, no. 8 (September 2001): 137–149.

2 The Globalization Process

1. See J. Szczesny, "Milestone: China Now General Motors' Biggest Market," *CNBC*, July 8, 2013, http://www.cnbc.com/id/100870316 (accessed May 11, 2015).

2. A maquiladora is manufacturing facility located within a free trade zone in Mexico. The principal purpose of a maquiladora is to manufacture products for export. The benefits of locating a maquiladora in Mexico are the tax benefits. Imported equipment and inputs as well as exported outputs are generally not subject to tax.

3. For details, see E. Araiza and P. Cardona Soriano, "LL Bean Latin America," IESE Business School, 2000.

4. For more on what I mean by currency risk, see chapter 5.

5. I continue with assumption no. 5, above (there is no residual value of the assets in which the company invests for its expansion to Newlandia—that is, the entire value of the Newlandia venture goes to $0 in year 6). I also continue with assumptions no. 6 (no currency risk) and no. 7 (no tax considerations).

6. Clearly, I am simplifying quite a bit for analytical convenience. For detailed information on how to calculate discount rates, I refer you to Aswath Damodaran's website (http://people.stern.nyu.edu/adamodar/). One common technique for generating the cost of capital that is appropriate to use as the discount rate in present value calculations comes from the capital asset pricing model (CAPM). CAPM can be expressed as $K_c = R_f + \beta_i (R_m - R_f)$, where K_c stands for the cost of capital used for discounting purposes; R_f is the risk-free rate (typically that associated with local US government bonds); β_i is the specific market beta of the company; and R_m is the market return (typically the return on some index like the S&P 500).

7. The generic present value formula can be expressed as $\{FV_n/(1+r)^n\}$ where FV_n is the future value (in this case, profit) in time period n, r is the discount (interest) rate, and n is the period (month, year, etc.).

3 The Impact of National Institutions on Globalization

1. Just a reminder that, throughout this book, when I refer to political institutions, I include legal and regulatory institutions as well. See chapter 4 for more explanation.
2. See D. C. North, "Institutions," *Journal of Economic Perspectives* 5, no. 1 (1991): 97–112.
3. Srilata Zaheer is widely credited for coining the phrase "liability of foreignness" in S. Zaheer, "Overcoming the Liability of Foreignness," *Academy of Management Journal* 38, no. 2 (1995): 341–363. The concept itself dates back at least to Stephen Hymer, who wrote about the disadvantages foreign companies face in his doctoral thesis. See S. Hymer, *The International Operations of National Firms: A Study of Direct Foreign Investment* (Cambridge, MA: MIT Press, 1960).
4. See "China Loses Its Allure," *The Economist*, January 23, 2014, http://www.economist.com/news/leaders/21595001-life-getting-tougher-foreign-companies-those-want-stay-will-have-adjust-china (accessed May 15, 2015).
5. Chapter 4 addresses individual kinds national institutions.
6. Typically, measures of institutional distance are calculated using Euclidean or Mahalnobis distance approaches. I will come back to measurement issues in later chapters.
7. See J. Campbell, "Ikea Shuts Down Lifestyle Website in Russia Over Fears It Promotes Gay Propaganda," *The Independent*, March 14, 2015, http://www.independent.co.uk/news/world/europe/ikea-closes-lifestyle-website-in-russia-over-fears-it-promotes-gay-propaganda-10108270.html (accessed May 26, 2015).
8. See J. Alcacer and J. Leitao, "Logoplaste: Global Growing Challenges," Harvard Business School Case 711–411, December 2010 (revised February 2013).

4 Political Institutions and Globalization

1. That is to say, when I speak of political institutions in this book, I refer generically to political, legal, and regulatory institutions as a set. It is perfectly reasonable to treat and measure political, governmental, legal, and regulatory institutions as distinct and separate institutional constructs. I simply collapse them here for analytical convenience and because they share significant theoretical and empirical overlap.
2. See First Read DMV, "Uber Wins Right to Operate in D.C.," *NBC Washington*, December 4, 2012, http://www.nbcwashington.com/blogs/first-read-dmv/Uber-Wins-Right-to-Operate-in-DC-182097951.html (accessed May 15, 2015).
3. See E. Badger, "How Airbnb Just Changed the Housing Laws in San Francisco," *The Washington Post*, October 8, 2014, http://www.washingtonpost.com/blogs/wonkblog/wp/2014/10/08/how-airbnb-just-changed-the-housing-laws-in-san-francisco/ (accessed May 15, 2015).
4. For examples of the difficulties experienced by Uber and Airbnb in Europe, see M. Scott and S. Plass, "German Court Lifts Ban on Uber Ride Service," *The New York Times*, September 16, 2014, http://www.nytimes.com/2014/09/17/business/international/uber-ban-in-germany-is-lifted-by-court.html?_r=0 (accessed May 15, 2015), or R. Minder and M. Scott, "Sharing Economy Faces Patchwork of Guidelines in European Countries," *The New York Times*, September 21, 2104, http://www.nytimes.com/2014/09/22/technology/sharing-economy-faces-patchwork-of-guidelines-in-european-countries.html (accessed May 15, 2015).

5. See U. Bhattacharya, N. Galpin, and B. Haslem, "The Home Court Advantage in International Corporate Litigation," *Journal of Law and Economics* 50 (2007): 625–659.

6. See Public Citizen, "Canadian Corporation Uses NAFTA to Sue the U.S.: The Loewen Group, Inc. v. The United States," http://www.citizen.org/trade/article_redirect .cfm?ID=1173 (accessed May 15, 2015).

7. For details, see K. Hyde, "Japanese Companies and U.S. Employment Law Liability: How to Avoid Court and Stay out of the Headlines," Japan Society website, September 13, 2011, http://japansociety.org/multimedia/articles/japanese-companies-us-employment -law-liability-how-to-avoid-court-stay-out-of-the-headlines (accessed March 25, 2015).

8. Even the most basic source—Wikipedia—makes clear that "The main institutions of law [are] courts...parliaments, ,, [the] executive [branch], the military and police, bureaucratic organization[s], the legal profession and civil society itself." Wikipedia, "Law," http://en.wikipedia.org/wiki/Law (accessed March 25, 2015).

9. For an excellent introductory overview of civil law and common law systems see the Robbins Collection "The Common Law and Civil Law Traditions," University of California at Berkeley School of Law website, https://www.law .berkeley.edu/library/robbins/CommonLawCivilLawTraditions.html (accessed May 15, 2015).

10. See K. Riesenhuber, "English Common Law versus German *Systemdenken*? Internal versus External Approaches," *Utrecht Law Review* 7, 1 (2011): 117–130.

11. See A. C. Bianculli, X. Fernández-i-Marín, and J. Jordana, "The World of Regulatory Agencies: Institutional Varieties and Administrative Traditions," EPSA 2013 Annual General Conference Paper 786.

12. Bianculli, Fernández-i-Marín, and Jordana, "The World of Regulatory Agencies."

13. See K. Kedl et al., *China Business Report* (The American Chamber of Commerce in Shanghai, 2015), http://www.amcham-shanghai.org/AmChamPortal/MCMS/Presentation /Publication/PublicationCustomization/Content.aspx?Type=1&GUID={E3337DDB -28FD-457D-96B7-2C77E21A2A90}&tb_Name=PublicationCustomization&origin=s horturl (accessed May 15 2015).

14. See Z. Wu and R. Salomon, "The Regulatory Liability of Foreignness: Enforcement Actions in the United States," New York University Stern working paper, 2015.

15. See B. Protess and D. Jolly, "French Bank Is Suspected of Violating Blacklistings," *The New York Times*, February 13, 2014, http://dealbook.nytimes.com/2014/02/13 /bnp-paribas-profit-falls-on-u-s-sanctions-troubles/ (accessed May 15, 2015); and B. Protess and J. Silver-Greenberg, "Bank of Tokyo Fined for 'Misleading' New York Regulator on Iran," *The New York Times*, November 18, 2014, http://dealbook.nytimes .com/2014/11/18/lawsky-fines-bank-of-tokyo-mitsubishi-ufj-another-315-million / (accessed May 15, 2015).

16. See H. Mance and K. Hille, "CNN to Pull Plug on Broadcasting in Russia," *Financial Times*, November 11, 2014, from http://www.ft.com/cms/s/0/a201f700–69b0-11e4-8- f4f-00144feabdc0.html#ixzz3IqvWwXgl (retrieved March 23, 2015).

17. See R. La Porta et al., "Law and Finance," *Journal of Political Economy* 106, 6 (1998): 1113–1155.

18. See Claudio Radaelli and Oliver Fritsch, "Measuring Regulatory Performance," OECD Expert Paper no. 2 (July 2012).

19. As I mentioned above, I make no value judgment about whether those numbers indicate better or worse political institutions. The absolute numbers mean very little to me; I leave such evaluations to political pundits.

5 Economic Institutions and Globalization

1. For more on the Kellogg's case, see M. Haig, *Brand Failures: The Truth about the 100 Biggest Branding Mistakes of All Time* (London: Kogan Page, 2003), chap. 5, 32–35.

2. See several sources for Daimler's market share data, including Statista, "Mercedes: Market Share of New Car Registrations in the EU from April 2014 to April 2015," http://www.statista.com/statistics/276309/mercedes-market-share-of-new-car -registrations-in-the-eu/ (accessed June 6, 2015); C. Hetzner, "European Automakers Seek Firmer Foothold in India," *Automotive News Europe*, September 1, 2014, http:// europe.autonews.com/article/20140901/ANE/140829857/european-automakers-seek -firmer-foothold-in-india (accessed June 6, 2015); and "What's Moving: U.S. Auto Sales—The U.S. Market," *Wall Street Journal*, June 2, 2015, http://online.wsj.com/mdc /public/page/2_3022-autosales.html#autosalesD (accessed June 6, 2015).

3. For a review of the onshoring trend, see R. Salomon, "Small Businesses in U.S. Reevaluate China Outsourcing Strategy," April 6, 2011, http://www.robertsalomon .com/small-businesses-in-u-s-reevaluate-china-outsourcing-strategy/ (accessed May 11, 2015); R. Salomon, "Offshores Coming Home," February 19, 2013, http://www .robertsalomon.com/offshores-coming-home/ (accessed May 11, 2015); or R. Salomon, "Revisiting Outsourcing…Again," August 9, 2011, http://www.robertsalomon.com /revisiting-outsourcing-again/ (accessed May 11, 2015).

4. Of course, in instances where a country officially adopts the currency of another (as Panama recognizes the US dollar [USD]) or pegs its currency to another (as Hong Kong does with the USD), exchange rates can remain relatively fixed by design.

5. See L. Thomas, Jr., "U.S. Strengths Buoy Consumers but Hurt Corporations with Business Abroad," *The New York Times*, January 27, 2015, http://dealbook.nytimes .com/2015/01/27/u-s-strengths-buoy-consumers-but-hurt-corporations-with-business -abroad/?_r=0 (accessed March 30, 2015).

6. There are a variety of ways to hedge currency risk, but currency hedging mechanisms are outside the scope of this book. I will leave that to international finance texts, which focus on a whole host of issues related to currency regimes, systems, differences, and risks as well as the management/hedging of those risks.

7. See BCG-K@W Report, "Overcoming the Challenges in China Operations," *Knowledge@Wharton*, March 22, 2005, http://knowledge.wharton.upenn.edu/special -report/bcg-kw-report-overcoming-the-challenges-in-china-operations/ (accessed May 28, 2015).

8. Of course, a country's economy and economic development is also influenced by its political, legal, regulatory, and cultural institutions. However, when it comes to measuring institutions in terms of their level of risk to a company seeking to globalize, it is important to distinguish between institutions that serve a specific economic function and those that serve a political, legal, regulatory, and cultural function. Although the lines between institutions can be blurred from time to time, I tend to distinguish economic institutions from other institutions by their more narrow relation to economic activity in a society.

9. Although I single out capitalism and command economies as prototypical economic systems since they are the most widely adopted the world over, they are not the only kinds of economic systems that currently exist or have existed.

10. The extent to which these systems are similar or different to capitalist/command economies is outside the scope of this book.

11. Data from the IMF World Economic Outlook Database, https://www.imf.org/external /pubs/ft/weo/2015/01/weodata/index.aspx (accessed on May 29, 2015).

12. See Statista, "Consumer Spending on Luxury Goods in China from 1998 to 2015," http://www.statista.com/statistics/235092/consumer-spending-on-luxury-goods-in-china/ (accessed March 30, 2015).

13. See, for example, the Heritage Foundation's Index of Economic Freedom (http://www.heritage.org/index/) or the Fraser Institute's Economic Freedom of the World Index (http://www.freetheworld.com/).

14. See, in particular, development indicators from the United Nations, the World Bank, and the International Monetary Fund.

15. See Aswath Damodaran's website (http://pages.stern.nyu.edu/~adamodar/New_Home_Page/data.html or http://pages.stern.nyu.edu/~adamodar/New_Home_Page/data.html), where he explains how he calculates cross-country economic risk spreads from sovereign bond ratings.

6   Cultural Institutions and Globalization

1. See D. Ricks, *Blunders in International Business*, 4th ed. (Malden, MA: Wiley, 2006).

2. See T. Watanabe, "Gerber Taking a Lesson from Foreign Babies," *Los Angeles Times*, May 27, 1991.

3. Michael Corleone is notorious for saying this line to Sonny in Francis Ford Coppola's 1972 film *The Godfather* (based on Mario Puzo's 1969 book of the same title).

4. Dow's then-president Robert Lundeen characterized the partnership as "an absolute disaster" and warned future foreign investors about the perils of investing with partners in South Korea. See T. Shorrock, "Dow Fights with Korean Partners, Slams Business Climate," *Multinational Monitor* 3, 9 (September 1982), http://www.multinationalmonitor.org/hyper/issues/1982/09/shorrock.html (accessed June 1, 2015).

5. For a detailed discussion of the Honda-Rover alliance, see J. K. Sebenius, A. Nanda, and R. S. Fortgang, "Honda-Rover (A): Crafting an Alliance," Harvard Business School Case No. 9–899–223 (1999), and subsequent updates B, C, and D.

6. Quoted from a 2002 working version (3.24) of Ron S. Fortang, David. A. Lax, and James. K. Sebenius, "Negotiating the Spirit of the Deal: Crafting the Social Contract," later published in *Harvard Business Review* (February 2003), product R0302E-PDF-SPA.

7. Michiyo Nakamoto and Christopher Lorenz, "It Doesn't Have to End in Tears," *The Financial Times*, March 7, 1994.

8. Michiyo Nakamoto and Christopher Lorenz, "Why We Can't Afford to Betray the Japanese," *Daily Mail*, February 22, 1994, p. 7.

9. See Roger Hallowell, Carin-Isabel Knoop, and David Bowenthe, "Four Seasons Goes to Paris," Harvard Business School Case No. 803069 (2002).

10. Philip Rosenzweig, "National Culture and Management," Harvard Business School Note 9–394–177 (1994).

11. See Geert Hofstede, *Cultures and Organizations: Software of the Mind* (New York: McGraw-Hill, 1999).

12. John Van Maanen and Andre Laurent, "The Flow of Culture: Some Notes on Globalization and the Multinational Corporation," in *Organization Theory and the Multinational Corporate*, ed. Sumantra Ghoshal and D. Eleanor Westney (New York: St. Martin's Press, 1993).

13. This is not to say that individuals within a country are homogenous; there is tremendous cultural variation within a country, and especially so in a large country like the United States. Some groups within a country may even relate more readily to the culture of another country. People who live close to the Canadian border in Michigan, for example,

might have more in common with Canadians who live just on the other side of the border than with some Americans who live in New Mexico. But this is more the exception than the norm.

14. Dow bases his calculations on Gordon's classification into language families, branches, and sub-branches. See Gordon's website *Ethnologue: Languages of the World*, http://archive.ethnologue.com/15/web.asp (accessed March 31, 2015).

15. Dow obtains the majority of his religion data from the *CIA World Factbook*, the *World Christian Encyclopedia*, and the Jewish Agency for Israel. He draws his definitions of major religions, denominations, and sects from the *World Christian Encyclopedia*, *Religion in Today's World*, *Contemporary Religions: A World Guide*, *The State of Religion Atlas*, and the *Concise Encyclopedia of Islam*. See Dow's website, https://sites.google.com/site/ddowresearch/ (accessed March 31, 2015).

16. See Hofstede, *Cultures and Organizations*, for a summary.

17. This raises a kind of "chicken or the egg" problem in terms of which came first: cultural institutions or political, legal, regulatory, and economic institutions. Attempting to answer that question is beyond the scope of this book.

7   Using Global Acumen to Account for Risk

1. These numbers are random and for illustrative purposes only. They are not drawn from any actual institutional data sources.

2. With a single institutional dimension, Euclidean distance approaches yield solutions that are equivalent to those that absolute value generates. It is easy to see this by applying the Euclidean distance technique to our simple example of the United States and China. Comparing the United States and China on simply one dimension—economic—results in a situation where the number of dimensions (n) is set to 1, and so the problem simplifies to $\sqrt{(5-2)^2} = 3$.

3. With a single institutional dimension, Mahalanobis distance approaches likewise yield solutions that are equivalent to those that absolute values generate. It is easy to see this by applying the Mahalanobis distance technique to our simple example of the United States and China. Comparing the United States and China on simply one dimension—economic—results in the following simplified calculation: $\sqrt{\{(5-2)*1*(5-2)\}} = 3$.

4. See R. Salomon and Z. Wu, "Institutional Distance and Local Isomorphism Strategy: Foreign Investment in the U.S. Banking Industry," *Journal of International Business Studies* 4, no. 43 (2012): 343–367.

5. Two countries that share the same institution scores will be indistinguishable on a scale of institutional distance, meaning it would be equally easy for a company from one country to do business in the other and vice versa.

6. "The discount rate...refers to the interest rate used in discounted cash flow (DCF) analysis to determine the present value of future cash flows. The discount rate in DCF analysis takes into account not just the time value of money, but also the risk or uncertainty of future cash flows; the greater the uncertainty of future cash flows, the higher the discount rate." See http://www.investopedia.com/terms/d/discountrate.asp#ixzz3XCnbSSVV (accessed March 9, 2015).

7. See A. Damodaran, "Valuing Young, Start-up, and Growth Companies: Estimation Issues and Valuation Challenges," New York University working paper (2009), http://people.stern.nyu.edu/adamodar/ (accessed March 9, 2015). Otherwise, the models I present in chapter 2—using domestic cost of capital to evaluate projects—would be perfectly valid for global activity.

8. See R. Salomon and Z. Wu, "Institutional Distance and Local Isomorphism Strategy: Foreign Investment in the U.S. Banking Industry."

9. As I discussed in chapter 5, this is in part because countries with more stable underlying economic institutions inspire more confidence in economic projections, and certain capital-market structures and interest-rate environments make it easier to raise capital.

10. You will recall that I consider political, legal, and regulatory institutions under the umbrella of political institutions. See chapter 4 for the rationale.

11. Although the Global Acumen approach is nuanced, the Euclidean and Mahalanobis distance approaches I describe above are generic, and you can apply them to any set of institutional measures. I describe the algorithmic procedures built into Global Acumen simply as a benchmark. Given the many ways to create risk spreads from country-specific measures of institutions, I would encourage anyone with a deep interest in data and measurement to experiment with various ingredients (individual institutional measures) and recipes (distance/risk formulas).

12. As of the writing of this book, I have developed version 2.1 of Global Acumen. The schematic does not vary much from version 2.0, though there are some slight differences. Work on version 3.0 is currently underway; it substitutes the standard Mahalanobis distance approach for the modified Euclidean distance approach I used in earlier models. So far, the output has been remarkably consistent with what I obtained from version 2.0.

13. I generated the Global Acumen spreads reported herein in January 2014. Because the sovereign debt component of Global Acumen changes instantaneously as sovereign debt is traded in real-time treasury markets, the exact Global Acumen spreads vary on a daily basis. GDP volatility (the other economic factor) changes annually, as do the political measures. The cultural measures are static (at least over the span of time for which I have data).

14. Assertions about the ease of doing business in the United States come from the *Doing Business* report series of the World Bank (http://www.doingbusiness.org/reports).

8 Global Acumen in Practice

1. You will recall that a more nuanced discussion in chapter 7 explained the specific (political, economic, and cultural) institutional elements that comprise Global Acumen; the algorithmic approach that combines those institutional elements to generate cross-country risk spreads; and how these risk spreads accurately and faithfully reflect cross-country institutional risk. I mentioned there how Global Acumen is only one approach to cross-country risk, and I therefore equipped interested readers to experiment with a variety of alternative approaches, merging other institutional measures in various ways using different distance and difference formulas.

2. See pages XX–XX and tables 2.1 through 2.3 for a reminder.

3. As before, we are assuming that business is conducted in USD and that there are no taxes, no depreciation expenses, and no debt. We also assume that the assets will have no residual value, which means that, at the end of the five-year period, the value of the initial investment (and the entirety of the business enterprise) is $0.

4. You will recall from chapters 2 and 7 that the discount rate is an interest rate based on some "reasonable" opportunity cost of capital—typically calculated using CAPM techniques that take into account the long-run average return (more or less) of the US stock market minus a "risk-free" rate of return on government bonds. CAPM can be expressed as $K_c = R_f + \beta_i (R_m - R_f)$, where K_c stands for the opportunity cost of capital; R_f is the risk-free rate (typically that associated with local US government bonds); β_i is the specific

market beta of the company; and R_m is the market return (typically the return on some index such as the S&P 500).

5. There is nothing inherently global about the original CAPM formula. R_f is typically the risk-free rate associated with local domestic government bonds; β_i is the market beta of the company in the domestic market; R_m is market return in the domestic market. It is therefore unclear if CAPM is appropriate for use in global settings. Some scholars have made an attempt to modify CAPM for global markets, but CAPM has been subject to criticism for generating arbitrary values. See P. Fernandez, "CAPM: An Absurd Model," SSRN (Social Science Research Network) working paper (2014).

6. I use 2014 Weighted Average Cost of Capital (WACC) calculations generated by http://www.stockresearching.com/ as my estimates for the opportunity cost of capital for Apple Inc. and Cisco Systems Inc. Given that WACC outputs are incredibly sensitive to their inputs and underlying assumptions, I present WACCs for illustrative purposes only. These WACCs are not necessarily the de facto WACCs for Apple Inc. and Cisco Systems Inc. Moreover, Apple Inc. and Cisco Inc. are likely to use their own internally generated discount rates for NPV and discounting purposes.

7. Although investors typically expect to receive returns in line with basic domestic cost of capital requirements (specific to the company and the industry) when companies expand globally, this assumption is admittedly an oversimplification. For example, in some cases industry risk profiles can change quite significantly from one country to another. I discuss variants to the Global Acumen model that address country-specific variation in chapter 9.

8. You will recall that, using the Global Acumen tool, I generated risk spreads that were approximately 19 percent for Russia, 15.5 percent for India, 14.5 percent for China, 10.5 percent for Japan, 4.5 percent for the United Kingdom, 4 percent for Canada, and 3 percent for Australia. See page XX.

9. You will recall the present value formula from chapter 2 as $\{FV_n/(1+r)^n\}$, where FV_n is the future value (profit) in time period n, r is the discount (interest) rate, and n is the period (month, year, etc.).

10. Slight modifications to the revenue projections in tables 8.2 and 8.3 help drive home the point. Slightly lower revenue projections of $980 (instead of $1,000), for example, in table 8.2 result in a negative NPV, even with a 10 percent Global Acumen risk spread and a 18.5 percent Newlandia-specific discount rate. Similarly, slightly higher revenue projections of $1,020 (instead of $1,000) will yield positive NPV results in Table 8.3, even with a 20 percent Global Acumen risk spread and a 28.5 percent Newlandia-specific discount rate.

11. Based on foreign direct investment flow data from the UN and OECD.

12. Belarus is not one of the 55 countries included in the Global Acumen database.

13. The Global Acumen database does not include Sudan, but see the Fragile States Index (FSI) (http://library.fundforpeace.org/fsi).

14. For an introduction to market risk premium adjustment techniques, see C. S. Eun and B. G. Resnick, *International Financial Management*, 7th ed. (New York: McGraw Hill, 2014), or L. L. Jaque, *International Corporate Finance: Value Creating with Currency Derivatives in Global Capital Markets* (Hoboken, NJ: Wiley, 2014).

15. See A. Damodaran, "Country Default Spreads and Risk Premiums" (January 2015), http://pages.stern.nyu.edu/~adamodar/New_Home_Page/datafile/ctryprem.html (accessed April 25, 2015).

16. One paper even laments how "Risk premiums are usually subjective and rarely justified in an analytical context." See R. E. Jensen "International Investment Risk Analysis: Extensions for Multinational Corporation Capital Budgeting Models," *Mathematical Modeling* 9, nos. 3–5 (1987): 265–284.

9 Using Global Acumen in Other Contexts

1. Stonewall Kitchen's product lines include jams and jellies; baking mixes for breads, desserts, and pancakes/waffles; dressings and sauces; candy and confectionary; and condiments. See www.hoovers.com for sales estimates.
2. You will recall that, as in earlier chapters, political risk also includes legal and regulatory risk.
3. Estimates from http://www.bayer.com/en/North-America.aspx
4. See Bayer CropScience website, "Close to US$ 1 Billion (EUR 700 million) Earmarked for Investments in the USA between 2013 and 2016," press release, Sept. 3, 2014, http://www.cropscience.bayer.com/Media/Press-Releases/2014/Close-to-US-1-billion-EUR-700-million-earmarked-for-investments-in-the-USA-between-2013-and-2016.aspx (accessed April 30, 2015).
5. Nonequity alliances are those in which neither party takes an equity stake in its partner firm. Equity alliances involve some sort of equity arrangement; one or both of the companies might take an ownership stake in the other. Joint ventures are a special kind of equity alliance that forms a new, separate legal corporate entity, in which each of the partners to the alliance take an ownership stake.
6. Under the terms of the joint venture arrangement, GM and SAIC each own 50 percent of the equity in Shanghai GM, the newly created corporate enterprise.
7. One of my studies addresses this topic. See X. Martin and R. Salomon, "Knowledge Transfer Capacity: Implications for the Theory of the Multinational Corporation." *Journal of International Business Studies*, 34 (2003): 356–373.
8. This fifty-fifty split in investment costs and profitability is a simplifying assumption. There are many ways in which joint venture partners can split investment costs and profitability. Joint venture partners need not, and often do not, split the investment costs and profitability precisely by the percentage of equity interest.
9. This application is more of an art than a science, and so managers need to use some intuition and think carefully about what level of correction to implement when conducting a financial analysis of exporting. The more a company is involved in the export market—exporting directly to foreign customers—the higher the risks it bears. The less a company is involved in the export market—using an import agent and distributor to reach foreign customers—the lower the risks it bears.
10. In a real-world situation, the revenues and costs would vary substantially for different entry modes. For example, shipping costs are typically greater when companies export than when they produce goods in the local market via a wholly owned subsidiary. Prudent managers would therefore be wise to generate precise revenue and cost projections for each entry mode scenario.
11. Although I discuss here only 100-percent equity subsidiaries, joint ventures, and exporting alternatives, it is important to note that we can also tailor Global Acumen to importing, franchising, licensing, and equity and nonequity alliances. Importing in many ways mirrors exporting, and so the appropriate Global Acumen adjustment is similar to that for exporting. Franchising, licensing, and alliances other than joint ventures fall somewhere along the spectrum between exporting and joint ventures; that is, the Global Acumen risk adjustment should fall somewhere between 10 and 50 percent.
12. The equal weighting of 33.3 percent is simply for expository purposes. I based the actual weights in the baseline Global Acumen algorithm on a combination of academic research findings and the underlying correlation structure among the constituent political, economic, and cultural variables.

13. You will recall from the previous discussion that Bayer North America currently generates about \$12–13 billion in sales from the Canadian and US markets.
14. As of January 2014.
15. Although this section discusses a company's experience in a particular country, individual managers of that company might also have experience in a particular country—having spent extensive amounts of time working, studying, or living there. An individual manager might also be a native of the country to which the company seeks to expand. To the extent that managers believe an individual's personal experience is relevant to a venture in a particular country, that experience can be factored into Global Acumen using a similar process.
16. For more details, see Pete Evans, "Target Closes All 133 Stores in Canada, Gets Creditor Protection," *CBC News*, January 15, 2015, http://www.cbc.ca/news/business/target -closes-all-133-stores-in-canada-gets-creditor-protection-1.2901618 (accessed April 30, 2015).
17. Of course, if a company has been operating in a certain country for a number of years, the managers might want to use the experience-adjusted risk spread for evaluation and performance benchmarking purposes.

10   The End of the Beginning for Global Acumen

1. You will recall from throughout the book that my references to political institutions subsume legal and regulatory institutions as well.
2. Symmetric risks are those in which the distance from country A to country B is equivalent to the distance from country B to country A. Refer to chapter 7 for a reminder about why this is important in generating useful institutional risk metrics.
3. Although I describe version 2.0 in this book, the most current version of Global Acumen is version 2.1. It is similar in many respects to version 2.0, except that I made some slight changes to the measures included as inputs, which modifies slightly the risk spread outputs. As I mentioned in chapter 7, work on version 3.0 of Global Acumen is currently underway. This substitutes Mahalanobis distance techniques for the modified Euclidean distance techniques used in versions 1 and 2 of Global Acumen.
4. As one example, Global Acumen currently assumes symmetry between countries for political and cultural dimensions and asymmetry for economic institutions. It need not. One could certainly explore other formulations assuming different levels of symmetry and asymmetry. Future algorithms could possibly allow for asymmetry in both economic and political institutions, or they could accommodate asymmetry across all institutional dimensions.
5. For example, Global Acumen currently expresses risk spread output in interest rate terms in a range of 0 to 30 percent, but it need not. We could tweak the algorithm to generate spreads in another form or over a different range. A manager could use these new spreads to generate liability of foreignness cost contingencies that are applied as a percentage of revenues or costs. Moreover, we could change the design to generate spreads over just about any range. Exploring these new uses of Global Acumen's risk spreads can yield insights into a host of real-world globalization problems.

Bibliography

Alcacer, J., and J. Leitao. "Logoplaste: Global Growing Challenges." Harvard Business School Case 711–411, December 2010 (revised February 2013).

Araiza, E., and P. Cardona Soriano. "LL Bean Latin America." IESE Business School Case FH-673-E, 2000.

Argote, L. *Organizational Learning: Creating, Retaining, and Transferring Knowledge*. Boston: Kluwer, 1999.

Bae, J. H., and R. Salomon. "Institutional Distance in International Business Research." In *The Past, Present, and Future of International Business and Management*, ed. T. Devinney, T. Pedersen, and L. Tihanyi, 327–349. Bingley: Emerald Group Publishing, 2010.

Badger, E. "How Airbnb Just Changed the Housing Laws in San Francisco." *The Washington Post*, October 8, 2014. http://www.washingtonpost.com/blogs/wonkblog/wp/2014/10/08/how-airbnb-just-changed-the-housing-laws-in-san-francisco/ (accessed May 15, 2015).

Barth, J. R., G. Caprio, Jr., and R. Levine. "The Regulation and Supervision of Banks around the World: A New Database." World Bank Policy Research working paper 2588 (2001).

Bartlett, C. A., and S. Ghoshal. *Managing Across Borders: The Transnational Solution*. Boston: Harvard Business School Press, 1989.

Bayer CropScience website. "Close to US$ 1 Billion (EUR 700 million) Earmarked for Investments in the USA between 2013 and 2016." Press release, September 3, 2014. http://www.cropscience.bayer.com/Media/Press-Releases/2014/Close-to-US-1-billion-EUR-700-million-earmarked-for-investments-in-the-USA-between-2013-and-2016.aspx (accessed April 30, 2015).

BBC News. "Tesco Plans Foray into US Market." February 9, 2006. http://news.bbc.co.uk/2/hi/business/4695890.stm (accessed June 24, 2015).

BCG-K@W Report. "Overcoming the Challenges in China Operations." *Knowledge@Wharton*, March 22, 2005. http://knowledge.wharton.upenn.edu/special-report/bcg-kw-report-overcoming-the-challenges-in-china-operations/ (accessed May 28, 2015).

Beck, T., et al. "New Tools in Comparative Political Economy: The Database of Political Institutions." *World Bank Economic Review* 15, no. 1 (2001): 165–176.

Berry, H., M. F. Guillén, and Z. Zhou. "A New Approach to Cross-National Distance." *Journal of International Business Studies* 41, no. 9 (2010): 1460–1480.

Bhattacharya, U., N. Galpin, and B. Haslem. "The Home Court Advantage in International Corporate Litigation." *Journal of Law and Economics* 50 (2007): 625–659.

Bianculli, A. C., X. Fernández-i-Marín, and J. Jordana. "The World of Regulatory Agencies: Institutional Varieties and Administrative Traditions." EPSA 2013 Annual General Conference paper 786.

Buckley, P., and M. C. Casson. *The Future of the Multinational Enterprise.* London: Holmes and Meier, 1976.

Campbell, J. "Ikea Shuts Down Lifestyle Website in Russia Over Fears It Promotes Gay Propaganda." *The Independent*, March 14, 2015. http://www.independent.co.uk/news /world/europe/ikea-closes-lifestyle-website-in-russia-over-fears-it-promotes-gay -propaganda-10108270.html (accessed May 26, 2015).

Caves, R. E. *Multinational Enterprise and Economic Analysis.* Cambridge, UK: Cambridge University Press, 1996.

Chen, Y., S. Matzinger, and J. Woetzel. "Chinese Infrastructure: The Big Picture." *McKinsey Quarterly* (June 2013). http://www.mckinsey.com/insights/winning_in_emerging _markets/chinese_infrastructure_the_big_picture (accessed May 11, 2015).

Cho, Y. "The Liability of Foreignness, R&D Investment, and Productivity Growth." New York University Stern working paper (2015).

Cho, Y., and J. Song. "Redefining the Liability of Foreignness and the Role of Experiential Learning in Overcoming the Liability of Foreignness." New York University Stern working paper (2015).

Damodaran, A. "Country Default Spreads and Risk Premiums" (January 2015). http:// pages.stern.nyu.edu/~adamodar/New_Home_Page/datafile/ctryprem.html (accessed April 25, 2015).

Damodaran, A. "Valuing Young, Start-up, and Growth Companies: Estimation Issues and Valuation Challenges." New York University Stern working paper (2009). http://people .stern.nyu.edu/adamodar/ (accessed March 9, 2015).

Dow, D. "Distance in International Business Research: Are We Really Making Any Progress?" In *Contributions to International Business,* ed. M. Laaksonen, A. Arslan, and M. Kontkanen, 119–140. Vaasa, Finland: Acta Wasaenia, 2014.

Dow, D., and A. Karunaratna. "Developing a Multidimensional Instrument to Measure Psychic Distance Stimuli." *Journal of International Business Studies* 37, no. 5 (2006): 575–77.

Economist. "A World of Pain: The Giants of Global Finance Are in Trouble." March 7, 2015. http://www.economist.com/news/finance-and-economics/21645807-giants-global -finance-are-trouble-world-pain (accessed May 11, 2015).

Economist. "China Loses Its Allure."January 23, 2014. http://www.economist.com/news /leaders/21595001-life-getting-tougher-foreign-companies-those-want-stay-will-have -adjust-china (accessed May 15, 2015).

Eden, L., and S. R. Miller. "Distance Matters: Liability of Foreignness, Institutional Distance and Ownership Strategy." In *Theories of the Multinational Enterprise: Diversity, Complexity and Relevance*, ed. M.A. Hitt and J. L. C. Cheng, 187–221. Bingley: Emerald Group Publishing, 2004

Eun, C. S., and B. G. Resnick. *International Financial Management.* 7th ed. New York: McGraw Hill, 2014.

Evans, P. "Target Closes All 133 Stores in Canada, Gets Creditor Protection," *CBC News,* January 15, 2015. http://www.cbc.ca/news/business/target-closes-all-133-stores-in-canada -gets-creditor-protection-1.2901618 (accessed April 30, 2015).

Fernandez, P. "CAPM: An Absurd Model." SSRN working paper (2014).

First Read DMV. "Uber Wins Right to Operate in D.C." *NBC Washington,* December 4, 2012. http://www.nbcwashington.com/blogs/first-read-dmv/Uber-Wins-Right-to -Operate-in-DC-182097951.html (accessed May 15, 2015).

Florida, R. "The World Is Spiky." *Atlantic Monthly*, October 2005.

Fortang, R. S., D. A. Lax, and J. K. Sebenius. "Negotiating the Spirit of the Deal: Crafting the Social Contract." *Harvard Business Review* (February 2003), product R0302E-PDF-SPA.

Friedman, T. L. *The World Is Flat: A Brief History of the Twenty-First Century.* New York: Farrar, Straus and Giroux, 2005.

Friedman, T. L. *Hot, Flat, and Crowded: Why We Need a Green Revolution and How It Can Renew America.* New York: Farrar, Straus and Giroux, 2008.

Galani, U. "No Froth in Starbucks' Buyout in Japan." *New York Times*, September 14, 2014. http://dealbook.nytimes.com/2014/09/24/no-froth-in-starbucks-buyout-in-japan (accessed May 11, 2015).

Ghemawat, P. "Distance Still Matters." *Harvard Business Review* 79, no. 8 (September 2001): 137–149.

Ghemawat, P. *Redefining Global Strategy: Crossing Border in a World Where Differences Still Matter.* Boston: Harvard Business School Press, 2007.

Ghemawat, P. "Why the World Isn't Flat." *Foreign Policy* (March–April 2007): 54–60.

Ghemawat, P. *World 3.0: Global Prosperity and How to Achieve It.* Boston: Harvard Business Review Press, 2011.

Ghoshal, S. "Global Strategy: An Organizing Framework." *Strategic Management Journal* 5 (1987): 425–440.

Gordon, R. *Ethnologue: Languages of the World.* http://archive.ethnologue.com/15/web.asp (accessed March 31, 2015).

Guiso, L., P. Sapienza, and L. Zingales. "Cultural Biases in Economic Exchange?" *The Quarterly Journal of Economics* 93, no. 3 (2009): 1095–1131.

Gupta, A., V. Govindarajan, and H. Wang. *The Quest for Global Dominance.* San Francisco: Jossey-Bass/Wiley, 2011.

Gupta, A., and V. Govindarajan. *Global Strategy and Organization.* Hoboken, NJ: John Wiley & Sons, 2004.

Haig, M. *Brand Failures: The Truth about the 100 Biggest Branding Mistakes of All Time,* chap. 5. London: Kogan Page, 2003.

Hallowell, R., C. Knoop, and D. Bowenthe. "Four Seasons Goes to Paris." Harvard Business School Case No. 803069 (2002).

Henisz, W. J. "The Institutional Environment for Economic Growth." *Economics and Politics* 12, no. 1 (2000): 1–31.

Henisz, W. J. "The Institutional Environment for Infrastructure Investment." *Industrial and Corporate Change* 11, no. 2 (2002): 355–389.

Henisz, W. J., and A. Delios. "Learning about the Institutional Environment." In *The New Institutionalism in Strategic Management,* ed. P. Ingram and B. S. Silverman, chap. 19, 339–372. Amsterdam: Elsevier, 2002.

Henisz, W. J., and B. A. Zelner. "AES-Telasi: Power Trip or Power Play?" Philadelphia: The Wharton School, 2006.

Hetzner, C. "European Automakers Seek Firmer Foothold in India." *Automotive News Europe,* September 1, 2014. http://europe.autonews.com/article/20140901/ANE/140829857/european-automakers-seek-firmer-foothold-in-india (accessed June 6, 2015).

Hofstede, G. *Cultures and Organizations: Software of the Mind.* New York: McGraw-Hill, 1999.

Hofstede, G. *Culture's Consequences: Comparing Values, Behaviors, Institutions, and Organizations Across Nations.* 2nd ed. Thousand Oaks, CA: Sage Publications, 2001.

Hyde, K. "Japanese Companies and U.S. Employment Law Liability: How to Avoid Court and Stay out of the Headlines." Japan Society website, September 13, 2011. http://japan-society.org/multimedia/articles/japanese-companies-us-employment-law-liability-how-to-avoid-court-stay-out-of-the-headlines (accessed March 25, 2015).

Hymer, S. *The International Operations of National Firms: A Study of Direct Foreign Investment.* Cambridge, MA: MIT Press, 1960.

Ingelhart, R., and W. E. Baker. "Modernization, Cultural Change and the Persistence of Traditional Values." *American Sociological Review* 65, no. 1 (2000): 19–51.

Inglehart, R., and C. Welzel. *Modernization, Cultural Change, and Democracy: The Human Development Sequence.* Cambridge, UK: Cambridge University Press, 2005.

Jaque, L. L. *International Corporate Finance: Value Creating with Currency Derivatives in Global Capital Markets.* Hoboken, NJ: Wiley, 2014.

Jensen, R. E. "International Investment Risk Analysis: Extensions for Multinational Corporation Capital Budgeting Models." *Mathematical Modeling* 9, no. 3–5 (1987): 265–284.

Jensen, R., and G. Szulanski. "Stickiness and the Adaptation of Organizational Practices in Cross-Border Knowledge Transfers." *Journal of International Business Studies* 35, no. 6 (2004): 508–523.

Johanson, J., and J.-E. Vahlne. "The Internationalization Process of the Firm-A Model of Knowledge Development and Increasing Foreign Market Commitments." *Journal of International Business Studies* 8, no. 1 (1977): 23–32.

Kaufmann, D., A. Kraay, and P. Zoido-Lobatón. "Governance Matters." World Bank Policy Research Working Paper 2196 (1999).

Kedl, K., et al., *China Business Report.* The American Chamber of Commerce in Shanghai, 2015. http://www.amcham-shanghai.org/AmChamPortal/MCMS/Presentation/Publication /PublicationCustomization/Content.aspx?Type=1&GUID={E3337DDB-28FD-457-D-96B7-2C77E21A2A90}&tb_Name=PublicationCustomization&origin=shorturl (accessed May 15, 2015).

Kirkman, B. L., K. B. Lowe, and C. B. Gibson. "A Quarter Century of Culture's Consequences: A Review of Empirical Research Incorporating Hofstede's Cultural Values Framework." *Journal of International Business Studies* 37, no. 3 (2006), 285–320.

Kogut, B., and H. Singh. "The Effect of National Culture on the Choice of Entry Mode." *Journal of International Business Studies* 19, no. 3 (1988): 411–432.

La Porta, R., et al. "Law and Finance." *Journal of Political Economy* 106, no. 6 (1998): 1113–1155.

Levitt, T. "The Globalization of Markets." *Harvard Business Review* (May 1983): 1–11.

Linders, G.-J. M., et al. "Cultural and Institutional Determinants of Bilateral Trade Flows." Tinbergen Institute Discussion Paper, TI 2005–074/3 (2005).

Mance, H., and K. Hille. "CNN to Pull Plug on Broadcasting in Russia." *Financial Times,* November 11, 2014. http://www.ft.com/cms/s/0/a201f700-69b0-11e4-8f4f-00144fe-abdc0.html#ixzz3IqvWwXgl (accessed March 23, 2015).

Martin, X., and R. Salomon. "Knowledge Transfer Capacity: Implications for the Theory of the Multinational Corporation." *Journal of International Business Studies* 34 (2003): 356–373.

Martin, X., and R. Salomon. "Tacitness, Learning, and International Expansion: A Study of Foreign Direct Investment in a Knowledge-Intensive Industry." *Organization Science* 14, no. 3 (2003): 297–311.

Mata, J., and P. Portugal. "The Survival of New Domestic and Foreign-Owned Firms." *Strategic Management Journal* 23, no. 4 (2002): 323–343.

Mezias, J. M. "Identifying Liabilities of Foreignness and Strategies to Minimize Their Effects: The Case of Labor Lawsuit Judgments in the United States." *Strategic Management Journal* 23, no. 2 (2002): 229–244.

Minder, R., and M. Scott. "Sharing Economy Faces Patchwork of Guidelines in European Countries." *The New York Times,* September 21, 2104. http://www.nytimes.com/2014/09/22 /technology/sharing-economy-faces-patchwork-of-guidelines-in-european -countries.html (accessed May 15, 2015).

Morck, R., and B. Yeung. "Why Investors Value Multinationality." *Journal of Business* 64, no. 2 (1991): 165–187.

Morck, R., and B. Yeung. "Internalization: An Event Study." *Journal of International Economics* 33 (1992): 41–56.

Nakamoto, M., and C. Lorenz, "It Doesn't Have to End in Tears." *The Financial Times*, March 7, 1994.

Nakamoto, M., and C. Lorenz. "Why We Can't Afford to Betray the Japanese." *Daily Mail*, February 22, 1994, p. 7.

North, D. C. *Structure and Change in Economic History*. New York: Norton, 1981.

North, D. C. "Institutions." *Journal of Economic Perspectives* 5, no. 1 (1991): 97–112.

Perkins, S. E. "Defining Institutional Similarity: The Multidimensions of Global Industry Regulation." Kellogg School of Management working paper (2011).

Perkins, S. E. "Cross-National Variations in Industry Regulation: A Factor Analytic Approach with an Application to Telecommunications." *Regulation and Governance* 8 (2014): 149–163.

Perkins, S. E. "When Does Prior Experience Pay? Institutional Experience and the Case of the Multinational Corporation." *Administrative Science Quarterly* 59, no. 1 (2014): 145–181.

Prahalad, C. K., and Y. L. Doz. *The Multinational Mission: Balancing Local Demands and Global Vision*. New York: Free Press, 1987.

Protess, B., and D. Jolly. "French Bank Is Suspected of Violating Blacklistings." *The New York Times*, February 13, 2014. http://dealbook.nytimes.com/2014/02/13/bnp-paribas -profit-falls-on-u-s-sanctions-troubles/ (accessed May 15, 2015).

Protess, B., and J. Silver-Greenberg. "Bank of Tokyo Fined for 'Misleading' New York Regulator on Iran." *The New York Times*, November 18, 2014. http://dealbook.nytimes .com/2014/11/18/lawsky-fines-bank-of-tokyo-mitsubishi-ufj-another-315-million / (accessed May 15, 2015).

Public Citizen. "Canadian Corporation Uses NAFTA to Sue the U.S.: The Loewen Group, Inc. v. The United States." http://www.citizen.org/trade/article_redirect.cfm?ID=1173 (accessed May 15, 2015).

Radaelli, C., and O. Fritsch. "Measuring Regulatory Performance." OECD expert paper, no. 2 (July 2012).

Ricks, D. *Blunders in International Business*. 4th ed. Malden, MA: Wiley, 2006.

Riesenhuber, K. "English Common Law versus German *Systemdenken*? Internal versus External Approaches." *Utrecht Law Review* 7, no. 1 (2011): 117–130.

Robbins Collection, "The Common Law and Civil Law Traditions." University of California at Berkeley School of Law website. https://www.law.berkeley.edu/library/robbins /CommonLawCivilLawTraditions.html (accessed May 15, 2015).

Rosenzweig, P. "National Culture and Management." Harvard Business School Note 9–394–177 (1994).

Salomon, R. "Offshores Coming Home," February 19, 2013. http://www.robertsalomon .com/offshores-coming-home/ (accessed May 11, 2015).

Salomon, R. "Revisiting Outsourcing…Again," August 9, 2011. http://www.robertsalo- mon.com/revisiting-outsourcing-again/ (accessed May 11, 2015).

Salomon, R. "Small Businesses in U.S. Reevaluate China Outsourcing Strategy," April 6, 2011. http://www.robertsalomon.com/small-businesses-in-u-s-reevaluate-china-outsourcing -strategy/ (accessed May 11, 2015).

Salomon, R. "So You Want to Do Business In a Developing Country?" September 15, 2009. http://www.robertsalomon.com/so-you-want-to-do-business-in-a-developing-country / (accessed May 11, 2015).

Salomon, R. "Tesco's American Foray," June 27, 2007. http://www.robertsalomon.com/2007/06/ (accessed May 11, 2015).

Salomon, R. "Update: Tesco's Venture into the U.S.," March 4, 2008. http://www.robertsa-lomon.com/update-tescos-venture-into-the-us/ (accessed May 11, 2015).

Salomon, R., and X. Martin. "Learning, Knowledge Transfer, and Technology Implementation Performance: A Study of Time-to-Build in the Global Semiconductor Industry." *Management Science* 54, no. 7 (2008): 1266–1280.

Salomon, R., and Z. Wu. "Institutional Distance and Local Isomorphism Strategy: Foreign Investment in the U.S. Banking Industry." *Journal of International Business Studies* 4, no. 43 (2012): 343–367.

Schwartz, S. H. "Beyond Individualism/Collectivism: New Cultural Dimensions of Values." In *Individualism and Collectivism: Theory, Method, and Application*, ed. U. Kim et al., 85–122. Newbury Park, CA: Sage, 1994.

Schwartz, S. H. "A Theory of Cultural Values and Some Implications for Work." *Applied Psychology: An International Review* 48, no. 1 (1999): 12–47.

Scott, M., and S. Plass. "German Court Lifts Ban on Uber Ride Service." *The New York Times*, September 16, 2014. http://www.nytimes.com/2014/09/17/business/international/uber-ban-in-germany-is-lifted-by-court.html?_r=0 (accessed May 15, 2015).

Scott, W. R. *Institutions and Organizations*. Thousand Oaks, CA: Sage Publications, 1995.

Sebenius, J. K., A. Nanda, and R. S. Fortgang. "Honda-Rover (A): Crafting an Alliance." Harvard Business School Case No. 9–899–223 (1999), and subsequent updates B, C, and D.

Shorrock, T. "Dow Fights with Korean Partners, Slams Business Climate." *Multinational Monitor* 3, no. 9 (September 1982). http://www.multinationalmonitor.org/hyper/issues/1982/09/shorrock.html (accessed June 1, 2015).

Siegel, J. I. "Lincoln Electric." Harvard Business School Case 707–445 (November 2006, revised August 2008). http://www.hbs.edu/faculty/Pages/item.aspx?num=33844 (accessed May 11, 2015).

Siegel, J. I., A. N. Licht, and S. H. Schwartz. "Egalitarianism and International Investment." *Journal of Financial Economics* 102, no. 3 (December 2011): 621–642.

Siegel, J. I., A. N. Licht, and S. H. Schwartz. "Egalitarianism, Cultural Distance, and Foreign Direct Investment: A New Approach." *Organization Science* 23, no. 5 (September–October 2012): 1174–1194.

Siegel, J. I., and B. Zepp Larson. "Labor Market Institutions and Global Strategic Adaptation: Evidence from Lincoln Electric." *Management Science* 55, no. 9 (September 2009): 1527–1546.

Statista. "Consumer Spending on Luxury Goods in China from 1998 to 2015." http://www.statista.com/statistics/235092/consumer-spending-on-luxury-goods-in-china/ (accessed March 30, 2015).

Szczesny, J. "Milestone: China Now General Motors' Biggest Market." *CNBC*, July 8, 2013. http://www.cnbc.com/id/100870316 (accessed May 11, 2015).

Thomas, L., Jr. "U.S. Strengths Buoy Consumers but Hurt Corporations with Business Abroad." *The New York Times,* January 27, 2015. http://dealbook.nytimes.com/2015/01/27/u-s-strengths-buoy-consumers-but-hurt-corporations-with-business-abroad/?_r=0 (accessed March 30, 2015).

Utpal, B., N. Galpin, and B. Haslem. "The Home Court Advantage in International Corporate Litigation." *Journal of Law and Economics* 50 (2007): 625–659.

Van Maanen, J., and A. Laurent. "The Flow of Culture: Some Notes on Globalization and the Multinational Corporation." In *Organization Theory and the Multinational Corporate*, ed. S. Ghoshal and D. E. Westney, 275–312. New York: St. Martin's Press, 1993.

Watanabe, T. "Gerber Taking a Lesson from Foreign Babies." *Los Angeles Times*, May 27, 1991.

Wikipedia. "Law." http://en.wikipedia.org/wiki/Law (accessed March 25, 2015).

Wu, Z., and R. Salomon. "Does Imitation Reduce the Liability of Foreignness? Linking Distance, Isomorphism, and Performance." New York University Stern working paper (2015).

Wu, Z., and R. Salomon. "The Regulatory Liability of Foreignness: Enforcement Actions in the United States." New York University Stern working paper (2015).

Xu, D., and O. Shenkar. "Institutional Distance and the Multinational Enterprise." *Academy of Management Review* 27, no. 4 (2002): 608–618.

Zaheer, S. "Overcoming the Liability of Foreignness." *Academy of Management Journal* 38, no. 2 (1995): 341–363.

Zaheer, S., and E. Mosakowski. "The Dynamics of the Liability of Foreignness: A Global Study of Survival in Financial Services." *Strategic Management Journal* 18, no. 6 (1997): 439–463.

Index

ABN-AMRO, 9
AES
  Georgia and, 3–5
  globalization and, 2, 7–8, 11
Airbnb, 50–2, 56, 60
Amazon, 38, 50
Apple, 27, 39, 41–2, 44, 147–8

Bangladesh, 99
Barclays, 62
Bayer AG, 164–7, 173
Best Buy, 39
Blunders in International Business (Ricks),
  96–7
BMW, 18, 101
Brazil, 13, 47, 74–6
Bremmer, Ian, 66
British Aerospace (BAe), 100–1

CAGE Comparative Data, 66–7, 91
capitalist economic systems, 80
Caterpillar, 75
Center for Systemic Peace, 64, 67, 134
China
  banking and, 61
  culture and, 37–9, 131
  economic institutions, 80–1, 86–8
  Fiat and, 97–8
  General Motors and, 165–6
  Global Acumen and, 118–22, 131, 135
  globalization and, 18–19
  institutional distance and, 13–14, 44
  manufacturing and, 19
  multinationals and, 78
  national institutions and, 37
  outsourcing and, 73

political institutions and, 55–6, 58, 68
regulatory structure, 61–2
U.S. and, 55–6, 130, 137–9, 153–4
Walmart and, 2, 6–8
CIA World Factbook, 66–7, 83, 90
Citibank, 9
Coca-Cola, 41–2
Corruption Perception Index, 65, 67, 134
credit default swap (CDS), 89
cultural institutions
  acquisition of culture, 104
  common business faux pas, 95
  coping with culture, 102
  cross-cultural differences, 100–1
  development of culture, 104–5
  erroneous cultural assumptions about,
    98–9
  explained, 102–3
  importance of, 93–4
  insensitivity to culture, 97–8
  language influences, 105
  learning cultural lessons the hard
    way, 96
  measuring, 108–11
  national culture, 107
  related to other institutions, 111–13
  religious influences, 105
  sharing a culture, 106–7
  social influences, 105
  sources of data on, 110–11
  transgressions of faith, 99
  what managers should know, 94–5
currency
  gaining money on exchange, 75–6
  hedging risk on, 76–7
  losing money on exchange, 74–5

Daimler, 71
Digest of Commercial Laws of the
    World, 65
Doing Business Index, 66–7, 91
Dow, Douglas, 108, 110–11, 134
Dow Chemical Company, 100, 166

eBay, 39, 50
economic infrastructure, 77–8
economic institutions
    anticipating economic shocks, 73–4
    bringing it all together, 91
    defining, 78–82
    economic actors, 79
    economic infrastructure, 77–8
    economic systems and structures,
        79–81
    impact of currency, 74–7
    managing institutional differences, 81–2
    measuring, 83–90
    misjudging quality, 72–3
    overestimating market potential, 70–1
    overview, 69–70
    see also measuring economic institutions
economic shocks, 73–4
economic systems and structures
    capitalist economic systems, 80
    combined economies, 81
    command economic systems, 80
    less common systems/structures, 80–1
    overview, 79–80
Eurasia Group, 66–7

Fiat, 97–8
flawed expansion
    AES in Georgia, 3–5
    IKEA in Russia, 5
    Tesco in the U.S., 5–6
    Walmart in China, 6–8
Florida, Richard, 10
foreign entry and ownership structure
    alliances, 165–6
    buy side, 161
    deeper foreign-market involvement, 161–6
    exporting and importing, 162–3
    investing in subsidiaries, 164–5
    modes of, 167–70
    sell side, 160–1
Foreign Law Guide, 65, 67

foreignness
    see liability of foreignness
Fresh & Easy, 6
    see also Tesco
Friedman, Thomas, 10–11

General Motors (GM), 18, 165–7
genetically modified organisms (GMOs),
    164
Georgia, Republic of, 2–4
Gerber, 98–9
Gere, Richard, 97–8
Ghemawat, Pankaj, 10, 66
GlaxoSmithKline, 39
Global Acumen
    algorithm, 133
    architecture, 134
    beyond U.S., 139–40
    as compliment instead of
        substitute, 147–8
    concrete example, 133–5
    dealing with uncertainty, 152–4
    devising cost contingency, 155–6
    as evaluation and monitoring tool,
        176–80
    existing alternatives vs., 154–7
    factoring experience into, 172–6
    factoring industry differences
        into, 170–2
    foreign entry and ownership
        structure, 160–70
    institutional vs. geographical
        distance, 135–6
    market risk premiums and risk-adjusted
        discount rates, 156–7
    Newlandia example, 144–52
    output, 135
    overview, 133
    in practice, 143–58
    symmetry in output, 136–9
    varying risks, 148–50
    weighing risks with, 167–70
    see also risk
globalization
    examples of flawed expansion, 3–8
    failures of, 8–10
    institutional distance and, 12–14
    overview, 1–3
    reimagining landscape of, 10–11

globalization, process of
  bottom line, 28–9
  bringing it all together, 32–3
  building alternative approach to, 31–2
  building business plans, 22
  costs, 27–8
  discount rate, 28
  examples, 22–6
  expansion, 19–21
  Mexican suppliers, 20–1
  niche markets, 20
  profits, 17–22
  real-world complexity, 26–9
  revenues, 26–7
GLOBE project, 110–11
Google, 39, 42, 44, 50, 111
Gordon, Raymond, 108

H&M, 19
Henisz, Witold, 64
Hofstede, Geert, 103, 109–11, 131, 134, 171
Home Depot, 39
Honda, 100–1
Hot, Flat, and Crowded (Friedman), 10
HSBC, 9, 62

IKEA
  culture and, 106
  globalization and, 2, 11, 41
  institutional distance and, 45–6
  intangibles and, 42–4
  Russia and, 5
  Walmart compared to, 7–8
Immelt, Jeff, 39
India
  Apple and, 27
  caste system, 105
  common law and, 58
  Daimler and, 71
  global acumen and, 115, 120, 135
  globalization and, 18
  institutional distance and, 13
  Kellogg's and, 71
  miscalculating local sales in, 71
  national institutions and, 36–7
  offshore outsourcing and, 72–3
  power distance and, 109
  risk and, 115, 120, 139–40, 153–4
  United States and, 72–3, 113, 137

individualism/collectivism, 109
institutional distance
  complex approaches to, 123
  Euclidian approaches to, 123–4
  Mahalanobis approaches to, 124–5
  subtraction vs. absolute value, 122–3
  using absolute value, 121–2
  using simple subtraction, 121
intangibles, 41–5, 112, 174
International Finance Corporation, 66
International Labor Organization, 83, 90
International Monetary Fund, 83, 90

Japan, 8, 19–20, 37, 53, 86, 95, 98–101,
    109, 115, 125, 130, 135, 137, 139–40,
    148, 153–4
Journal of International Business Studies,
    125, 130

Kellogg's, 71, 162
Kering, 39
Korean Pacific ChemicalCorporation
    (KPCC), 100, 166

L.L. Bean, 20
language, measuring, 108
Laurent, Andre, 104
liability of foreignness
  currency risk and, 77
  dangers of seeing globalization
      everywhere, 41
  experience and, 173–5
  Global Acumen and, 154–7, 173
  individuals and, 39–40
  institutional difference and, 37, 46, 48
  intangibles and, 42, 46
  minimizing through personal
      experience, 174
  overcoming, 43–4
Logoplaste, 19, 46–7
L'Oréal, 39
LVMH, 39

Mahalanobis distance, 124–5
market potential, overestimating, 70–1
Markit, 89, 91
masculinity/femininity, 110
Mattel, 19
McDonald's, 41

measuring economic institutions
  comparing using capital market
    structure, 86
  comparing using credit default swaps,90
  comparing using GDP components, 86
  comparing using sovereign bond spreads,
    89–90
  detailed risk factors, 85–90
  direct measures, 85
  economic data sources, 90
  hypothetical example, 84
  indirect measures, 87
  using macro-level data, 83–4
  volatility of, 87–9
Microsoft, 41, 75

national institutions
  bringing it all together, 47–8
  danger of "seeing" successful
    globalization, 40–7
  foreignness and, 39–40, 43–4
  importance of, 36–9
  institutional distance and, 44–7
  intangibles and, 41–3
  overview, 35–6
Nation Master, 66–7
niche markets, 6, 20
North American Free Trade Agreement
  (NAFTA), 19, 53, 136
NYU Stern School of Business, 76, 157

Organization for Economic Cooperation
  and Development (OECD), 65, 84

payback methods, 128–9
Penn World Table, 83, 90
Piergallini, Alfred, 98
Political Constraints (POLCON) Index,
  64, 67
political institutions
  analyzing, 54–5
  bringing it all together, 66–8
  civil law, 57–8
  combined legal systems, 59
  common law and, 58
  cultural differences and, 55–6
  globalization and legal institutions,
    59–60
  legal institutions, 57–60
  managers and, 49–52

  measuring, 63–6
  navigating, 53
  overview, 49
  regulatory institutions, 60–3
  religious legal systems, 58–9
power distance, 109
Proctor & Gamble, 47, 75
PRS Group, 66–7

quality, misjudging, 72–3

religion, measuring, 108–9
RGE Macroanalytics, 66–7
Richemant, 39
Ricks, David, 96
risk
  cultural institutions and, 131
  economic institutions and, 132
  Global Acumen, 125–30, 133–41
  higher risk entry modes, 164–5
  incorporating difference and distance,
    130–1
  institutional distance, 121–5
  lower risk entry modes, 162–3
  moderate risk entry modes, 165–6
  moving from institutions to institutional
    distance, 117–19
  overview, 115–17
  payback methods, 128–9
  political institutions and, 132
  symmetry and measurement, 129–30
  venture capital, 127–8
  what managers are missing, 120
Roubini, Nouriel, 66
Rover, 100–1
Royal Bank of Scotland, 9, 62

SAIC, 165–6
Schein, Henry, 81–2
Schwartz, Shalom, 111
Schweppes, 97
Selkirk Group, 19, 21
Shanghai, 7, 84, 122–3
Shanghai GM, 165
  see also General Motors
social structure, measuring, 109–10
Spain, 13, 29–30, 40, 47, 58, 60, 75, 94,
  105, 162–3, 166, 174
Standard and Poor's (S&P), 89
Stonewall Kitchen, 162–3, 166–7, 169

Tesco, 2, 5–8, 11, 14, 39, 186
Thom McAn, 99
Thomson Reuters, 89, 91
Tiffany, 39
Transparency International, 65, 134

Uber, 50–2, 56, 62
uncertainty avoidance, 109–10
US Bureau of Labor Statistics, 84, 91

van Maanen, John, 104
venture capital (VC), 127
Vitro, 73–4

Walmart
   China and, 2, 6–8, 38, 78
   Fresh & Easy and, 6
   globalization and, 11
Wharton School of the University of
   Pennsylvania, 64

Whole Foods, 6
World Bank
   Country Policy and
      InstitutionalAssessment
      (CPIA), 85
   Database of Political Institutions (DPI),
      64, 134
   Doing Business Index, 66
   macro-level data, 83–4
   World Development
      Indicators, 86
World Economic Forum, 65
World Is Flat, The (Friedman), 10
World Justice Project, 65
World Values Survey, 110–11
Worldwide Governance Indicators
   (WGI), 63–4
Wu, Zheying, 125, 130

Yahoo, 50